The Water in the Glass
Body and Mind in Psychoanalysis

Nick Totton

Rebus Press
76 Haverstock Hill
LONDON
NW3 2BE

ISBN 1 900877 12 0

For my parents, who always thought I would.

In depth psychology, the analyst operates with drives, but he is rather like the man who wants to drink water from a glass which he sees reflected in a mirror.

Wilhelm Reich, *The Function of the Orgasm*

Acknowledgments

This book had its origins in my dissertation for an MA Degree in Psychoanalytic Studies at Leeds Metropolitan University. I want to thank everyone connected with the course, in particular the course leader, Alison Hall, and my dissertation supervisor, Christine Bousefield; and the course members, especially the small group with whom I talked and argued over many of the themes of the book: Christine Bostock, Colin Buckle, Anne Marie Jones, Teresa Norman, and Penny Tharratt. Mary Swale read and commented on a draft of Chapter Nine, and Richard House contributed several helpful references and thoughts. No one, of course, is responsible for my mistakes and misapprehensions other than myself.

I am grateful to many other people for interesting conversations and support; to my original trainer in Reichian therapy, William West, and to all my colleagues and trainees over the years; and to my clients. I also want to thank my daughter, Zoë Edmondson, for her tolerance of the many hours spent working on this book rather than doing more interesting things with her.

It would be inadequate to 'thank' my partner, Em Edmondson. Rather, I need to acknowledge that all my ideas on these matters are inextricably bound up with hers - and that, although I wrote all the words, this book also belongs to her.

A Note on Language and Translation

In line with many recent writers, I have throughout silently corrected the translation of Freud's *'trieb'* to 'drive' (rather than 'instinct'). I have done the same with other psychoanalytic texts translated from the German. For a justification of this measure, see Ornston 1992: 93-5.

Whenever the occasion arises, I have used 'she' and 'her' to represent the so-called 'neutral' third person pronoun.

A Note on Texts

Wherever possible, I have quoted Freud's texts from the Penguin Freud Library as well as the Standard Edition, the Penguin page number preceding the Standard Edition page number. A single reference is used when a text is only available in the Standard Edition.

All quotations from Sigmund Freud, Sándor Ferenczi and Georg Groddeck are reproduced by permission of Mark Paterson and Associates and Sigmund Freud Copyrights Limited.

CONTENTS

Introduction

Soul.

O who shall, from this dungeon, raise
A soul enslaved so many ways?
With bolts of bone, that fettered stands
In feet; and manacled in hands:
Here blinded with an eye; and there
Deaf with the drumming of an ear:
A soul hung up, as 'twere, in chains
Of nerves, and arteries, and veins:
Tortured, besides each other part,
In a vain head, and double heart.

Body.

O who shall me deliver whole
From bonds of this tyrannic soul?
Which stretched upright, impales me so,
That mine own precipice I go;
And warms and moves this needless frame
(A fever could but do the same);
And, wanting where its spite to try,
Has made me live to let me die:
A body that could never rest
Since this ill spirit it possest.

Andrew Marvell, 'A Dialogue Between the Soul and Body'

What is a body?

Most of us probably feel we have some intuitive grasp of the answer to this question. It takes philosophers and psychoanalysts to throw this certainty into doubt. The doubt is often fruitful; but it can make us wonder whether we have bodies, whether we *are* bodies. What follows is an attempt to re-balance our thinking around these issues - suggesting among other things that our doubts about the body, our sense of alienation from it, themselves reflect a problem of a psychoanalytic nature. This problem is well illustrated by the quotation above, from Marvell, which is itself strikingly reminiscent of passages from

Freud's *Beyond the Pleasure Principle*.

My principle aim in this book is to suggest ways in which we can reassure ourselves, on every level from the primal to the metaphysical (and, really, the two are closely linked), that we in fact *are* bodies; that it is with, in and through our bodies that we both feel and think; and that this way of experiencing is profoundly 'psychoanalytic', and in fact restitutive of something important that has gone missing from psychoanalysis.

Looking at the literature from this point of view, it is very striking how many of the key themes and questions of psychoanalysis we are immediately led to by thinking about the body; or, conversely, how we are led to the body by thinking about these questions. Examples from metapsychology include affect, the drives, the place of biology in general, repression, the status of the unconscious, and character. On the more clinical side, we can instance hysteria, masochism, the question of parameters, and transference and countertransference. In what follows I shall touch on all of these, and look in detail at several.

In Chapter 1, 'Foreign Body', I introduce the whole book and indicate why I believe there is a problem: how psychoanalysis is distorted and limited by the concepts of 'mind' and 'body' which it has inherited from mainstream Western thought. I apply this to both theoretical and clinical topics, and end by considering the possibility of a 'bodymind-centred analysis'. I also say something about the relationship of my ideas to those of language-centred analytic theory and practice, and introduce the idea of the List - a set of binary dichotomies such as 'mind/body', 'thought/feeling', 'male/female' and so on, which act as powerful constraints on thinking in our culture.

Chapter 2, 'Body Represented', begins by looking at Freud's *Project for a Scientific Psychology* (1895) and how it portrays mind as a representation of body: body mapped onto brain, so to speak. It is widely recognised that this very early, 'pre-analytic' work contains in germ many of the great themes and issues of Freud's career - ideas to which he returns explicitly in *Beyond the Pleasure Principle*. I go on to show Freud's ambiguous attitude to mind and body operating throughout his work, in relation to the concepts of drive, affect and the unconscious - how he consistently strives to bring psyche and soma together, yet simultaneously wedges them apart. I suggest that from this viewpoint we can cast light on some of the knotty issues of metapsychology.

In Chapter 3, 'Hysterical Body', I examine the interaction of clinical and theoretical versions of hysteria in the work of Freud, Ferenczi and Reich. I argue that Reich and Ferenczi attempted to restore to a central place in analytic theory the idea of a 'fundamental hysteria', which precedes all other diagnostic categories, and is basic to our experience as embodied beings in culture. If we stop trying to fit hysteria into a mind-privileging, language-privileging model, then this concept - once more - becomes fruitful in a number of new ways.

Chapter 4, 'Body as Id, Body as Ego', begins by exploring the work of Georg Groddeck, another of the 'eccentrics' of psychoanalysis whose ideas I am trying to bring back toward the centre of the picture (or perhaps rather to move the picture so that its centre comes closer to these ideas). I explore Groddeck's fascinating personal/intellectual relationship with Freud, and move on to look in more detail at Reich's thinking about 'mind' and 'body', relating his work to Groddeck's and make the distinction between the two. I centre my discussion on Reich's fundamental discovery of the somatic anchoring of repression in the musculature, and end the chapter with an appraisal of Reich's strengths and weaknesses as a theoretician and clinician.

Chapter 5, 'Bodywork', outlines the practical application of the ideas I have been describing, for the benefit of those readers who know little or nothing about bodymind-centred psychotherapy. I give a detailed paraphrase of one of Reich's case histories, and discuss some of the problems and pitfalls of bodymind-centred work. I am not trying to argue here that all analysts or therapists should work directly with the body, but only to make the idea of doing so seem rather less wholly unacceptable, and to indicate how it might be done in a way which honours the goals and meets the demands of analytic/psychodynamic work.

In Chapter 6, 'Body as Death', I suggest some possibly unexpected similarities between the ideas of Reich and those of

Lacan, focusing on their respective portrayals of the ego, sexuality, and the death drive. In the course of this I also discuss some of the differences, and indeed complete incommensurabilities, in their theories. In this chapter our understanding deepens of how and why the ego, identifying itself as 'mind', can experience bodily impulses and experiences as alien and dangerous to it.

Chapter 7, 'Bodymind', is the centre of the book: here I draw upon other disciplines, such as neuroscience, information theory, and developmental psychology, which seem to me potentially useful in developing a more workable metapsychology. I also address the theoretical problems of relating analytic discourse to other discourses. In this chapter I offer my own formulations on 'body' and 'mind', and discuss in more detail the question of language and what is or is not 'outside' it.

Chapter 8, 'Body as Character', looks at Reichian and post Reichian work in this area, both as an example of the theoretical achievements of bodymind-centred analysis - since this work on character seems to me far more powerful than that within mainstream analysis - and as a theoretical framework which we can use to understand differences between the various styles of psychotherapeutic practice and theory.

Chapter 9, 'Sexed and Gendered Body', was in many ways the most difficult to write, and remains, I feel, the least complete. Here I try to address the implications, if we place the body at the centre of our work of, and for, sexual difference. I argue that we do not have to fall back into 'biologism', and that, in fact, there is a need for a new kind of 'human biology' which *brings together* our embodiment and our power of symbolisation.

Chapter 10, 'Body of Knowledge', tries to suggest some paths forward for those who accept the arguments put forward in this book - paths towards a theory and practice which gives a more honourable place to 'the body'.

I put quotation marks around 'the body' because I find the phrase so irritating, so hypostatising in its thrust. What I want to talk about is not 'the body' but *bodies* - actual human organisms, whose thought and speech are bodily functions - or what Teresa Brennan powerfully calls 'the Flesh' (Brennan 1992). *'The* body' is already a mental concept rather than a physical experience: in a sense, once we talk of 'the body', the pass has already been sold. However, to avoid the phrase entirely, or to score through ' the ' in Lacanian style as I am tempted to do, would involve a degree of novelty perhaps more distracting than illuminating. As a minimal gesture, I have eliminated 'the' from chapter titles.

In writing this book, I have tried to assume as little prior knowledge as possible in its readers: although it does seem reasonable to expect an interest in the topic, and in its background field of psychoanalysis, which doesn't actually begin with opening this book! I myself am by no means a specialist in all the areas I discuss; it is hard to see how anyone could be, when they include along with psychoanalysis the fields of philosophy, cognitive science and information theory.

Even within the area of psychoanalysis, I need to own some definite limitations. To begin with, unfortunately I know neither German nor French well enough to read analytic texts in the original. The Freud discussed here is Strachey's Freud, as realigned by Ornston, Mahoney et al (Ornston 1992), Laplanche and Pontalis (1988), and others. Even more seriously, the Lacan I describe is the author of those *Écrits* and *Seminars* which have been englished, however inadequately, together with other works presented as quotation or hearsay by commentators and exegesists.

This latter point is particularly serious because those who do 'know Lacan' emphasise that his views, much like Freud's, change and develop over time; and stress how little of that development can be grasped through reading what is available in English. However, I believe that there is a place for the 'bad' English reader of Lacan, who may have interesting things to say from outside the encampment - things, in part, which highlight the immense value of Lacan's formulations. As this book progressed, it became clearer to me that the really fruitful dialogue is with Lacan - or possibly 'Lacan', the translated, Anglo-Saxonised figure who features here. And this is, after all, basically an 'Anglo-Saxon' book (to use another Lacanian term), though with a few 'Continental' bells and whistles: Anglo-

Saxon in its style (mostly), its philosophical outlook, and its general sympathy with the Independent stream in psychoanalysis.

It is Anglo-Saxon even though it does not (except occasionally, in passing) address the work of Melanie Klein, which may seem surprising to some readers. In one sense, Kleinian analysis is very body-focused; many of its central terms and concepts derive from early bodily experiences. But it is the body *image*, the body as taken up and transformed through mental phantasy, on which Kleinian theory focuses, and this is a very different (and very important) topic. The fleshly body, it seems to me, does not appear in Klein[1].

It would also be fair to say that this book is Anglo-Saxon in the sense of being (whisper it:) *empiricist* - not a 'positivist' or 'five senses' empiricism, but an *empiricism of cultural production*. By this I mean that I draw on a wide range of disciplines, but ultimately as cultural phenomena. Pieces of neuroscience, of developmental psychology, or indeed of psychoanalytic theory, are positioned as examples of *how things seem to us*, rather than of how things, in some ultimate and incoherent sense, 'are'. I am suggesting two things here: that cultural products inform us about the state of the unconscious, and that psychoanalysis, as a cultural product which claims a particular perspective from which it *comments on* culture, cannot seal itself off from adjacent discourses. Psychoanalysis must articulate itself *in relation to* psychology and neuropsychology; not because the findings of these disciplines are more 'true', but because they are parts of the same body, so to speak. (I say more about this in Chapters 7 and 10.)

Because of all this, I am constantly engaged in what follows in a work of translation between discourses. One strand of Lacanian thinking which I do not accept is the view that translation between languages, in the final analysis, is impossible:

> Psychoanalytic theories are languages… Each psychoanalytic theory articulates these terms in a unique way, as well as introducing new terms of its own, and is thus a unique language, ultimately untranslatable. (Evans 1996: ix)

This slide from 'imperfect' to 'impossible' can only end up in some form of linguistic solipsism. In reality, translation is constant, inevitable, and essential, not only between the 'languages' of psychoanalysis, but between all the many languages in which we talk, and try to talk about being human.

I have therefore chosen not to play safe, but to explore fields of discourse where my understanding is definitely amateur at best. Lacan is one example; another is neuroscience, where I lack the solid base which would allow me, for instance, to distinguish confidently between work at the centre of the discipline, work at the leading edge, and work which is either speculative or outdated. An investigation of body and mind must be multidisciplinary if it is to address the most interesting issues; but in any case, the 'unsound' and 'unorthodox' may speak as much or more for the unconscious as any more central text. And it is the voice of the unconscious which I am trying to hear - and to which I return in my final chapter.

In *The Plural Psyche*, Andrew Samuels suggests that 'when analysts argue, the plural psyche is speaking. Differing points of view reflect the multiplicity of the psyche itself' (Samuels 1989: 5). And again:

> The texts of the depth psychologists, taken as a whole, may unwittingly provide us with documents of the soul. What was intended to be about psyche is of psyche. ... [W]hat gets revealed ... are the central characteristics of psyche itself. This is where clashes between theory are so useful, because the actual clash contains the definitive psychic issue. (Samuels 1989: 217)

I am writing very much from this viewpoint[2] - and extending it beyond what Samuels calls 'depth psychology' to the whole field of human cultural production. If western culture, including much of depth psychology, clashes so strongly and repeatedly on the question of 'mind' vs. 'body', then we must conclude that our unconscious experience contains such a clash:

that the psyche - the Western psyche certainly, but I think not only Western - contains figures much like the 'Soul' and 'Body' of Marvell's extraordinary poem, each regarding the other as gaoler, as mortal enemy.

If this situation is healable, it is certainly not through the 'victory' of one aspect or the other! And this book is not advocating such a victory, even in the limited sphere of psychoanalytic studies. It is written to redress a balance which has swayed too far towards the hegemony of 'mind'; to restore to our awareness the equal centrality of 'body'.

No doubt readers will attempt to work out what position within psychoanalytic theory I represent, what school I identify with. To save you the trouble, I'm playing for a fantasy team: the Reich-Ferenczi All Stars, who coulda been contenders, but got knocked out at an early stage in the tournament. A part of my fantasy is that many prominent figures of the Independent Group would have been signed up to the team, along with others who in reality made their way outside psychoanalysis entirely.[3]

However, the current mood of psychoanalysis, as of psychotherapy in general, seems to be one of making connections and links; of recovering and re-appraising what has been obscured from history; and of moving towards a pluralism of both psyche and psychotherapy. (Of course there is, as always, another, simultaneous but probably more superficial, move towards faction and purges.) Ferenczi's ideas have already been rehabilitated to some considerable extent. I hope to support this process, and extend it to the even more worrisome figure of Reich. Who knows? In a few years the old team, with new players, may be back in action again - and this time not as a fantasy.

To those Reichians, post Reichians and neo-Reichians who take up this book, I should acknowledge that it covers Reich's work only up to the end of the 1930s, and leaves aside entirely his investigation of orgone energy, which he himself saw as his central achievement. I want to emphasise that this is not yet another attempt to discriminate between an early, sane Reich and a later, 'crazy' one. His later work is important to me personally, and, I believe, in the long run for all of us, but it doesn't belong in this particular context.

Chapter One - Foreign Body

> We must presume rather that the psychical trauma - or more precisely the memory of the trauma - acts like a foreign body which long after its entry must continue to be regarded as an agent that is still at work... (Freud and Breuer 1893:56/6)

Missing body

In the index of Etchegoyen's massive work, *Fundamentals of Psychoanalytic Technique* (Etchegoyen 1991), there is no entry for 'body'. Nor is there an entry for 'emotion'. Revealingly, however, there is one entry for 'emotional development, primitive'. The only entry for 'affect' is 'affect, and insight' - in other words, *thinking* about affect. There is no entry for 'instinct', no entry for 'drive', and one entry for 'drives, aggressive, in negative therapeutic reaction'.[1]

How, in a major contemporary analytic textbook (by a subsequent president of the IPA), can the body be wholly ignored, and important body-linked concepts such as affect and drive appear only in a negative and marginal role - as 'primitive', 'aggressive' forces to be tamed by 'insight'? This may be where psychoanalysis has ended up, but it is not how psychoanalysis started out. Freud's initial theory was very much a bodily one, insisting - and this was a considerable part of its shock effect - that mental process up to the most rarefied levels of intellectuality is in fact preoccupied with, and dependent upon, the basic demands of the human organism.

The last sentence of the previous paragraph has embedded within it a metaphor of height and depth so familiar in Western thought as to be semi-invisible: mind/high/advanced ('up to the most rarefied levels'), body/low/primitive ('basic').[2] We sense the same metaphor in Etchegoyen's index; and find it throughout analytic discourse. The goal of psychoanalysis is typically seen as learning to *think feelings*, to keep impulses to action internal, to mentalise and verbalise the somatic. The analyst, as Freud puts it, is:

> in a perpetual struggle with his patient to keep in the psychical sphere all the impulses which the patient would like to direct into the motor sphere. (Freud 1914: 153)

In Freud's day it was intellectually respectable to consider these goals synonymous with 'higher' civilisation. This is no longer a very convincing way to think about culture - it is widely recognised that Western civilisation privileges the mental, the verbal and the physically inexpressive, and that to judge other societies by these standards is cultural imperialism - yet the goal remains welded to psychoanalysis, its implications largely unconsidered. I shall be arguing that psychoanalysis, beginning with aspects of Freud's own work, has repressed the body, allowing it into awareness only in sublimated form, as the *idea* of the body, the 'body image' rather than the physical organism itself and our experience of it. In the terms of my epigraph, this is the water in the mirror rather than the water in the glass.

There are deep paradoxes here. Psychoanalysis, at least from one point of view, is centrally the study of how the human mind confronts the impulses of the body - how it denies, represses, ablates, compromises with, permits into split and partial representation those impulses. At the same time, though, analytic theory lacks any coherent account of the articulation each upon the other, of these two great realms or registers, 'mind' and 'body'.

Perhaps this is not so strange, though, considering that Western thought itself lacks such a coherent account. As Robert M. Young flamboyantly puts it:

> a philosophical scandal lies at the heart of modern thought. Cartesian dualism says that humans are made up of two utterly basically ... different kinds of substances: body and mind. Yet they are defined so that interaction

between them is literally inconceivable.
(Young 1994: 5)

This may be simplified, but it is hardly exaggerated, as a look at more specialist accounts of the 'mind-body problem' demonstrates.[3] And this 'scandal', the 'sheer nonsense of the official account of the relations between body and mind' (Young, 4-5), gives rise to a consequent scandal of analytic metapsychology: the scotomisation of the body.

Psychology and biology

> For the psychical field, the biological field does in fact play the part of the underlying bedrock. (Freud 1937: 252)

This imposing statement from one of Freud's last works falls apart as soon as we look at it closely. How can a 'field' be a 'bedrock'? Well, actually it only 'plays the part of' a bedrock, which leads to the question: why does it 'in fact' play this part, on whose behalf - and what would it be doing if it stopped playing a part and acted naturally? And what is a 'bedrock', anyway? Something one cannot excavate, presumably; something with nothing more fundamental to be found beneath it. An odd state of affairs: if we are going to reduce matters to biology, then why not reduce them to physics - a position Freud often adopts elsewhere. Why shouldn't the *physical* field play the part of the underlying bedrock? And what, in any case, is a 'field'?

Without torturing this unfortunate sentence any further, I want to suggest that its very indefiniteness represents something fundamental (a bedrock?) about Freud's attitude towards the body. Although he consistently portrays the dependence of psychoanalysis upon the body, he also constantly interposes barriers and hurdles between the two, like the bundle of interposed phrases - 'does in fact', 'play the part', 'underlying' - between the psychic and the biological in the sentence above. Examples of these interposed concepts, as we shall see in Chapter Two, are drive, affect, conversion - and the unconscious itself.

Freud's fascination with 'the biological field', his recurring use of models and metaphors drawn from it, exists in parallel with a rigorous insistence on the *absolute difference* between psychoanalysis and biology: an insistence that has been taken up with, if anything, greater energy by later analytic writers.[4]

Freud has repeatedly been attacked as too biological: Frank Sulloway's entire book is devoted to portraying Freud as a 'crypto-biologist' who 'frequently failed to appreciate how extensively biological, Darwinian, and particularly biogenetic assumptions pervaded his psychoanalytic thinking' (Sulloway 1980: 443). Writing from a very different viewpoint, Laplanche tries to 'flush out' Freud's 'pseudo-biology' (Laplanche 1989: 26), with examples of his 'puerile' use of false anatomical and physiological analogies (Ibid 6-7, 17-29). Here and elsewhere Freud is being used as something to identify over and against, so as to establish a psychoanalysis on 'new foundations' - foundations which are other than the biological.[5]

Well, of course psychoanalysis is not biology. In fact there seems so little danger of anyone making this misidentification that one is entitled to ask what is being so sternly defended against. Why would it be so disastrous to allow any close contact between the two? If one thing led to another, what dreadful miscegenation might occur? Or, as the sexual imagery suggests, is it possible that something is being defended against in the analytic sense: that in some way biology has been repressed by and from psychoanalysis?[6]

Touch and abstinence

Certainly analytic theory itself *portrays* such a repression. This is how the psyche itself is shown dealing with the pressure of biology in the form of the drives (see Chapter Two). But more immediately, analytic practice places the body of the client (and conversely, the body of the analyst) most strictly out of bounds. In his presidential address to the 34th International Psychoanalytic Conference in Hamburg, 1985, Adam Limentani said:

It is very easy, though, for psychoanalysts to introduce harmless parameters still compatible with… the analytic process, such as prolonging the session a little; inviting the patient to sit up; offering a tissue to a patient in distress; taking an occasional telephone call, etc. It is another matter to introduce parameters in the form of holding a patient's hand; touching his or her forehead, or any other physical contact… What concerns me here is that psychoanalysts *still wish to claim that it is psychoanalysis when direct and persistent physical contact has been permitted.*
(Limentani 1989: 244, my italics)

What concerns *me* here is to discover the precedent for the idea that 'direct and persistent physical contact' (and what a precisely-chosen word, 'persistent'!) is Just Not Psychoanalysis. (There is an obvious further question as to whether or not it is ethically or technically acceptable or desirable.) Two obvious questions arise: at whom is this stricture aimed, and from whom does it draw its authority?

One target is presumably D W Winnicott, whom many would rate as an authority on the practice of psychoanalysis, and who touched certain clients as an aid to and a support through regression ('literally, through many long hours he held my two hands clasped between his, almost like an umbilical cord' - Little 1990: 44). As we shall see in Chapter Seven, Winnicott also has acutely relevant things to say about 'mind' and 'body'. As for the anti-touch authority, it can hardly be Freud: in his papers on technique he says nothing directly about it, though he clearly does not practice it himself (Freud 1913, 1914, 1915a, 1919). In his correspondence with Ferenczi, he strongly advises against physical contact of a basically affectionate, reassuring kind, and indeed refers to Ferenczi's supposed habit of kissing patients as 'disgraceful', but does not actually forbid it. (Grosskurth 1991: 206-9.) He seems to have been mainly worried about bad publicity, and about how young

analysts might develop the practice. As Anna Freud wrote to
Lou Andreas-Salomé:

> it (touch) is not troubling so long as this
> method is confined to Ferenczi, for he has the
> necessary restraint for it. (Quoted in
> Grosskurth 199: 206n)

Freud's overarching pronouncement on this and all issues of
technique is the following:

> What I am asserting is that this technique is
> the only one suited to my individuality; I do
> not venture to deny that a physician quite dif-
> ferently constituted might find himself dri-
> ven to adopt a different attitude to his
> patients and to the task before him. (Freud
> 1912: 111)

  I will be arguing that the historical development of psychoanalysis has been towards a practice which attracts almost
exclusively those of a single 'constitution', one which has no
room for touch - one shared by its founder.
  It has been surprisingly difficult to find out much about how,
when and where the rejection of touch became canonical. It
seems as though this must have happened in the training pro-
grammes, through ideas passed down in lectures and seminars,
without the issue ever being fully argued, given the answer was
assumed to be already clear. Certainly the analysts and analytic
therapists whom I have heard talking about the question of
touch all seem to use a narrowly stereotypical set of arguments
which probably stem from the same original source.
  The strongest argument against touch (and this is also
Limentani's position) is generally derived from Freud's statement that analysis should be carried out, so far as possible, in a
state of *abstinence*.

> I shall state it as a fundamental principle that
> the patient's need and longing should be

allowed to persist in her [*sic*] in order that
they may serve as forces impelling her to do
work and make changes, and that we must
beware of appeasing these forces by means of
surrogates. (Freud 1915b: 165)

It is suggested, therefore, that touch offers a gratification of
the analysand's desires which is therapeutically counter-pro-
ductive: that it constitutes, in effect, a sort of acting-out. Now it
seems clear that therapy always involves a tension between
some degree of 'privation', and some degree of 'gratification'
(for example, saying 'Hallo' at the start of the session - or, less
trivially, conveying that one understands what is being
expressed to one); and also, that the analysand's unconscious
process will, out of whatever material comes to hand, construct
experiences of 'privation' and of 'gratification' (of coldness and
warmth, hate and love) appropriate to that analysand's history
and expectations - appropriate, in other words, to unfolding the
transference. Ferenczi makes essentially the same point in his
description of a 'twofold method of frustration and indulgence':

However great the relaxation, the analyst will
not gratify the patient's actively aggressive or
sexual wishes or many of their other exaggerated demands. There will be plenty of oppor-
tunity to learn renunciation and adaptation.
(Ferenczi 1930: 301)

In other words, decisions about touch, along with a whole
range of other parameters, must be made on technical grounds
alone; they cannot be treated as pre-ordained and unthinkable,
however distressing this may be for therapists 'of a certain constitution'. The question of abuse is, of course, quite distinct from
this. It may well be that some therapists as well as clients are
unable or unwilling to handle (so to speak) their feelings around
touch - and, therefore, are very wise to avoid it.[7] On the other
side of the coin, it may equally well be that some therapists are
only able to maintain their liberal position on sexual matters,

fantasies, and so on in a 'state of abstinence' - the analyst as priest. (See also the discussion in Chapter Five below.)

Freud and Ferenczi famously disagreed on these matters, and this disagreement recreates itself in modern controversies around regression, an issue deeply bound up with physical and symbolic holding (Stewart 1989). We should note at this point how thinking about the body leads directly into thinking about the therapeutic relationship, transference and countertransference, and related issues.

Oddly enough, the person who introduced touch as a therapeutic technique, Wilhelm Reich himself, unlike most of his 'descendants' was rather unwilling to use touch as support and comfort. In this and several other ways, he was in fact a psychoanalyst of the old school. Perhaps this is partly because Reich's own work - again, unlike many 'Reichians' - was never regressive in orientation.

> In my view, it was a remnant of Reich's psychoanalytic superego and reflected his fear of association with pornography that he only occasionally used physical contact in a supportive, comforting way. In the 1940s, Alexander Lowen, then a young therapist in training with Reich, mentioned that he had inadvertently left his hand resting on the patient's back, and the patient had commented on how good it felt. Reich reflected, then commented without committing himself: 'The analysts would call that seductive.' (Sharaf 1983: 235)

Much more important for my purpose, though, is the use of physical intervention *as technique*, as an alternative to or extension of free association and resistance interpretation. One might imagine that this was unthought of by Freud, were it not for this passage from the Freud-Fliess letters:

> Yesterday Mrs K again sent for me because of

cramplike pains in her chest; generally it has
been because of headaches. In her case I have
invented a strange therapy of my own: I
search for sensitive areas, press on them, and
thus provoke fits of shaking that free her.
(Freud to Fliess, March 13th 1895, Masson
1985: 120)

Towards a body-centred analysis?

As we shall see, touch as an analytic technique rather than simply as comfort was introduced by Wilhelm Reich. My own original training was as a Reichian therapist; and my practice still
includes a good deal of body contact between therapist and
client, both supportive and as 'bodywork'. The history of
Reich's anathematisation by the IPA - long-forgotten by analysts
- was part of my therapeutic inheritance. (See for an account
Sharaf 1983: 175-91, summarised below in Chapter Four.) My
training introduced me to Reich as a humanistic psychotherapist, a 'growth work' practitioner (Totton and Edmondson
1988). What I did not understand until re-reading Reich in the
context of my study of analytic theory, was just how much of an
analyst he was - and, indeed, remained, even after the break with
institutional analysis; how deeply his work and thought was
informed by the themes and issues of Freudian therapy - and, in
turn, how much Freudian therapy needs some of Reich's
insights.

As examples of Freudian themes in Reich's writings, Freud's
image of the protoplasmic vesicle in *Beyond the Pleasure Principle*
becomes central to Reich's vision and mode of thinking. Freud's
statement in *The Ego and the Id* that the ego is 'first and foremost
a bodily ego' (Freud 1923: 364/26) is equally strongly taken up
(see Chapter Three); and Reich rescues and foregrounds Freud's
original concepts of 'actual neurosis', of physiological libido, of
anxiety as converted libido, and of affect discharge. The question of what Reich can offer psychoanalysis forms one of the
major themes of this book.

Within psychoanalysis, however, the situation is more conflictual than it may at first appear. Looking deeply at analytic theory and practice - particularly in the earlier years of the century - we can make out the cloudy shape of an 'alternative psychoanalysis' - analysis as it might have become, and to some extent, in some practitioners' hands, still is: a body-centred, body-honouring theory and practice, which would have as its goal a reconciliation of the different experiences, the 'split complementarities' (Benjamin 1996, passim), which we tend to label 'mind' and 'body'. We can see how crucial, and in many ways disastrous, were the few years in the early 1930s when Ferenczi was suppressed, Reich was expelled, and a mentalistic ego psychology took central stage. (During the same period, we may note, Lacan gave his first Congress paper.)

In the early 30s, then, institutional psychoanalysis had its own 'psychical trauma'. When the smoke had cleared and the blood had been mopped up, analysis showed a very different face to the world. By the end of World War Two, the process of becoming respectable was more or less complete. This of course meant that very different kinds of people became psychoanalysts, a process that Maxwell Gitelson laments in a perceptive paper from the 1950s, 'Therapeutic Problems in the Analysis of the "Normal" Candidate' (Gitelson 1954), where he points out that the new status of analysis in the USA was attracting clients for whom:

> normality, a symptom, actually is not suffered from as such. On the contrary, it is capable of earning social rewards of which the first is acceptance as a candidate. To no other symptom does such a large quota of secondary gain attach. (Gitelson 1989: 418)

Gitelson quotes Robert Knight in his 1952 Presidential Address to the American Psychoanalytic Association:

> In the 1920s and early 1930s those who undertook psycho-analytic training were of a somewhat different breed from the current crop of candidates... Many analysts were

trained who might today be rejected. Many training analyses were relatively short, and many gifted individuals with definite neuroses or character disorders were trained... In contrast, perhaps the majority of students of the past decade or so have been 'normal' characters, or perhaps one should say had 'normal character disorders'. They are not introspective, are inclined to read only the literature that is assigned in institute courses, and wish to get through with the training requirements as rapidly as possible. (Gitelson 1989: 414)

This state of affairs can certainly be extended to the present (and applied to other forms of psychotherapy besides psychoanalysis). Among its many effects has been a lack of interest in metapsychology (so that the parlously incoherent base of psychoanalysis is unrecognised[8]); a tendency to unquestioningly identify with the 'normal' values of our culture; and a positive disinterest in questioning orthodoxy - most particularly, around 'scandalous' issues like touch and body-centred work. These effects combine with the amnesiac effects of trauma - the institutional traumatisation of psychoanalysis through the process of expulsion and splitting to which I have referred. Elizabeth Kurzweil talks of 'the method of *Totschweigen* (deathly silence) about dissidents' practiced within psychoanalytic institutions (Kurzweil 1993: 8). This is of course on one level a process of political control, paralleled in Stalinist Russia and other totalitarian societies, but I would suggest that it is at the same time a process of shock-induced scotomisation. As Freud and Breuer suggested (1893: 56/6), 'the memory of the trauma... like a foreign body... long after its entry must continue to be regarded as an agent that is still at work'.

Therapies and character strategies

There is a personal, passionate side to this argument, and my indignation at Reich's treatment by the psychoanalytic institutions is only the smallest part of it. What is most important to me is my awareness of the immense gains that I and numerous clients have derived from a body-centred form of therapy. I think particularly of two client groups: those whose primary experience is bodily, proprioceptive - who 'live in their bodies', and must be met there for useful work to take place - and, on the other hand, those who 'live in their heads', whose primary experience is mental, cognitive, and whose bodies are crying out to be recognised and valued and communicated with.

It is in the second group that I place myself: a 'natural' intellectual - which, of course, means someone who has learnt to experience the intellect as their 'natural' habitat! I believe one of Reich's great contributions is his theory of character (see Chapter Eight), which potentially offers a systematic, body-centred, developmentally-based, non-judgmental way to understand differences in human modes of perception and experience.

The belief - the experience - that mind is 'higher' and of more value than body is hegemonic in our culture. In fact, the whole 'higher' valuation of 'highness' may derive from the fact that the head is physically higher than the body. The head is important not because it contains the brain (the physical location of which is irrelevant, since it models the whole body), but because it contains the eyes and ears, the most abstract and 'mental' of our senses. But this higher valuation is also a character position: a predilection, a core strategy alongside other core strategies, and no more or less true than other strategies which privilege, for example, bodily experience, or emotion, or intuition.

> It is commonly assumed that human intellect has a solely objective function and that it is directed towards the world... Two things are overlooked here: 1) the intellectual function itself is a vegetative [i.e. bodily] activity; and 2) the intellectual function may have an affective charge whose intensity is no less than

any purely affective impulse... Intellectual
activity can be structured and directed in
such a way that it looks like a most cunning-
ly operating apparatus whose purpose is precisely to avoid cognition. (Reich 1972: 305-6)

The character structure ('constitution' is Freud's word)
which privileges intellectual experience, however, is dominant
in analytic circles. It sets up a circularity of theory and experience which attracts those of similar structure and repels (or
expels) all others. Thus, inevitably, other forms of therapy develop to accommodate those who privilege, or feel the need to
experience, other aspects of human existence. Unfortunately,
these other therapies tend to be as one-sided as psychoanalysis:
they tend to exclude and devalue the intellectual. As with any
groups that speak different languages, communication tends to
be minimal.

Thus my hope is to contribute something towards bridging
the abyss of fundamental incomprehension which opens so easily between different worldviews - the more so when they are
deeply anchored in character structure, of which we are largely
unconscious.

Two sorts of unconscious

I have just used the term 'unconscious' in a way which bestrides
two meanings that may, or may not, be viewed as quite distinct.
The 'Freudian unconscious' is repressed: we do not know it
because we *will* not know it, *must* not know it. What we may call
the 'cognitive unconscious', the sense in which the term is
nowadays employed in thinking about intelligence and its prop-
erties, is unconscious rather in the sense of 'non-conscious' (not
quite 'preconscious' in Freud's sense, since it may be structural-
ly inaccessible to consciousness). It refers instead to all those
aspects of our internal neurological/perceptual/decision-mak-
ing functioning which operate 'automatically'.

This covers everything from brainstem homeostatic control
of heartbeat and peristalsis, up through semi-autonomic func-

tions like breathing, to complex processes of perceptual analysis and evaluation of data, where we are aware only of the end result - the image of 'tree', 'woman', 'danger', or whatever - not at all of the process. (See e.g. Hunt 1982.) There is overwhelmingly clear experimental evidence[9] that preconscious evaluation of sensory data - the whole 'decision' about whether and how to allow it into conscious representation - is influenced by unconscious factors (in the full Freudian sense). In other words, perceptual information which associates with repressed material, and thus produces anxiety, tends to be kept from entering conscious awareness.

What we conclude about the relationship between 'mind' and 'body' has a lot to do with how we view the relationship between these two kinds of unconscious. For example, the preconscious processes of evaluation can be considered physiologically, as bodily (neurological) events (Dixon 1981: 166). When we get to this kind of level, the mind/body frontier becomes impossible to police. *Perception itself* is processed and filtered in accordance with the ego's defensive mechanisms, so no line can be drawn between the Freudian unconscious and the cognitive non-conscious - or between either of these, and the physiology and neurology of the body.

Freud himself has more than one view on this issue. At times he certainly portrays the unconscious as 'the proper mediator between the somatic and the mental' (letter to Groddeck, Groddeck 1977: 38) - in other words, as something that might include subliminal perceptual processes, and even autonomic bodily functions. This is the view which Reich takes up.

At other times, Freud has a much more 'mind-centred' view of the unconscious as a linguistic function - the aspect of his work which has been taken up and made central by Lacan, for whom the unconscious has really nothing to do with the body, being structured instead like a language. So really we have three 'kinds of unconscious' on the table: the data-processing unconscious, the Freud/Reich bodily unconscious, and the Freud/Lacan linguistic unconscious. One question before us is: how do these three relate? Are they three different (hypothetical) entities - in which case, could all three exist? Or are they three ways of looking at the same thing - in which case, what are the different functions of each approach?

I want to suggest, though, that all these arguments - and the whole philosophical controversy about the 'mind-body problem' - are irremediably behind the times, conducted either before or in ignorance of enormously important research and thinking which redefines the central terms of the debate.

I am referring on the one hand to information theory and systems theory[10], with their redefinition and re-description of 'mind' as an intrinsic function of any sufficiently complex organisation (see Bateson 1973 e.g. 458); and on the other hand (though not unconnectedly) to recent and ongoing explorations of the *observable* - as opposed to hypothetical - capacities and discriminations of human infants[11], best summarised in an analytic context by Daniel Stern (Stern 1985). Chapter Seven explores all this in more detail.

Looked at in these two lights, the best we can say of a lot of analytic metapsychology is 'this turns out not to be the case'. Of course, current thinking will certainly be supplanted by new ideas - and probably soon, since it has very much the flavour of work in progress. But we will not be going back to Cartesian dualism, nor to materialist reductionism, nor to a view of the human infant as not fully human in the absence of language, as in some way merged with mother and environment. Like phlogiston and the crystalline spheres, these things have turned out not to be the case.

To take just one example of research which is enormously relevant to analytic ideas about infancy, Meltzoff and Moore have established that infants as young as 42 *minutes* are capable of imitating adult expressions. From a series of experiments with babies in this and older age-ranges, Meltzoff and his associates demonstrate that imitation is a voluntary, goal-directed, self-correcting act. (For example, when adults protrude their tongue to the side, infants either do the same, or protrude their tongue forward while turning their head to the side, to achieve the same effect by an easier route.) They hypothesise that our intuitive view of what is going on is in fact valid: that 'infants see other people in terms of human acts and, in imitating them, intend to match these acts.' (Meltzoff & Moore 1995: 54). Babies also respond positively to *having their own expressions imitated* by adults.

This and much other work demolishes the traditional view of 'profound adualism between infant and environment' (Butterworth 1995: 90), a view which psychoanalysis has until very recently incorporated into its conceptual base. It has become clear that infants differentiate *from the start* between their own bodies and the world (Butterworth 1995: 93-5), and that their development *from the start* is organised around (working both out of and towards) a distinction from, and a relationship with, other human beings.[12]

So is psychoanalysis salvageable? Much modern, within-the-paradigm, conventional analytic theory, I would argue, is not salvageable, or only with so much reworking as to not be worth the trouble. It incorporates assumptions about human beings so centrally insupportable, incoherent, and at odds with other disciplines as to render its theories useless. Clinical effectiveness, of course, is a quite separate issue; but there too, as I have already indicated, I believe psychoanalysis to be seriously faulty because of what it excludes.

Both theoretically and clinically, though, Freud and his immediate followers are a different case. I will be seeking to show that Freud, in the absence of an information-based model of 'mind' and 'body', was in effect working as if he had one, was struggling to say something very different from what his vocabulary allowed him to say. If 'the body' became repressed, and hence unconscious, it was also struggling to return, struggling to take control of the language of psychoanalysis. My whole argument is that to give a central place to 'the body' is not to demote 'the mind', but to exit the whole illusory Cartesian dichotomy between the two. This is where the 'other psychoanalysis' whose lineaments I am tracing will tend. There is something here very much worth saving, that offers a central and vital contribution to the revolution in our understanding of human beings which is currently (and always) in progress.

Body Talk

It may appear that I am ignoring that point of view - both within and outside psychoanalytic thought - which privileges the linguistic as definitional of the human, and argues that since we can never leave language once we enter it, never talk to ourselves without using words, it makes no sense to speak of a non-linguistic reality. The Lacanian version of this position would be that to speak of the organismic body as anything other than an object of external perception is to speak of the Real, of which we cannot speak, in much the same sense that we cannot know what is happening beyond the Einsteinian Event Horizon, or cannot discover both the mass and the movement of an electron.[13]

It is not my task here to do justice to this approach. But I need to make clear that, although I disagree with it, I recognise its force, and the great richness of its results. The domain of language is enormous, and, *from its own perspective*, universal. My position, though, is that there are other perspectives - not necessarily conflicting, but simply different. Within the human territory, there are a number of places to stand, and each of them is the centre while we are standing there.

Certainly, I am using language to describe this situation, which can only be experienced as such in and through language. But when all is said and done, so to speak, the map is still not the territory. The fact that we can (and, in order to register them in consciousness[14], must) *say things about* non-linguistic experiences does not mean that they are 'really' linguistic. I return to this in Chapters Seven and Ten, but it seems to me to say a great deal about the state of affairs in psychoanalytic studies that I have to labour this point simply in order to clear a space to start.

The List

One aspect of linguistic experience to which we must attend is its tendency to dichotomise, to digitalise analogue experience (Wilden 1972). Earlier in this chapter I referred to the persistent metaphor of height/depth, and the way in which it is consistently linked to the polarity of mind/body in such a way that 'mind' and 'height' are seen to correspond and, conversely, 'body' and 'depth', due to an implied logic that 'as a is to b, so x is to y'[15]. 'Height/depth' and 'mind/body' are both part of a much longer list, part of which runs:

> mind/body
> adult/infant
> civilised/primitive
> conscious/unconscious
> psychology/biology
> culture/nature
> male/female

This list is *very* long, and no-one in our culture can fail to recognise how it is supposed to proceed - no-one would accidentally (though they might deliberately and subversively) reverse any of the pairs and, for instance, align 'mind' with 'female' or 'conscious' with 'infant'. A considerable proportion of supposed theoretical production consists simply in humming along with this tune, using the list as a sort of thinking-machine, reading off various supposed correspondences and drawing out the implications. Freud was uncritically committed to this list and sometimes used it to do his thinking for him (see the discussion in Chapter Two of Freud's metaphors for the unconscious), even though some features of his work problematise it.

Another section of the List - it deserves capitalisation - is crucially relevant for discussing the body/mind issue:

> body/mind
> body/brain
> feeling/thought
> feelings/words
> experience/language
> infant/adult

A number of confusions derive from treating these pairs as

interchangeable; for example, the idea that the relationship between *brain* and body is analogous to that between *mind* and body; and also, that the relationship between feeling and thought is analogous to that between experience and language. In the following chapter, we shall begin to see some of the effects of these assumptions.

Chapter Two - Body Represented

> The theory of the drives is so to say our
> mythology. Drives[1] are mythical entities,
> magnificent in their indefiniteness. In our
> work we cannot for a moment disregard
> them, yet we are never sure that we are see-
> ing them clearly. (Freud 1932: 127/95)

'Like other natural things'

As we have seen, Western thought even today lacks a coherent
account of the mind-body relationship. If Freud had waited for
philosophy, he would never have got started. Any great theory
depends for its greatness on what it *assumes*, what it leaves
'magnificent in [its] indefiniteness'. And what Freud assumes -
the assumption itself is magnificent - is precisely this: 'mind'
and 'body' are both *real, distinct,* and *related*[2].

Like every assumption, this one performs work; work which
takes its shape in the opening words, scribbled in ecstatic haste
on the train from Berlin, of what is arguably the first analytic
text: the *Project for a Scientific Psychology*. These words deserve
careful reading.

> The intention is to furnish a natural-scientific
> psychology: that is, to represent psychologi-
> cal processes as quantitatively determinate
> states of specifiable material particles, thus
> making those processes perspicuous and free
> from contradiction. (Freud 1950: 295, transla-
> tion slightly modified)

Although Freud soon abandoned this 'intention', he never abandoned his position that it was in principle *possible*: that the psychological is wholly material - or, more precisely (crucially so),
that it can be *represented* as such. To do so, for Freud, would be
to render the psyche 'perspicuous' - to render it clear, transpar-

ent, to achieve a gnosis wherein:

> the barriers were suddenly raised, the veils
> fell away, and it was possible to see through
> from the details of the neuroses to the deter-
> minants of consciousness. Everything
> seemed to fit together, the gears were in
> mesh, the thing gave one the impression that
> it was really a machine and would soon run
> itself... Of course I cannot contain myself
> with delight. (Letter to Fliess 20.10.1895, in
> Masson 1985: 146)

Not only is the *theory* a machine that can 'run itself', so is
what it models: the human psychic apparatus *as a representation
of* the human somatic apparatus. This capacity for representation, in fact, *is* the relationship between psyche and soma. The
unstated, intermediate model is clearly the representation of the
body in the brain (the '"cortical homunculus" of the anatomists'
to which Freud refers in *The Ego and the Id* [Freud 1923: 365/26]).
In the same way that the localisation of brain function inscribes
a distorted homunculus on the surface of the cortex so, in
Freud's view, the psyche is a reinscription of somatic processes
in neuronal processes (themselves, of course, specialised somatic elements).

To put it succinctly: in the *Project*, Freud represents Mind as
Body mapped onto Brain, by means of an operation which
transforms quantity into quality. 'Mind' here would be another
word for the qualitative transcription of somatic experience
(i.e., perceptual data). The defining attribute of the central nervous system is its ability - and requirement - to 'keep off *quantity*' (1950: 309, original italics).

Although this representation (so Freud believes) clarifies the
psyche, it is itself not clear *to* the psyche. For the first of many
times, Freud tells us that we do not know what we are.

> It follows, from the postulate of conscious-
> ness providing neither complete nor trust-

> worthy knowledge of the neuronal processes,
> that *these are in the first instance to be regarded*
> *to their whole extent as unconscious* [*unbewusst*]
> and are to be inferred like other natural
> things. (1950: 308, my italics)

Precisely those data on which an account of consciousness is to
be founded are themselves unavailable to consciousness -
unknown, *unbewusst*, in shadow. It is rather as if the cortical
homunculus were self-aware - yet, obviously, unconscious of its
own status as a representation. (Nowadays the image would be
of an artificial intelligence lodged on a computer hard disk.)

It is an interesting paradox or 'contradiction': in representing
the psyche *as* soma ('quantitatively determinate states of speci-
fiable material particles'), Freud is giving an account of the psyche as a representation (transcription) *of* soma - but one which is
occult to itself. A mirror in which no-one is looking. As he puts it
much later in 'The Unconscious':

> In psycho-analysis there is no choice for us
> but to assert that mental processes are in
> themselves unconscious, and to liken the per-
> ception of them by means of consciousness to
> the perception of the external world by
> means of the sense-organs. (Freud 1915a:
> 172/171)

Freud here moves away from the natural-scientific 'third-person' viewpoint, but not quite to a phenomenological 'first-person' viewpoint (see Dennett 1990: 70). He no longer just looks at
the psyche from the *outside* (so that subjective evidence becomes
only hearsay), but neither can he rely on just experiencing it
from the *inside*, since we do not know what we are. Much later
he describes very clearly and acutely the synthesis, the doubled
perspective, crucial to the unfurling of psychoanalysis away
from its natural-scientific stem. His procedure, he says in the
Autobiographical Study, is only 'treating one's own mental life as
one had always treated other people's.' (Freud 1925a: 215/32; cf.
1926b: 320/219.)

'Between the two'

'It will be observed,' writes Strachey in a footnote to the passage quoted above, about unconscious neuronal processes, 'that this is a statement made about *physiological* entities - "neuronal processes". Some time was to elapse before Freud could make exactly the same statement about *psychical* events.'

Strachey greatly underestimates the importance of the fact that for Freud, this is indeed 'exactly the same statement'. What changes is the third person/first person viewpoint. Just before the passage quoted, Freud underlines that he is 'treating psychical processes as *something that could dispense with this awareness through consciousness*, as something that exists independently of such awareness'. Consciousness, therefore, is a secondary representation of the unconscious (unknown) psychic - a *faulty* representation, which Freud hopes to rectify, to make 'perspicuous'.

The *Project*'s account of the relationship between soma and psyche represents a bridging-point in Freud's thinking. In 'The Neuro-Psychoses of Defence', written the previous year, Freud assigned quite complex phenomena - the splitting of idea and affect in neurosis - entirely to the somatic realm.

> These are processes which occur without consciousness. Their existence can only be presumed, but cannot be proved by any clinical-psychological analysis. Perhaps it would be more correct to say that these processes are not of a psychical nature at all, that they are physical processes whose psychical consequences present themselves as if what is expressed by the terms 'separation of the idea from its affect' and 'false connection' of the latter had really taken place. (Freud 1894: 53, my italics)

By the time of writing the *Project*, Freud is becoming clear that making a distinction between what we might call 'psychical mental processes" and 'physical mental processes' contributes nothing. What allows him to do without this distinction is the concept of the psychical unconscious, which emerges out of his new emphasis on *representation*:

> ...to represent psychological processes as quantitatively determinate states of specifiable material particles, thus making those processes perspicuous and free from contradiction. (1950: 295, translation slightly modified)

Freud, then, is already carving out a space (one more commodious, in fact, than he sometimes allows himself later [see Freud 1915a: 170]) for unconscious mental events, for the fundamental analytic experience of discovering ourselves to consist of something other than what we know and perceive. In this context, in fact, unconscious mind - thought without a 'thinker' - is far easier to 'represent' than conscious mind, which he is describing as basically a neural monitoring system, a reflexive device for 'keeping off quantity' (Freud 1950: 309), for minimising internal and external stimulus. The reflexivity of consciousness is a by-product of its homeostatic goal:

> It would seem as though the characteristic of quality (that is, conscious sensation) comes about only where quantities are as far as possible excluded. (Freud1950: 309)

Only by 'complicated and far from perspicuous' - that word again - 'hypotheses', Freud admits, is he able to model consciousness in neurological terms.

> No attempt, *of course*, can be made to explain *how it is* that excitatory processes *bring consciousness along with them*. It is only a question of establishing a coincidence between the characteristics of consciousness that are known to us and processes... which vary in parallel with them. (Freud 1950: 311, my italics)

Here is Freud's assumption at its grandest. The 'coincidence' he seeks to establish is one of *representation* - one might almost say, a rhetorical one- a capacity to *describe* consciousness in a certain way. But Freud realises he can't quite leave it there:

> A word on the relation of this theory of con-
> sciousness to others. According to an
> advanced mechanistic theory, consciousness
> is a mere appendage to physiologico-psychi-
> cal processes and its omission would make
> no difference to the passage. According to
> another theory, consciousness is the subjec-
> tive side of all psychical events and is thus
> inseparable from the physiological mental
> process. *The theory developed here lies between*
> *the two.* Here consciousness is the subjective
> side of one part of the physical processes in
> the nervous system... and the omission of
> consciousness does not leave psychical
> events unaltered... (Freud 1950: 311, my ital-
> ics)

We could spend a lot of time on this passage. What I want to stress here is the characteristic of *lying between* which is so cru-cial to Freud's approach to body-mind relations. Not only his theory of consciousness, but consciousness itself, is seen as lying between - not wholly either 'body stuff' or 'mind stuff', but the 'subjective *side of*' - whatever that may be - 'brought along by' a bodily process. It is clear how Freud's terminology, though cutting-edge for its time, *prevents him from thinking what he is trying to think,* which I believe to be a theory of information in complex systems.

Confronted with the limits of his terminology Freud soon, very sensibly, starts trying to think something else. He drops his whole embedding of the psychic in the neurological ('the phys-iological mental process'), while keeping up the imagery, the *representation* of the *Project*: the neurological *metaphor*: networks, paths, *Bahnung, Besetzung,* preserving the basic view of consciousness as a *faulty representation* - gapped, scarred, blurred, erased, reinscribed, bandaged, screened... But if he drops neurology, he cannot drop the body. The body is what the psyche 'represents', the 'quantity' from which 'quality' is refined. Over and over again, Freud describes how the psyche seeks to deal with 'endogenous stimuli' - with energy originating in the body, energy which must be *stepped down*, as electrical current is stepped down between power station and socket, in a gradual transition between soma and psyche.

It is clear that we are dealing with more than one model of the body-mind relationship. In one picture, *energy* moves from one system to another system, passing barriers and filters as it does so. (Like water making its way from reservoir to glass.) In the other picture, one system, together with changes that occur in it, is *represented* in, modelled by, mapped onto, another system. What moves is, therefore, in contemporary terminology, *information*. (Like the image of the glass of water reflected in the mirror.) Are these two versions compatible? Can both 'glass' and 'mirror' hold water? We need to find out more about the relationship between them - by looking at some of the concepts that Freud interposes between soma and psyche: drive,[2] affect, and conversion.

It is important to realise that the unconscious *itself* is, among other things, such a bridging concept - 'the proper mediator between the somatic and the mental, perhaps the long-sought "missing link"' as Freud wrote to Groddeck (Groddeck 1977: 38). As we shall see when we look at this letter again, Freud never actually wants to *close* the gap between the two. Each 'link' or 'mediation' he proposes acts also as a wedge to push the two apart. Again, what is noteworthy is the way in which Freud's mind-body theory *itself models the relationship it hypothesises*. In the letter to Groddeck, Freud is identifying the unconscious as 'proper mediator' both in the *theory*, and in the *human being*. This collapse of theory into its own object, along with the wedging-apart of psyche and soma, are constant features of Freud's approach to mind and body, giving his portrayal a curiously elastic quality.

Drive

> The theory of the drives is the most impor-
> tant but at the same time the least complete
> portion of psychoanalytic theory. (Freud 190:
> 83n/168n)

This is a footnote added in 1924 to the following passage (itself
added in 1915) in the *Three Essays on Sexuality*:

> By a 'drive' is provisionally to be understood
> the psychical representative of an endoso-
> matic, continuously flowing source of stimu-
> lation... *The concept of drive is thus one of those
> lying on the frontier between the mental and the
> physical.* The simplest and likeliest assump-
> tion as to the nature of drives would seem to
> be that in itself a drive is without quality,
> and, so far as mental life is concerned, is to be
> regarded as a measure of *the demand made
> upon the mind for work...* The source of a drive
> is a process of excitation occurring in an
> organ and the immediate aim of the drive lies
> in the removal of this organic stimulus.
> (Freud 1905: 82-3/121-2, my italics)

The origins of this passage in the *Project*[3] are apparent - for
example, the reference to 'quality', and the portrayal of the
drive as seeking to restore a lower level of stimulus, 'demanding' that the mind performs the 'work' necessary for this purpose. The concept of 'frontier' (*Grenz*) is an important one for
Freud - crucial to both the topographic and the dynamic models of the psyche; it already appears in the *Project* on the neuronal level, as the 'contact-barrier' (what we now call the neural synapse):

> ...the structure of neurones makes it probable
> that the resistances are all to be located in the
> contacts, which in this way assume the value
> of barriers. (Freud 1950: 298)

Here, in germ, in the ambiguity of 'between' - both a connection and a separation, a 'contact' and a 'barrier' - is the dialectic of the symptom, both a barrier *against* and a contact *with* unconscious desire. Freud's vision of the symptom seems to have its origin in the discovery of the synapse. Truly, as he says, 'the hypothesis of contact-barriers is fruitful in many directions' (Freud 1950: 298).

But the exact positioning of the drive in relation to this 'frontier' is highly variable. In the passage just quoted from the *Three Essays*, the drive aims to remove the organic stimulus. Elsewhere, however, it is *identified with* the organic stimulus, becoming itself the pressure which the psyche is trying to transform, the energy it is trying to step down. Sometimes the drive is a mental entity, at other times only the 'drive representative', the 'drive idea', is mental in nature - the glass of water reflected in the mirror that Reich describes in my epigraph. (See Strachey's footnote at the beginning of Freud 1915d: 108-9/143-5.) There is a multiplication of entities, in other words, which in effect *thickens* the 'frontier', making it more of a no-man's land, a territory rather than a dividing line, putting the glass *beyond* the mirror...The more Freud tries to use the drive to separate psyche and soma, the more he interconnects them; the more he tries to interconnect them, the more he separates them - again, that elasticity.

The footnote quoted above refers us to *Beyond the Pleasure Principle* and *The Ego and the Id* for 'further contributions' to drive theory. What we find there, of course, is a recasting of the fundamental polarity of the drives as between, not survival and sexuality, but Life and Death. The specific character and vicissitudes of the drives are not our concern here but what is relevant is that, as Freud tiptoes into metaphysics, he simultaneously wishes he could:

> ...replace the psychological terms by physiological or chemical ones. It is true that they too are only part of a figurative language; but it is one with which we have long been familiar and which is perhaps a simpler one as well. (Freud 1920: 334/60)

He yearns to reinstate the project of the *Project*, to represent the psychic as material - but in the full knowledge that this is only replacing one representation, one discourse, with another. This, in a sense, would constitute Freud's answer to Laplanche's powerful critique of the 'pseudo-biology' which is the controlling metaphor of *Beyond the Pleasure Principle* (Laplanche 1976 52: 1989: 27)[4]: essentially that he is speaking in metaphors. Yet in the next sentence, Freud reverses his ground and reveals the full ambivalence of his own relationship with biology:

> On the other hand it should be made quite clear that the uncertainty of our speculation has been greatly increased by the necessity for borrowing from the science of biology... [The] answers it will return in a few dozen years to the questions we have put to it... may be of a kind which will blow away the whole of our artificial structure of hypotheses. (Freud 1920: 334/60, my italics)

This was, of course, exactly what happened, though Freud's 'artificial structure' was not 'blown away', but simply decoupled from a biology which no longer supported it - if indeed it ever had. The casting-adrift of Freud's ideas from their supposed objective grounding in biology allows us to see more clearly the nature of this 'artificial structure'. The unexpected modern reformulation of biology in terms of information theory has reopened the space for a fertile connection with Freud's early thinking, which I am suggesting gropes in this same direction. At least one modern neurologist, Karl Pribram, has identified the Project as 'a psychobiological Rosetta Stone'. (Pribram 1968: 398).

Here and elsewhere, it is constantly in relation to the *drives* that Freud appeals to the 'figurative' nature of scientific terminology. In *Why War?* he writes:

> It may perhaps seem to you as though our theories [of the drives] are a kind of mythol-

ogy, and in the present case not even an
agreeable one. But does not every science
come in the end to a kind of mythology like
this? (Freud 1933: 358/211)

These are not just momentary or late thoughts, however little
Freud normally casts himself as a relativist. For instance, the
whole opening section of *Instincts and Their Vicissitudes* aims at
providing an epistemological justification for the 'magnificent
indefiniteness' of the concept of the drive:

Such ideas - which will later become the basic
concepts of the science... must at first necessarily possess some degree of *indefiniteness*;
there can be no question of any clear delimi-
tation of their content... Thus, strictly speaking, they are in the nature of conventions -
although... determined by their having significant relations to the empirical material, relations that we seem to sense before we can
clearly recognise and demonstrate them.
(Freud 1915c: 113/117, my italics)[5]

He proceeds to give a description of the drives which is very
similar to those we have already examined: a *continuous endogenous stimulus*, originating in an *organ*, and giving rise to the need
for *mental work* to restore a *lower level of stimulation*.

We have seen that Freud's picture of the drives, however
'indefinite', is also highly complex. It appears in at least three
versions:

(1) The drive as a *pressure* from the biological into the psyche
- a force which requires stepping down and breaking up into
more manageable pieces. (Energy model: the water in the glass.)

(2) The drive as a *representation* of biological energy in psychic terms; this picture being *itself* a representation in psychic
terms of what is happening in (1). (Information model: the
water in the mirror.)

(3) The drive, in *Beyond the Pleasure Principle*, as a sort of

instantiation of psychic/cosmic processes in biological, cellular processes, which Freud justifies by saying that these terms are, themselves, merely 'figurative', merely representations. (Metaphysical model: a hall of mirrors reflecting water and glasses, glasses and water.)

We can also see that Freud establishes a sort of Jacob's ladder of intermediate concepts or entities (and the ambiguity between the two is precisely one of my points) as the channel through which energy or information flows between soma and psyche. It is striking that traffic 'up' the ladder from body to mind seems to Freud obvious and not in need of explanation - though it does require (and constitute) *representation*, which the *Project* attempts to provide. This sort of 'conversion', of soma into psyche, while complex, is not seen as basically mysterious; it is simply in the nature of somatic stimulus, it seems, to 'rise' into mental representation. Flow of information or energy *downwards*, however - as in hysterical conversion - strikes Freud as mysterious, *unheimlich*[6]. All of this - including the metaphor of 'upwards' and 'downwards' which is quite clearly embedded in Freud's thinking - will bear careful examination.

Affect

> What is alone of value in mental life is rather the feelings. No mental forces are significant unless they possess the characteristic of arousing feelings. Ideas are only repressed because they are associated with the release of feelings which ought not to occur. (Freud 1907: 49/49)

Freud has striking difficulty with the concept of affect, and my argument is that this difficulty has to do with its unavoidably *bodily* quality[7]. Although right from the start the eliciting of affect is a necessary condition of analytic cure (Freud and Breuer 1893: 57-8/7-8), Freud spends very little time exploring what affect *is*, certainly compared with its enormous, if cloudy, role in later analytic and psychotherapeutic theory. When he does deal with it, what he has to say is hardly 'perspicuous and free from contradiction'.

The Unconscious includes a whole section on 'unconscious feelings', in which Freud links affect with drive, asking himself 'are there... unconscious drive impulses, emotions and feelings...?' He begins his answer with the drives, making the distinction we have outlined above between the drive itself and its psychic representation:

> I am in fact of the opinion that the antithesis of conscious and unconscious is not applicable to drives. A drive can never become the object of consciousness - only the idea that represents the drive can... If the drive did not attach itself to an idea or manifest itself as an affective state, we could know nothing about it. (Freud 1915a: 179/177)

The drive, in other words, is fundamentally somatic, physiological;[8] it can no more be an unconscious mental process than it can be a conscious one. Although the *idea* attached to a drive can be unconscious, the same is not true, Freud says, of 'unconscious feelings, emotions and affects'.[9]

> It is surely of the essence of an emotion that we should be aware of it, i.e. that it should become known to consciousness. Thus *the possibility of the attribute of unconsciousness would be completely excluded as far as emotions, feelings and affects are concerned.* (Freud 1915a: my italics)

It must be said this argument makes very little sense. Having spent a considerable part of this and other works arguing against the view that an unconscious *thought* is a contradiction in terms (Freud 1915a: Section I), Freud suddenly grants exactly this point in relation to unconscious *feelings*.[10] There is no obvious reason why unconsciousness should be any less a possible quality of feelings than of ideas. In fact, we know very well that affect can be unconscious; we have all had the experience many times of realising 'Oh, so *that* is what I have been feeling, without knowing it.' This is so obvious, in fact, that a majority of later analysts have simply assumed the point, apparently without realising how strongly Freud argues otherwise.

But as so often when Freud appears to be arguing badly, one needs to look at where he is trying to get to. He is positioning himself for a *pièce de resistance,* the description of neurosis as the *splitting of idea and affect,* in other words, for an account of the different vicissitudes possible for these two components of the drive. This is one of Freud's most fundamental ideas, originating even before the *Project,* in 'The Neuro-Psychoses of Defence', where Freud describes how in hysteria the 'excitation' (or affect) of an idea is 'transformed into something somatic', while in obsessional neurosis idea and affect are split[11] (Freud 1894: 49-53).

It is doubtful whether this version of the relationship between idea and affect - between reason and emotion, one might say - can be maintained. As Cavell (1993: 139-40) points out, Freud himself repeatedly talks in a clinical context of finding the *rational justification* for a feeling - for example of guilt, in *Civilization and its Discontents* (Freud 1930: e.g. 328/135, 332/139). [12] More generally, he claims that:

> Psychoanalysis can put [neurotics] upon the right path by recognising the emotion as being... justified and by seeking out the idea which belongs to it but has been repressed and replaced by a substitute. (Freud 1900: 597/461)

He goes on from this passage to his well-known description of affect and idea as 'two separate entities' which 'may be merely soldered together'. His own argument seems to establish, however, that the relationship of affect and idea is no merely arbitrary soldering, but that there is a profound connectedness between the two, that their separation is a condition of neurosis, and that the restoration to an affect of its appropriate idea is a - or even *the* - curative process.[13]

For Freud, '*to suppress the development of affect* is the true aim of repression' (Freud 1915: 180/177, my italics; cf. Freud 1900: 762/582). While 'ideas are cathexes - basically of memory traces', and therefore *qualitative* - affect is *quantitative*. '[A]ffects and emotions correspond to processes of discharge, the final manifestations of which are perceived as feelings' (Freud 1915: 181/178). In other words, although Freud acknowledges the very obvious link between affect and the body (after all, we use the same word - 'feeling' - for both affect and sensation, and 'pleasure' and 'pain' can be a 'feeling' in either sense), he sees the body as *responding to* ideas *with* feelings.

> Repression results not only in withholding things from consciousness, but also in preventing the development of affect and the setting-off of muscular activity. *As long as the system* Cs *controls affectivity and motility, the mental condition of the person in question is spoken of as normal*... Whereas the control by the Cs over voluntary motility is firmly rooted... even within the limits of normal life we can recognise that a constant struggle for primacy over affectivity goes on between the two systems Cs and Ucs. (Freud 1900: 181/179, my italics; cf. Freud 1915d: 152-3/152-3)

Unconscious and body

Thus Freud installs one of the leading therapeutic goals of psychoanalysis: to strengthen and safeguard this control of system Cs over emotion and action, of 'mind' over 'body' - what Brennan (1991: 2) calls 'the machinations of the flesh'. This is a goal which, I am arguing, is carried forward by the *theory* as well as by the *clinical practice* of analysis.

However, the passages just quoted directly call into question the equation *unconscious = body*. The pattern is one of struggle between conscious and unconscious systems for control of the body in its dual aspects of feeling and movement.

> Thus it is the ego's business not to permit any release of affect, because this at the same time permits a primary process. (Freud 1950: 358)

We shall see later how Reich reframes the issue, and sees repression as fighting against not the development of affect, but its *expression* (which he equates with its becoming conscious). In this - as so often - he returns to the earlier Freudian position:

> What is alone of value in mental life is rather the feelings. No mental forces are significant unless they possess the characteristic of *arousing* feelings. Ideas are only repressed because they are associated with the *release* of feelings which ought not to occur. (Freud 1907: 49/49, my italics)

One of the ongoing themes in this book is the relationship between the unconscious and the body. There is a strong tendency in analytic thought to identify the two, a tendency which rests on the culture-specific List of aligned polarities that we considered in Chapter One. Freud often included in his personal edition of the List the polarity 'conscious/unconscious', aligned so that an identity could be read off between 'conscious' and 'mind', 'unconscious' and 'body'.

Lacan disputes this equation, aligning the unconscious with the symbolic, with language, with the mental. The 'real of the body' he regards as ineffable and undiscussable; what we might call the 'emotional body' he categorises as imaginary, and to be deconstructed. I want to show that Freud, in contrast, consistently aligns the body with the unconscious - and, indeed, with affect.

Necessarily and explicitly, Freud describes the unconscious through metaphor. Looking through the whole of Freud's work, one can distinguish four major groups of metaphor - frequently overlapping - which he uses for this purpose: metaphors of space (the unconscious as a place, a country, a stratum);[14] of power (the unconscious as a slave, a domesticated animal, a non-white race);[15] of history (the unconscious as archaic, primitive, prehistoric);[16] and of body (the unconscious as somatic, internal, visceral). All of these metaphoric sets relate to The List, and they all tend to portray the unconscious as *lower* in one or other sort of hierarchy.

As we have already seen, the body is widely understood as 'lower' than the mind, and the lowliness of the body supports that of the unconscious - system *Ucs* descends from the mind into the body. At times Freud imagines the relationship of psyche and soma as a tube with a mouth onto the world at one end, and receding infinitely 'inwards'/'downwards' towards the body at the other end. The tube mouth is not freely open to the world, however. The psyche, and in particular system *Pcpt-Cs*, exists as a barrier - semitransparent by necessity - between the outside world and the interior depths.

Curiously enough, a more explicit metaphor used by Freud for the mind/body relationship is that of - the body! In *The Ego and the Id* he argues that:

> ...consciousness is the surface of the mental
> apparatus... we have ascribed it as a function
> which is spatially the first one reached... and
> spatially... also in the sense of anatomical dis-
> section. (Freud 1923: 357; see also 1920: 295)

Repeatedly, and at greatest length in *Beyond the Pleasure Principle*, Freud uses the image of a primitive organism or 'vesicle' protected from its environment by a 'skin', or 'crust' .Consciousness, here, is a hardened and only partially alive armouring between the living core of the organism (the id) and external reality (Freud 1920: 297 ff.; cf. 1923: 357 ff.).

System *Ucs* is *inside*, therefore, a crucial component of Freud's vision. But his favourite of all bodily images - indeed, perhaps his favourite image for unconscious process - is that of pathways:

> At the roots of drive activity the systems
> communicate with one another most exten-
> sively... Normally all the paths from percep-
> tion to the Ucs remain open... (Freud 1915a:
> 198)

> There are two paths by which the contents of
> the id can penetrate into the ego. (Freud
> 1923a: 397)

In these examples the 'path' image is used to describe relations
between *Cs*/ego and *Ucs*/id. It can also be used to describe the
structure of the unconscious itself:

> All mental acts which are truly unconscious...
> are paths which have been laid down once
> and for all, which never fall into disuse and
> which... are always ready to conduct the exci-
> tatory process to discharge. (Freud 1900: 704)

The neurological metaphor is here explicit, and refers straight
back to the *Project*: the 'pathways' which recur in Freud's writing were originally neurological 'paths of conduction'.
However, the 'pathway' image translates very readily between
neurology and topography, and in fact works to knit the two
together, especially when combined with the familiar 'frontier'
image (the 'contact barrier'):

> The Ucs is turned back on the frontier of the
> Pcs... all the paths... leading on from the Ucs
> are subject to blocking by repression. (Freud
> 1915: 197-8)

Three important streams of visualisation in Freud's thinking
come together in the pathway/frontier metaphor: the neurology of the *Project*, which he allows to become, not exactly a 'dead
metaphor', but a sleeping one; the walking holidays which
were such an important part of his life, not only for 'relaxation'
but as the occasion for crucial intellectual exchange, first with

Fliess, later with Ferenczi and others; and the political map of Central Europe, with its *Grenze* and *Grenzpolizei* who feature in several of Freud's dreams and analogies. The image of the pathway is particularly important in *The Interpretation of Dreams*, and could be seen as the controlling image of this most richly metaphorical of Freud's works. Freud uses the term 'path' (*Bahn*) to move easily between neurological and topographical visualisations. But it is important to grasp that when Freud talks of 'pathways', he is at least vestigially describing a *bodily* process. Along with the 'paths of conduction', the 'contact barrier' endures as a key image throughout Freud's work, and re-appears in his concept of the symptom as simultaneously expression and repression. The project of the *Project* is taken up in Freud's later work as a mode of *representation*.

Chapter Three - Hysterical Body

'To grief from one's own body'

Freud's original engagement with the body was practical, passionate - sometimes even directly physical. According to Ferenczi, he would, if necessary, spend 'hours lying on the floor next to a person in a hysterical crisis' (Ferenczi 1988: 93)[1]. Similarly he involved himself in 'pinching', 'pressing' and 'kneading' Frau Elizabeth von R's legs (Freud 1895: 204-5/137-8), 'getting rid' of Emmy von N's gastric pains by 'stroking her' (Freud 1895: 110/54) and 'massaging her whole body twice a day' (Freud 1895: 106/50), and, as is well-known, in pressing patients' heads with his hands to help them remember (Freud 1895: 173-4/110). The Freud-Fliess letters, the *Studies on Hysteria*, the dreams analysed in *The Interpretation of Dreams* - all are saturated in bodily reference. In his letters to Fliess, Freud runs through one theory after another of an immediate, organic causation for neurosis: masturbation, sexual toxicity, menstruation, nasal problems - and, of course, bodily sexual abuse. All circulate in a vivid, hallucinatory whirl, together with the essentially 'mental' theories of defence, phantasy and repression.

Take for example this passage from a letter of January 1st 1896, where Freud is seeking an explanation of migraine:

> Olfactory substances - as, indeed, you yourself believe, and as we know from flowers - are breakdown products of the sexual metabolism; they would act as stimuli on both these organs [Schneider's membrane and the *corpora cavernosa*]. During menstruation and other sexual processes the body produces an increased Q[uantity] of these substances and therefore of these stimuli. It would have to be decided whether these act on the nasal organs through the expiratory air or through the blood vessels; probably the latter, since

one has no subjective sensation of smell
before migraine. Thus the nose would, as it
were, receive information about internal
olfactory stimuli by means of the corpora
cavernosa, just as it does about external
stimuli by Schneider's membrane; *one would
come to grief from one's own body.* (Masson
1985: 161, last italics mine)

As an account of migraine,[2] this might be read as simply another eccentric nineteenth-century hypothesis. As Freud says 'a
whole number of obscure and ancient medical ideas would
acquire life and value' (Masson: 1985, 162). However, the passage needs to be read as part of an intricate, never-completed
theory which linked migraine, hysteria, menstruation, periodicity and noses - the Freud-Fliess Olfactory Theory, we might be
calling it, had Freud not broken with Fliess and changed it into
psychoanalysis.

I have often had the suspicion that something organic plays a part in repression; I
was able once before to tell you that it was a
question of the abandonment of former sexual zones... [T]he notion was linked to the
changed part played by sensations of smell:
upright walking, nose raised from the
ground, at the same time a number of for-
merly interesting sensations attached to the
earth becoming repulsive... We must assume
that in infancy the release of sexuality is not
yet so much localised as it is later, so that the
zones which are later abandoned (and perhaps the whole surface of the body as well)
also instigate something that is analogous to
the later release of sexuality. The extinction
of these initial sexual zones would have a
counterpart in the atrophy of certain internal
organs in the course of development. A
release of sexuality (as you know, I have in
mind a kind of secretion...) comes about,

then, not only (1) through a peripheral stimulus upon the sexual organs, or (2) through
the internal excitations arising from these
organs, but also (3) from ideas - that is, from
memory traces - therefore also by the path of
deferred action. (Masson 1985: 279)

To put it crudely, the memory actually stinks.
(Masson 1985: 280)

Here Freud has shifted - a shift of emphasis only, not of causal
level - from the *physiological* nose of the earlier letter to a *symbolic* nose, a nose which can smell out stinking memories. This
is the first appearance of an idea to which Freud in fact held
throughout his career: that there is something foundational for
humanity in our learning to stand upright and separate our
sense of smell from our (and other people's) genitals and anus,
from:

the coprophiliac instinctual components
which have proved incompatible with our
aesthetic standards of culture, probably
since, as a result of adopting an erect gait, we
raised our organ of smell from the ground.
(Freud 1912(b): 189/258)

The letter to Fliess makes clear that it is not only the smell of
faeces which erect humanity finds disgusting, but the smell of
sexual secretions - in particular, of menstrual blood. More than
thirty years later, in *Civilization and Its Discontents*, Freud
returns, using almost identical terms, to the connection of
human culture with our 'rising above' the smell of menstrual
blood:

The taboo on menstruation is derived from
this 'organic repression', as a defence against
a phase of development that has been sur-
mounted. (Freud 1930: 288n/99n)

Menstruation is related to the nose not only through the theme of smell, but by Fliess's theory of the 'Nasal Reflex Neurosis'[3] - with symptoms including headaches (from which both men suffered badly), vertigo, widely distributed neuralgia, and disturbances of the circulation, respiration, digestion, and sexual functions. Fliess's theory draws on the recognised physiological connection that makes the turbinal bones of the nose swell and sometimes bleed during menstruation.

Without venturing too far into the enormous mass of material,[4] we can see the basic outlines of a theory of neurosis which relates it to menstruation, and to an equivalent periodicity in men, 'releasing' libido and creating a crisis of repression.

> It is only now that I dare to understand my [sic] anxiety neurosis: the menstrual period as its physiological model; the anxiety neurosis itself as an intoxication, for which an organic process must furnish the physiological foundation.[5] (Masson 1985: 174)

Freud and Fliess supported each other in their tendency to formulate daringly speculative syntheses, of which psychoanalysis was only one among several siblings. *At the time* it by no means stood out as more sensible, meaningful, or 'scientific' than their other theories. The notions which assembled themselves into psychoanalysis originated in a stew of other ideas which to most contemporary eyes are cranky indeed. Freud is clearly drawn to the 'olfactory theory', partly by his intense relationship with Fliess, and also partly by his own nasal and neurotic symptoms in this period (and his use of cocaine to control those symptoms). But these ideas also attract him because they allow him to think about the relationship between physical sexuality and neurosis, with the nose standing in for a psychic representation/transformation of the bodily drive, an intermediate point between soma and psyche.

We can see here just how greatly the episteme has changed within a century. For Freud, at this stage in his career, there is no particular *difference of level* between physiological and psychological theories. It is not that he perceives himself oscillating between bodily and mental accounts, but that the distinction between the two kinds of theory is nowhere near as crucial then as it is now taken to be. As we have seen, Freud himself is a major figure in this epistemic shift, to a new Cartesianism which rigorously distinguishes mental from bodily explanation - a shift which is perhaps at last approaching the end of its dominance.

These ideas concerning a somatic account of neurosis never fully drop out of Freud's thinking. For example, in *The Question of Lay Analysis*, he portrays menstruation, along with menopause, as 'normal models' of neurosis, just as in *Inhibition, Symptoms and Anxiety* he portrays affect as a normal model of hysteria (see below). These early formulations remain encysted, so to speak, in the body of psychoanalysis, as material that can be neither absorbed nor eliminated by the general theory.

But what is changed and what is conserved in the shift from the 'olfactory theory' to psychoanalysis? What drops out (to bob up again in *Civilization and Its Discontents*) is the nose itself; everything else remains surprisingly similar, except that gradually Freud elides, rather than resolves, the problematic of the mind/body relationship, the *how* of repression. Perhaps the biggest shift is that Freud *generalises* his conception of neurosis as stemming from conflict between the biological and the psychological spheres. In the Freud-Fliess letters, he is experimenting with various innate, specific factors, either psychological (e.g. innate disgust, particularly in supposedly non-libidinal woman) or biological (e.g. periodicity), as causative of neurosis. As his thinking develops, the picture becomes wider, but is basically the same: neurosis is caused by more (somatic) stimulus than we can (psychically) bear.

Conversion

The version of this theory which becomes psychoanalysis - situating the origin of neurosis in the repression of sexual desire - is itself a *bodily* theory. It describes how bodily stimulation is transformed and transvalued through psychical representation, the fundamental purpose of which, as we have seen, is to eliminate that stimulation.

> The source of a drive is a process of excita-
> tion occurring in an organ and the immedi-
> ate aim of the drive lies in the removal of this
> organic stimulus. (Freud 1905: 83/168)

The *Three Essays*, which sets out to 'discover how far psychological investigation can throw light upon the biology of the
sexual life of man' (Freud 1905: 41/131) traces the migrations
and transformations of sexual energy across a real fleshly
human body:

> Any... part of the skin or mucous membrane
> can take over the function of an erotogenic
> zone... the quality of the stimulus has more
> to do with producing the pleasurable feeling
> than has the nature of the part of the body
> concerned. A child who is indulging in sen-
> sual sucking searches about his body and
> chooses some part of it to suck... [In hysteria]
> repression affects most of all the actual geni-
> tal zones and these transmit their suscepti-
> bility to stimulation to other erotogenic
> zones... Any other part of the body can
> acquire the same susceptibility to stimula-
> tion... (Freud 1905: 100/183-4)

For example:

> Like the labial zone, the anal zone is well
> suited by its position to act as a medium
> through which sexuality may attach itself to
> other functions... We learn with some aston-
> ishment from psychoanalysis of the trans-
> mutations normally undergone by the sexu-
> al excitations arising from this zone... (Freud
> 1905: 102/185)

And so on. One could produce pages of equivalent quotation, documenting the absolute *concreteness* of Freud's vision -

> [t]he retention of the faecal mass, which is thus carried out intentionally by the child to begin with, in order to serve... as a masturbatory stimulus upon the anal zone or to be employed in his relation to the people looking after him, is also one of the roots of... constipation (Freud 1905: 104/186-7)

- and also, equally, his grand assumption of the power of libido to 'transmute', 'attach itself', 'transmit itself' from one organ or skin area to another.

As the first passage quoted above makes clear, the plasticity and lability of libido in infancy is parallel to (and, in the development of Freud's theory, *modelled* on) hysteria. 'Erotogenic and hysterogenic zones show the same characteristics' (Freud 1905: 100/184). Hysteria, however, introduces a further factor: the phenomenon of conversion. The hysterical symptom is itself only a special form of the 'hysterical attack' (Freud 1909), a more gradual and continuous form in which the body is taken over by a memory. This parallels the distinction between a continuous endogenous excitation and a sudden exogenous excitation.

Once we think about it, erogenous zones themselves exhibit a sort of 'conversion'. Sexual arousal itself is, more often than not, a physical response to psychological stimulus, which we would have difficulty in distinguishing from conversion, except for the fact that the psychological state involved is not removed from awareness. Libido itself becomes a sort of 'normal hysteria'. Actually, Freud argues in *Inhibitions, Symptoms and Anxiety* that *emotion* is normal hysteria. Affects are:

> *universal, typical and innate hysterical attacks,* as opposed to the recent and individually acquired attacks which occur in hysterical neurosis and whose origins and significance

as mnemic symbols have been revealed by
analysis. (Freud 1926a: 290/133, my italics)

This alternative theory of affect to the main one described in
Chapter Two states that that all feelings are in some sense *memories*: 'precipitates of primaeval traumatic experiences' (Freud
1926a: 244/93). They repeat and re-perform 'very early, perhaps even pre-individual experiences of vital importance'
(Freud 1926a: 289/133). Instead of being the 'discharge' of
drive impulse, affect is here portrayed as the result of *exogenous*
stimulus - the taking over of the body by a scene of unconscious origins. Thus, all feelings are hysterical!

This is not, in fact, a new idea for Freud. It is also articulat-
ed, for instance, in the *Introductory Lectures*:

An affective state would be constructed in
the same way as an hysterical attack and,
like it, would be *the product of a reminiscence*.
A hysterical attack may thus be likened to a
freshly constructed individual affect, and a
normal affect to the expression of a general
hysteria which has become a heritage.
(Freud 1916-17: 444)

It is not immediately obvious what problem Freud is trying to
solve with this remarkable theory. It has a clear connection with
Darwin's theory of emotion, which Freud refers to most directly in *Studies on Hysteria*:

All these sensations and innervations [like
being 'slapped in the face' or 'stabbed to the
heart'] belong to the field of 'The Expression
of Emotions', which as Darwin [1872] has
taught us, consists of actions which originally had a meaning and served a purpose...
[I]n all probability the description was once
meant literally; and hysteria is right in
restoring the original meaning of the words
in depicting its unusually strong innerva-

tions.[6] (Freud 1895: 254/181)

Interestingly, this is actually a very misleading account of Darwin, who suggests 'three great principles' to account for emotional expression, only one of which corresponds to Freud's point. One of the others concerns 'the direct action of the excited nervous system on the body' which is often 'quite independent of the flow of nerve-force along the channels which have been rendered habitual' (Darwin 1934 : 166-7). This 'principle' is directly opposite to Freud's, since it implies a transcultural and physiological basis for at least some human emotional expression.[7]

Freud's later theory of anxiety is of exactly the kind he outlines here: an affect imprinted on the body by a prototypical experience, in this case birth.

> We assume, in other words, that an anxiety-state is the reproduction of some experience which contained the necessary conditions for such an increase in excitation and a discharge along particular paths, and that from this circumstance the unpleasure of anxiety receives its specific character. In man, birth provides a prototypic experience of this kind, and we are therefore inclined to regard anxiety-states as a reproduction of the trauma of birth. (Freud 1926a: 289/133)

He proceeds immediately to align anxiety with affect in general:

> This does not imply that anxiety occupies an exceptional position among the affective states. In my opinion the other affects are also reproductions of very early, perhaps even pre-individual, experiences of vital importance; and I should be inclined to regards them as universal, typical and innate hysteri-

cal attacks... (Freud 1926a: 289-90/133; see
also up to 295/138; 245/93; and Freud 1917,
235/199)

It is extraordinary from our modern viewpoint how Freud
slides so easily from the individual experience to the 'pre-individual' - in other words, from the idea that individual trauma
affects the emotional disposition, to the idea of an *inherited*
species predisposition.

From one point of view, Freud is using a general theory of
affect to back up a specific theory of anxiety. But this is using a
hammer to crack a nut - however stubborn a nut anxiety was
for Freud. We should also consider why Freud felt the need to
drop his original theory of anxiety, which, as we shall see, was
maintained by Reich as a central platform of analysis - anxiety
as the expression of undischarged sexual excitement:

> that neurotic anxiety arises out of libido, that
> it is the product of a transformation of it, and
> that it is thus related to it in the same kind of
> way as vinegar is to wine. (Freud
> 1905:147/224: fn added 1920)

In *Inhibitions, Symptoms and Anxiety*, Freud does not flatly
reject his earlier view of anxiety. He writes: 'It might still be
true... that in repression anxiety is produced by the libidinal
cathexis of the drive impulses' (Freud 1926a: 264/110).
However, he cannot reconcile this idea with his view that anxiety belongs to the ego, is a signal of danger - primarily of the
danger of castration - and that, therefore, 'it does not proceed
out of repression but, on the contrary, sets repression in motion'
(Freud 1926a: 264/110; see also 284/128-9). But he acknowledges difficulties with this latter view also - for example, anxiety in women, where 'we can hardly speak with propriety of
castration *anxiety* where castration has already taken place
[*sic*!]' (Freud 1926a: 278/123).

We will not be able to make sense of these incoherences until
we look at the death drive and Reich's theory of orgasm anxi-

ety. However, the underlying issue is Freud's presentation, in both his theories, of affect as a *disturbance*, as something in a sense unnatural - an invasion or attack upon reason, like an hysterical attack.

What, then, is this hysterical attack, which Freud treats as a known entity with which affect can be compared? The answer to this question is less than straightforward. Although we can readily say what an hysterical attack *looks like*, it is a lot harder to say what it *is*. Above all else, though, it is a *bodily* experience.

The puzzling leap

In his important 1919 paper 'The Phenomena of Hysterical Materialisation', Ferenczi focuses on the problematics of hysterical conversion:

> The unconscious will of the hysteric brings about motor manifestations, changes in the circulation of the blood, in glandular function and in the nourishment of the tissues, such as the conscious will of the non-hysteric cannot achieve. The smooth musculature of the alimentary canal, of the bronchi, the tear and sweat glands, the nasal erectile tissue, etc., are at the disposition of the hysteric; he can bring about individual innervations, for instance, of the musculature of the eyes and Adam's apple, that are impossible for healthy persons; his capacity for manifesting local haemorrhages, blisters, and cutaneous and mucous swellings, though certainly rarer, is also well-known.[8] (Ferenczi 1994a: 91)

As we shall see, not only Ferenczi but also Reich and Groddeck give these phenomena a central place in their theory of mind/body relationship. Straight away, Ferenczi situates them within the range of *normal* human capacities.

> We do not forget, however, that it is not only

> hysteria which is capable of such achieve-
> ments, but that it is also possible to evoke
> similar manifestations by hypnotism and
> suggestion to which the normal person also
> is more or less accessible. There are, too, peo-
> ple otherwise normal who make a habit of a
> few such super-achievements in childhood,
> for instance the individual control of mus-
> cles which ordinarily contract symmetrically,
> the voluntary control of the cardiac, gastric,
> and intestinal functions, of the muscles of
> the iris, etc., which they finally display as
> though endowed with some special gift. *A
> great part of the education of a child consists of
> breaking away from such tricks and acquiring
> others.* (Ferenczi 1994a: 91-2, my italics; see
> also Ferenczi 1994a: 283-4)

If Ferenczi were writing now, he would certainly refer also
to biofeedback and yoga. We now have a great deal more evidence available to us of the capacity of human beings mentally
to influence their somatic state. The final sentence is particularly interesting, bringing in as it does the role of social conditioning, which will be taken up strongly by Reich. Ferenczi continues:

> The education of a child presupposes a psy-
> chic control of certain organ-activities which
> later apparently occur 'automatically' or as
> 'reflexes', but which are really command-
> automatisms active since childhood; for
> example the regular functioning of the
> sphincter and expulsive muscles of the
> bowel and bladder, going to sleep and awak-
> ening at regular intervals of time, etc. An
> increase of capacity due to affects which can
> influence the most varied circulatory and
> excretory processes is equally well known.
> (Ferenczi 1994a: 92)

The mystery, Ferenczi is arguing, is not just in hysterical conversion, but rather in *the entire relationship of mental and bodily phenomena*, our basic situation as incarnate beings. He talks about 'materialisation phenomena', under which he includes not only hysterical conversions but 'a great many of the so-called expressional movements that accompany the emotions of the human mind - blushing, pallor, fainting, anxiety, laughter, crying, etc.' (Ferenczi 1994a: 96)

There is something paradoxical, or at least circular, happening here. If we posit a radical separation of the mental from the physical, then many everyday phenomena will appear extraordinary - will seem, as Ferenczi puts it, to 'leap across' this imaginary barrier (Ferenczi 1994a: 97). We will then be led to elaborate theories that try to account for this 'puzzling leap' (Ferenczi 1994a: 97) - for instance, Ferenczi suggests a regression to 'autoplastic' rather than 'alloplastic' stages of development, to the 'protopsyche'.

> Those primitive vital processes which hysteria seems to fall back upon consist of bodily changes which are quite natural and habitual, although when they are psychogenic they impress one as supernormal. The movement of the smooth muscle fibres of the vascular walls, the functioning of glands, the entire process of tissue nourishment, are regulated infra-psychically [i.e. in the brain?]. In hysteria all these physiological mechanisms are at the disposal of unconscious wish-impulses so that, by a complete reversal of the normal path of excitation, a purely psychic process can come to expression in a physiological bodily change. (Ferenczi 1994a: 97-8)

One could add to Ferenczi's list of 'materialisation phenomena' - reducing it to complete absurdity - that of bodily sexual excitement which follows on from thoughts and fantasies. It is the axiom that the 'normal path of excitation' flows in one direction only which must fall. Ferenczi is struggling to break through an unnoticed barrier in his own thinking: a barrier which produces bizarre explanations similar to Freud's theory of the hysterical nature of affect in general.

Ferenczi's final thoughts on these issues appear in his *Clinical Diary*:

> If the psychically dormant substance [i.e. the material substance of the body] is rigid, while the nervous and mental systems possess fluid adaptability, then the hysterically reacting body can be described as semifluid, that is to say, as a substance whose previous rigidity and uniformity has been partially redissolved again into a psychic state, capable of adapting. Such 'semisubstances' would then have the extraordinarily or wonderfully pleasing quality of *being both body and mind simultaneously*, that is, of expressing wishes, sensations of pleasure-unpleasure, or even complicated thoughts, through changes in their structure or function (the language of organs). (Ferenczi 1988: 7)

It should be clear how much Ferenczi - uniquely among analysts - is in active dialogue with Freud's 'biological mythology'. In the light of his earlier paper, there seems no good reason why Ferenczi should restrict to the *hysteric* body this 'quality of being both body and mind simultaneously'. Later, I hope to reframe this idea in more useful terms. In the meantime, we shall examine how, for Ferenczi, hysteria had an important and universal role.

'Fits of shaking which free her'

> Ferenczi, that highly gifted and humanly outstanding man, was well aware of the desolateness in the field of therapy. He sought for the solution in the body. (Reich 1973: 151-2)

This is Wilhelm Reich's strongest acknowledgement of Ferenczi's influence on his own work. Though sympathetic, it seems hardly complete, continuing with a brief reference to Ferenczi's 'active technique' and making no mention of the 'materialisation' paper which strikingly anticipates many of Reich's positions, and with which Reich must undoubtedly have been familiar.[9] Like Freud himself, and many other original thinkers, Reich tended not to keep track of the sources of his own ideas.

It is much more doubtful whether Reich would have been aware of the startling anticipation of his techniques by Freud himself, which I have already highlighted:

> Yesterday Mrs K again sent for me because of cramplike pains in her chest; generally it has been because of headaches. In her case I have invented a strange therapy of my own: I search for sensitive areas, press on them, and thus provoke fits of shaking which free her. Formerly, these areas were supraorbital and ethmoid; now they are (for the breast cramps) two areas on the left chest wall, wholly identical with mine. (Masson 1985:120)

This 'strange therapy' which Freud used, it seems, with one patient only and then forgot, was rediscovered forty-five years later by Reich, when he began using his hands to help loosen tight musculature in his patients:

> The loosening of the rigid muscular attitudes produced peculiar body sensations in the patients: involuntary trembling and twitching of the muscles, sensations of cold and hot, itching, the feeling of pins and needles, prickling sensations, the feeling of having the jitters, and somatic perceptions of anxiety, anger and pleasure. (Reich 1973: 271)

He describes even more dramatic reactions:

> violent convulsions of the pelvic muscula-
> ture... turned out to be the warding off of
> blows... kicking of the feet followed by vio-
> lent pelvic movements... (Reich 1973: 304)

> Acute manifestation of vegetative shock. The
> pallor of his face changed rapidly from white
> to yellow to blue. His skin was spotted and
> motley. He experienced violent pains in the
> neck and back of the head. His heartbeat was
> rapid and pounding. He had diarrhoea, felt
> tired, and seemed to have lost control...
> Affects had broken through somatically...
> (Reich 1973: 269)

Without the element of physical pressure, but by emphasis
on 'relaxation',[10] the same sort of phenomena were elicited by
Ferenczi and described in his Clinical Diary and elsewhere:

> Hysterical physical symptoms would sud-
> denly make their appearance... paresthesias
> and spasms, definitely localised, violent
> emotional movements, like miniature hys-
> terical attacks, sudden alterations of the state
> of consciousness, slight vertigo and clouding
> of consciousness often with subsequent
> amnesia for what had taken place. (Ferenczi
> 1994b: 118)

> Breathing disturbances when in relaxation...
> Preceded by fierce pains in abdomen, in and
> around the uterus. Face is quite haggard,
> sensation of being crushed; Cheyne-Stokes
> [i.e. alternation of deep, rapid breathing with
> no breath at all], face pale, head subjectively
> hot. (Ferenczi 1988: 134)

Almost hallucinatory cathartic abreactions of repressed, traumatic events... violent twistings of her hands at the wrists, a feeling of trying to push off with her palms the weight of a gigantic body... (Ferenczi 1988: 21-2)

The patient sinks into a jumble of hallucinations, emotional outbursts, physical and psychical pain... (Ferenczi 1988: 54)

As Ferenczi indicates, these phenomena are recognisably very similar to what Freud (following the tradition of Charcot) had long before described as the 'hysterical attack' (cf. Freud and Breuer 1893, 64-8/13-17; Freud 1909 passim). They are similar not only in terms of the bodily experiences involved (*attitudes passionnelles*, 'generalised clonic spasms', 'cataleptic rigidity', 'a frenzy of rage' [1893, 64/14]), but also in the integral connection with *memory*.

The memories which emerge, or can be aroused, in hysterical attacks correspond to the precipitating causes which we have found at the root of chronic hysterical symptoms. (Freud and Breuer 1893: 66/15)

As is well-known, Freud's and Breuer's original, spectacular claim was that the restoration of memory - *with affect* - removed the hysterical symptom.

Each individual hysterical symptom immediately and permanently disappeared when we had succeeded in bringing clearly to light the memory of the event by which it was provoked and in arousing its accompanying affect, and when the patient had described the event in the greatest possible detail and had put the affect into words. (Freud & Breuer 1893: 57/6)

It is noticeable how even within this sentence, an initial optimism - 'each... symptom immediately and permanently disappeared' - is steadily qualified by a series of 'and... and... and' clauses. Of course, this was the clinical fate of the 'cathartic technique': it turned out to depend on a positive transference which could not always, or often, be mobilised. In a brilliant switch of emphasis, Freud pointed out that negative transference was itself a recapitulation of past traumatic experience. Learning to work with the transference became the core of the analytic process.

It is startling, then, to find Ferenczi - one of the leading figures in psychoanalysis, and specifically in the development of transference analysis (Ferenczi and Rank, 1986) - in his final years as an analyst returning to and recapitulating Freud and Breuer's work of the 1880s, repeating the attempt to facilitate affect discharge as a core method of treatment - to induce, in effect, a therapeutic hysterical attack.

> In certain cases these hysterical attacks actually assumed the character of *trances*, in which fragments of the past were relived... Without my making the least attempt to induce a condition of this sort, unusual states of consciousness manifested themselves, which might also be termed autohypnotic. Willy-nilly, one was forced to compare them with the Breuer-Freud *catharsis*. (Ferenczi 1994b: 119)

In fact, Ferenczi was as startled as anyone else - and not particularly enthusiastic:

> I must confess that at first this was a disagreeable surprise, almost a shock, to me. Was it really worthwhile to make that enormous detour of analysis of associations and resistances, to unravel the maze of the elements of ego-psychology, and even to tra-

verse the whole metapsychology in order to
arrive at the good old 'friendly attitude' to
the patient and the method of catharsis, long
believed to be discarded? (Ferenczi 1994b:
119)

In part, this emergence of 'neocatharsis' (Ferenczi 1994b: 119)
is to do with the kind of analysand that Ferenczi finds himself
working with - people who would now be described as suffering from profound trauma, and whom Ferenczi portrays in
terms strikingly similar to contemporary models of dissociation:[11]

Actual trauma is experienced by children in
situations where no immediate remedy is
provided, and where adaptation, that is, a
change in their own behaviour, is forced on
them... From then on, neither subjective nor
objective experience alone will be perceived
as an integrated emotional unity... If a trauma
strikes the soul, or the body, unprepared...
then its effect is destructive for body and
mind, that is, it disrupts through fragmenta-
tion. (Ferenczi 1988: 69)

Compare this with recent trauma research:

It has been our experience with infants and
young children that the behaviors exhibited
in the acute and post-acute trauma include
numbing, compliance, avoidance, and
restricted affect, all consistent with a primary
dissociative response pattern. Traumatized
children use a variety of dissociative techniques. Children report going to a 'different
place,' assuming persona of heroes or animals, a sense of 'watching a movie that I was
in' or 'just floating' - classic depersonaliza-

tion and derealization responses. Observers will report these children as numb, robotic, non-reactive, 'day dreaming', 'acting like he was not there', 'staring off into space with a glazed look'. If immobilization, inescapability or pain are involved, the dissociative responses will become more predominant. (Perry *et al*, 1995: 282)

What Ferenczi does, though, is to generalise *backwards* from his overtly abused and traumatised patients to the normal situation of children in our culture, seeing a universal abuse in the 'projection of our own passions or passionate tendencies onto children' (Ferenczi 1988: 155).[12] He insists to Freud that the original analytic picture was the correct one:

> In *all* cases where I penetrated deeply enough, I found uncovered the traumatic-hysterical basis of the illness... Where the patient and I succeeded in this, the therapeutic effect was far more significant... Psychoanalysis deals far too one-sidedly with obsessive neurosis and character-analysis - that is, ego-psychology - while neglecting *the organic-hysterical basis of the analysis.* This results from overestimating the role of fantasy, and underestimating that of traumatic reality... (Letter to Freud 25.12.1929, quoted in Ferenczi 1988: xii; second italics mine)

In a strange way, we are brought back round to Freud's notion of affects as 'products of reminiscence' - 'universal, typical and innate hysterical attacks'. Except here Ferenczi is saying something more precise - that many affects which appear and need to appear in analysis represent memories not of primal and prehistoric traumas of the species, but of actual traumatic attacks experienced by the analysand in childhood. This is perhaps a partial explanation of Freud's odd slide from the individual to the 'pre-individual', which we have already noticed; as well as being pulled by his consistent interest in Lamarckian ideas, Freud is also pushed by an unwillingness to think too much about actual trauma.

As with Freud, though, Ferenczi's hopes that discharge, expulsion of the traumatic 'foreign body' (Freud and Breuer 1893: 57), will lead to cure are not fulfilled.

> Psychoanalytical expectations until now allowed us to hope that with each such outburst a certain quantity of the blocked affect would be lived through emotionally and muscularly, and that when the entire capacity is exhausted the symptom will disappear of its own accord...[13] But in reality... one encounters more and more disappointments... (Ferenczi 1988: 106)

Instead, Ferenczi experienced 'an almost endless series of repetitions', 'a somewhat tedious rehashing' of the traumatic material. In other words, he goes through a similar process of 'disappointment' to Freud himself - but he revises his theory in a distinctly different way. He contests the whole 'mature' direction of psychoanalysis, and the whole edifice of ego-psychology by arguing that, in the simplest possible terms, people become neurotic because bad things happen to them. (As we shall see, this is also Reich's position.) But in that case, why does the simple discharge model not work, but lead to 'endless repetitions'? Ferenczi finally concludes that:

> an abreaction of quantities of the trauma is not enough: the situation must be different from the actually traumatic one in order to make possible a different, favourable outcome. *The most essential aspect of the altered repetition is the relinquishing of one's own rigid authority and the hostility hidden in it.* (Ferenczi 1988: 108, my italics)

This, in a nutshell, is where Ferenczi parts company with Freud. He believes that the *therapeutic posture* of psychoanalysis is unproductive, more than that, cruel; what would now be called *re-traumatising*.[14] It is clear that one part of his quarrel with the analytic mainstream is *his refusal to abandon the body*, and the crucial role of bodily discharge of affect - 'the organic-hysterical basis of the analysis'. For Ferenczi, near the end of his career, the importance of the transference relationship is in its effect on the analysand's ability to experience and express emotion, to access bodily memory.

Anatomy and destiny

The theory of somatically bound affect is not restricted to hysteria. In fact hysteria, where the symptoms are capable of being turned back into affect, is in some senses less obscure than other forms of 'psychosomatic' ailment which are not so easily budged. Reich describes an organic paralysis with an emotional meaning:

> What impressed me most about this case was the fact that *a psychic experience can cause a somatic response which produces a permanent change in an organ.* Later I called this phenomenon the physiological anchoring of a psychic experience. It differs from hysterical conversion by virtue of the fact that it cannot be psychologically influenced. (Reich 1973: 64, original italics)

With his usual concrete approach, Reich seeks to know *how* the body is changed by psychic processes - not only in neurosis but also in ordinary life.

> Emotion originates in the drives, thus in the somatic realm. An idea, on the other hand, is a purely 'psychic', non-physical formation. What, then, is the relation between the 'non-physical' idea and the 'physical' excitation? (Reich 1973: 93)

What was necessary was a functional, biologically substantiated theory of psychic structure. (Reich 1973: 150)

He is led gradually into a body-centred analysis by the conver-
gence of this train of enquiry with his theory of character.
'Character' is defined precisely as the effect on a person's present choices and perceptions of affect-laden memories from the
past.

> The entire world of past experience was
> *embodied* in the present in the form of charac-
> ter attitudes. A person's character is the func-
> tional sum total of all past experiences.
> (Reich 1973: 145, my italics)

> A person's character conserves and at the
> same time wards off the function of certain
> childhood situations. (Reich 1973: 305)

Reich turns around Freud's view of affect. For Reich, the
question is not 'why emotional expression?' but: 'why *not* emotional expression?' The answer he gives is that childhood experiences have made the discharge of affect unsafe. Character is
understood as an ensemble of 'affect-blocks', a set of defensive
inhibitions on emotional expression. This is of course not a novelty in analytic thinking, though Reich does put much more
emphasis on object relations than was common at this period.

But *how*, Reich again asks, does character structure inhibit
expression of affect? If, as Freud says, 'to suppress the development of affect is the true aim of repression' (Freud 1915:
180/177), then how does repression carry out its aim? Reich
finds his answer - and this is his great original discovery - in the
voluntary musculature.

> Until now, analytic psychology has merely
> concerned itself with *what* the child suppress-
> es and what the motives are which cause him
> to learn to control his emotions. It did not

enquire into the *way* in which children habitually fight against impulses. *It is precisely the physiological process of repression* that deserves our keenest attention... It can be said that *every muscular rigidity contains the history and meaning of its origin.*[15] (Reich 1973: 300, original italics)

For Reich, there is a continuity between conscious inhibition of emotional expression - like stopping oneself from crying - and repression in the full analytic sense. Repetition of the former gradually becomes the latter.

The spasm of the musculature is the somatic side of the process of repression, and the basis of its continued preservation. It is never individual muscles which become spastic, but rather muscle groups which belong to a functional unity... When, for example, an impulse to cry is to be repressed, it is not solely the lower lip which is tense but also the entire musculature of the throat and jaw, as well as the corresponding musculature of the throat... (Reich 1973: 302, original italics)

Reich here makes coherent sense of Freud's intuition that 'something organic plays a part in repression'. Freud may have been thinking of chemistry, but Reich finds an answer in physiology. Interestingly, we see the return of a feature of hysteria which Freud mentions several times in *Studies on Hysteria*, but without being able to make much of it: the *muscular stiffness* and pains from which his hysterical patients frequently suffered (Freud & Breuer 1893: e.g. 129/55, 151/90-1, 246ff/174ff).

Reich also, deliberately or not, takes issue with one of Freud's famous observations about hysterical somatisation:

Hysterical paralyses must be completely independent of the anatomy of the nervous

system, since in its paralyses and other manifestations hysteria behaves as if anatomy did
not exist or as though it had no knowledge of
it. (Freud & Breuer 1893:)

For Reich, the exact opposite point is significant:

We are reminded in this connection of the
well-known phenomenon that hysterical persons demarcate their somatic symptoms not
according to anatomical but according to
functional areas ...The vegetative body function is ignorant of the anatomical demarca-
tions, which are artificial designations.(Reich
1973: 302)

Freud's position was that hysterical symptoms do not recognise anatomical reality, and are therefore *artificial* (linguistic).
Reich turns this on its head: hysterical symptoms do not recognise anatomical artifice, and are therefore *natural* (expressive).
This is part of his consistent anti-nominalism: 'Words can lie.
The expression never lies' (Reich 1973: 171).[16]
    For Reich and - as we have seen - for Ferenczi, hysteria is a
fundamental condition, a traumatised 'layer' which must be
reached in any analysis. Ferenczi's critique of a 'one-sided'
emphasis on character analysis, in fact, does not apply to Reich.
In a summary of the 'typical phases' of successful character-
analytic work, Reich moves through ego interpretation towards
a

breakthrough of the deepest layers of strongly affect-charged material: *reactivation of the
infant hysteria...* (Reich 1972: 292, my italics)

In Reich's developed work, the approach to this fundamental
'infant hysteria' - Ferenczi's 'organic-hysterical basis of the
analysis' - is through releasing the tension of the voluntary
musculature, and the feelings and memories 'contained' in the
muscles. Words like 'contained' and 'held' do a good deal of

work here. Muscular tension holds *back* emotional expression, and contains it in the same sense that a sea wall contains water. It also holds *onto* the emotion - the functional equivalent of the unconscious holding onto repressed impulses. We shall see in Chapter Five, looking at one of Reich's case histories, how the specific details of muscle tension perform both the expression and the repression of buried impulses, therefore, by acting as symptoms or 'contact-barriers'.

The Freudian repressed unconscious thus emerges as a special case of the habitual unconscious - what Ferenczi called 'command-automatisms', ingrained patterns of denial which appear as 'natural'. In his 1925 paper 'Psycho-Analysis of Sexual Habits', Ferenczi develops a theory of habit as a sort of bridge between drive and ego - a foundation-stone of character:

> Habits would then, represent, so to speak,
> the cambium layer of drive-formation where
> even now the transformation of voluntary
> into instinctive action takes place and can
> still be observed. (Ferenczi 1988a: 286)

Ferenczi treats habits as a place where id, ego, and superego come together in an uneasy balance. Many of his examples relate to Reich's ideas about patterns of muscle tension. Both men are portraying certain types of 'habit' as nodal points where preconscious patterns of automatic action or inaction are affected by the gravitational pull of drive and repression.

Active technique and relaxation technique

We can begin to see how Reich's 'vegetotherapy' emerges out of Ferenczi's 'active technique' and 'relaxation technique', and then becomes an independent parallel to Ferenczi's 'neocatharsis'. Specifically, the 'active technique' consists of the use of strategic and tactical instructions and prohibitions, to maximise libidinal tension in the analytic situation. When these ideas are viewed from a historical perspective, though, it seems not unfair to make the same 'mistake' Ferenczi complained about in some of his contemporaries, and use the term 'active technique' as a name for a more general analytic style, one which favours intervention and confrontative interpretation, and which focuses strongly on the transference relationship and on bodily tensions, inhibitions and compulsions.

Ferenczi gives his own account of how the 'relaxation technique' grew out of the 'active technique':

> Subsequent reflection has convinced me that my explanation of the way in which the active technique worked was really a very forced one: I attributed everything that happened to frustration, i.e. to a 'heightening of tension'. When I told a patient, whose habit it was to cross her legs, that she must not do so, I was actually creating a situation of libidinal frustration, which induced a heightening of tension and the mobilization of psychic material hitherto repressed. But when I suggested to the same patient that she should give up the noticeably stiff posture of all her muscles and allow herself more freedom and mobility, I was really not justified in speaking of a heightening of tension, simply because she found it difficult to relax from her rigid attitude. It is much more honest to confess that here I was making use of a totally different method which, in contrast to the heightening of tension, may safely be called relaxation. We must admit, therefore, that psycho-analysis employs two opposite methods: it produces heightening of tension by the frustration it imposes and relaxation by the freedom it allows. (Ferenczi 1988b: 433)

Reich's work takes up Ferenczi's relaxation technique, and encourages patients to 'give up the noticeably stiff posture of all [their] muscles and allow [themselves] more freedom and mobility.' 'Muscular rigidity', then, is the phenomenon which brings together memory, affect, habit, the unconscious, 'hysterical attack' and the body into a powerful and practical theory, and which allows Reich to assert that

> *the psychic structure is at the same time a bio-physiological structure.* (Reich 1973: 301, original italics)

This takes us definitively beyond Freud's struggles with the relationship between psyche and biology, into what Reich calls a 'unitary-functional' approach (Reich 1973: 72). Reich recalls that

> at a meeting of the inner circle of analysts, Freud once exhorted us to be cautious. We had, he said, to be prepared to expect dangerous challenges to the psychic therapy of the neurosis by a future organotherapy. There was no way of knowing what it would be like, but one could already hear its exponents knocking at the door. Psychoanalysis must one day be established on an organic basis. This was a genuine Freudian intuition! (Reich 1973: 114)

It is this 'intuition' of Freud's which Reich sought to put into practice, not as an attack on psychoanalysis - that is, seeking to replace it by an 'organotherapy' - but as the fulfilment of the deepest goals of analytic therapy and theory, a 'functional unity' of psyche and soma, which brings our gaze back from the water in the mirror, to the water in the glass in our hands.

Chapter Four - Body as Id, Body as Ego

> For him [Freud] there is just as little division
> between body and soul as there is for me and
> every human being. But for the purposes of
> his profession as a specialist in mental illness
> he named these things in different ways,
> more appropriate for his purposes...
> (Groddeck, 'The It and Psychoanalysis', quot-
> ed in Groddeck 1977: 14)

Groddeck: 'Body and mind are one'

We can approach Reich's theory from a different angle through
another analytic figure who used touch - Georg Groddeck.
Throughout his career Groddeck extensively massaged his
patients. There is a degree of mystery surrounding his inten-
tions, but it was clearly not 'just' a medical procedure.
According to Hermann Graf Keyserling, it was 'a technically
controlled form of torture': a 'special kind of massage during
which he conducted an analysis based on my expressions of
pain' (Groddeck 1977: 21). In Groddeck's own account, the pain
is partly a by-product of physical work to relieve oedema
(Groddeck 1977: 238-9) and to enhance breathing (Groddeck
1977: 238-240). At the same time, though:

> the patient's changing expressions reveal hid-
> den secrets of his soul that in no other way
> could come to the knowledge of his doctor.
> Unconscious impulses and deeply buried
> traits of character betray themselves in his
> involuntary movements... (Groddeck 1977:
> 236)

To divide the 'psychotherapeutic' side of Groddeck's massage work from its 'medical' side would be to traduce the whole
spirit of his thought in the way that so many people have done,

starting with Freud himself. Groddeck gives one of his clearest self-accounts in his first letter to Freud, writing as someone who has independently come to many of the views of psychoanalysis.

> The distinction between body and mind is only verbal and not essential... body and mind are one unit... they contain an It, a force which lives us while we believe we are living... In other words, from the first I rejected a separation of bodily and mental illnesses, tried to treat the individual patient, the It in him, and attempted to find a way into the unexplored and inaccessible regions. (Groddeck 1977: 33)

Groddeck is, quite appropriately, ambivalent as to whether these views give him 'the right to call myself a psychoanalyst publicly' (Groddeck 1977: 33). It almost seems as though - ever since his first contact with Freud in 1917 - he is striving to be repudiated by Freud and psychoanalysis:

> I hope I may assume that you, dear Professor, will understand from these hints that I intend in my book to put forward the idea that all human illness like all human life, comes under the influence of an unconscious and that in this influence sexuality can always be traced, at the very least. I can well imagine that you might disavow anyone who held such a theory as somebody who does not fit into the analytic circle in your sense of the term were he to call himself a psychoanalyst. I would be very grateful, therefore, if you would let me know what you think of this. I shall... give *a clear description of what excludes me* from the official school of psychoanalysis. (Groddeck 1977: 36, my italics)

Freud responds in a scintillating, charming, *seductive* letter which, deliberately or otherwise, overlooks the enormous difference in viewpoint between himself and Groddeck.

> I have to claim you, I have to assert that you are a splendid analyst who has understood for ever the essential aspects of the matter. The discovery that transference and resistance are the most important aspects of treatment turns a person irretrievably into a member of the wild army. No matter if he calls the unconscious 'It'. (Groddeck 1977: 36)

Freud is both right and wrong here. He is clearly correct in pointing out to Groddeck that 'you are requesting me urgently to supply you with an official confirmation that you are not a psychoanalyst... and will be able to call yourself something special, and independent' (Groddeck 1977: 36). He is also clearly right that Groddeck, in the passage just quoted, fails to distinguish his work from psychoanalysis - a belief in the unconscious and in infantile sexuality scarcely defines a difference! Groddeck struggled unsuccessfully for the rest of his relationship with Freud - that is, for the rest of his life - to 'give a clear description of what excludes me', to make a proper distinction between his own work and Freud's.

Groddeck's failure in this respect results from what he calls 'a kind of exact paradoxicalness that resembles unreasonableness closely and in a certain sense is unreasonableness,' which means that 'I cannot see the demarcation between objects, only their fusion' (Groddeck 1977: 64). This characteristic of his work only disguises the fact that there is a very real and important difference between his position and that of Freud.

It is precisely this preference for 'fusion' over 'demarcation' which constitutes the difference. Freud spots this in his very first letter to Groddeck:

> Why do you jump from your beautiful basis into mysticism, cancel the distinction

> between mental and somatic, commit your-
> self to philosophical theories which are not
> called for? ...It seems to me as wilful to com-
> pletely spiritualise nature as radically to de-
> spiritualise it. Let's leave it its extraordinary
> variety which reaches from the inanimate to
> the organic and living, from the physical life
> to the spiritual. Certainly the unconscious is
> the proper mediator between the somatic
> and the mental, perhaps the long-sought
> 'missing link'. Yet because we have seen this
> at last, should we no longer see anything
> else? (Groddeck 1977: 37-8)

In this beautifully eloquent passage, Freud describes perhaps
more clearly than anywhere else in his work his essential vision
of the relationship between psyche and soma. Yet he also seems
to contradict himself, or at least to cloud the issue: is he
describing a break between the 'mental and somatic', or a continuum? Behind this passage is the useful paradox of the 'contact barrier', the process of simultaneous connection and separation which we examined in Chapter Two.

The issue on which Groddeck tries to focus in his initial letter, and which he raises repeatedly with Freud (e.g. Groddeck
1977: 97-8) is his use of psychoanalysis to understand and treat
physical illness. It is fair to say that Freud never opposed this
idea, and in some ways supported it, though unemphatically.
In fact, in his initial response to Groddeck, as well as 'claiming'
the man himself, Freud wants to claim his views on the analysis of organic illness.

> In my article on the unconscious that you
> mention there is an inconspicuous footnote:
> 'We are reserving for a different context the
> mention of another notable privilege of the
> *Ucs.*' I shall tell you what was not mentioned
> here: the assumption that the unconscious
> exerts an intensive, decisive influence on

somatic processes such as conscious acts never do. My friend Ferenczi who knows about this has a paper on pathoneurosis waiting to be printed in the *Internationaler Zeitschrift* which is very close in its ideas to yours. (Groddeck 1977: 37)

Ferenczi's paper, 'Disease- or Patho-Neuroses' (Ferenczi 1994a: 78-9), actually takes the exact opposite view to Groddeck; it is concerned with the effects on unconscious phantasy of physical illness or injury! Whether or not Freud is being disingenuous here (he may possibly be thinking of the 'Hysterical Materialisation' paper, though this was not published in the *Zeitschrift*), he certainly does, systematically and throughout their relationship, misrepresent Groddeck's views and their connection with his own theories. This culminates in his breathtaking appropriation of Groddeck's *Es* to designate one element of his own topography (Freud 1923: 362/23). As Groddeck wrote in 1926:

Freud honoured me by drawing attention to me in his book *The Ego and the Id* as the person who was the first to use the expression 'the It' and said that he had taken it over from me. This is true, except that the term 'It' as used for my purposes was unusable to him and he turned it into something different from what I meant... He has not changed the nature of psychoanalysis with it, neither adding nor subtracting anything. It remained what it was, the analysis of the conscious and of the repressed parts of the psyche. But *the It cannot be analysed*, whether it is Freud's It or mine which share a common name... (Groddeck 1977: 14-15, my italics)

In 1927 Freud makes his point again, but more critically, accusing Groddeck of 'a position of cancelling all distinctions... An unsatisfactory monotony with regard to the It mythology' (Groddeck 1977: 96). It is true that Groddeck's work is largely an endlessly brilliant, endlessly ingenious repetition of a single thesis, which can be seen as essentially mystical. Because he spins such a fine and endless thread, Groddeck tempts one to quote at enormous length - but here is one typical passage, from 'On the It':

> The It knows neither body nor soul since they are both manifestations of the same unknown entity... the I, individuality, becomes a doubtful concept since the It can be traced right back to the moment of fertilisation and even beyond this to the chain of parents and ancestors... Life and death... are turned into arbitrary, artificial concepts as nobody can know when the It makes death or life. There is no spatial separateness of the It either; it is fused with the environment; it is not possible to mark the point when a piece of bread, a sip of water, a breath of air, an object of sight, hearing, smell, taste, becomes the property of the It. The differences of sex are blurred; male and female are one in the human It from time immemorial and are mixed anew in the act of fertilisation... the consciousness of man loses its central position and yields it up to the unconscious, yet there is no definite dividing line between the two... The route I have taken leads clearly to the sentence: All things are one. (Groddeck 1977: 135-6, my italics)

It would not be hard to mistake this for some Buddhist, Taoist or alchemical text. In many ways Groddeck's It is close to the 'Archeus' of the sixteenth-century magus Paracelsus, which

makes bread become blood, though there was
no blood in the bread; likewise we do not
have to eat hair to grow a beard. (Sudhoff,
1922-5: 173, trans. the author)

What is outside is also inside; and what is not
outside man is not inside. The outer and the
inner are one thing... For this is the limbus,
the primordial matter which contains all creatures in germ... (Sudhoff, 1922-5: 189, trans.
the author)

Paracelsus calls by many names - archeus, iliaster, firmament,
the star in man, mumia - something absolute, constitutive,
whole and unknowable which is very similar to Groddeck's It.
He makes an attempt - like Groddeck - to insert this mystical
entity into a secular discourse; and, like Groddeck, he applies it
centrally to human illness.[1]

It is not possible here to formulate a full argument on how far
Groddeck is caught up in the phantasies of the unconscious, and
how far he is radically explicating them. But we can certainly
agree that Freud, in speaking of Groddeck's 'jump into mysticism', is pointing to a defining difference between two theories.
In another letter Freud takes a different approach, almost apologetic yet subtly self-praising:

I understand very well why the unconscious
is not enough to make you consider the It dis-
pensable. I feel the same. Yet I have a special
talent for being satisfied with the fragmen-
tary. For the unconscious is merely something
phenomenal, a sign in place of a better
acquaintanceship... (Groddeck 1977: 58)

Freud spots the difference between himself and Groddeck,
but treats it as non-defining. In his first letter to Groddeck he
makes a false identification which becomes central to the relationship: 'No matter if he [Groddeck] calls the unconscious "It"'.

Your central concept is the same as mine, Freud insists. And what is more, you cannot have conceived it independently from me:

> There is only one disturbing circumstance, the fact that you have not managed to overcome the trivial ambition of claiming originality and priority... Can you be sure in this respect? ...Could you have absorbed the main ideas of psychoanalysis in a cryptamnesic way? ...What's the use of struggling for priorities against an older generation? (Groddeck 1977: 36-7)

Coming from someone for whom that 'trivial ambition' was always of consuming importance, this is a bit rich - and must, in fact, be understood as projection. There are no reasons other than intuitive judgement of probability to doubt that Groddeck did, as he asserts, independently arrive at many of the central findings of psychoanalysis: unconscious mental processes, infant sexuality, transference and resistance (Groddeck 1977: 31). But Freud chooses - in the most charmingly persuasive way - to make this a bridge that Groddeck must cross, in order to do what Freud wants him to do: to enter the psychoanalytic community. So, with one hand Freud wipes out a real substantive difference, yet with the other he sets up a potential difference of great personal importance to himself, but which he ascribes to Groddeck!

Groddeck's response is to try again to define the point of difference he wants to sustain.

> Even in psychoanalytic circles many phenomena of life are apparently still claimed as pure products of consciousness, as if the unconscious had nothing to do with them. I am of the opinion that consciousness is merely a form of expression used by the It... that ultimately everything is created by the

unconscious. Consciousness is merely a tool of the unconscious, serving essentially similar purposes of communication as language or gesture. It often seems to me also as if the unconscious... is playing a very gay yet also very cruel game with us, i.e. with itself... occasionally the observer succeeds in seeing something which looks like the face or hand of the unconscious... Life exists before the brain. (Groddeck 1977: 39-40.)

We can perhaps see here why Ferenczi and Groddeck had such a friendly relationship; both men were drawn to the biological, to what Reich calls the 'vegetative', and placed a high value on the non-intellectual functions. Groddeck insists on a fully radical meaning of the unconscious: consciousness, he seems to be saying, is how the unconscious talks to itself - perhaps in the same way that a person is a means for the germ plasm to move around.

Freud's reply is curt and oddly commanding. Brushing aside Groddeck's specific points, he says:

I believe you should consider yourself somebody who is close to us in spite of the fact that your position on the question of the distribution between the somatic and the mental is not quite ours, and that you should help us in our work. Our journals are open to you. (Groddeck 1977: 41)

There is a long pause while Groddeck digests these instructions. In October 1917, he responds by sending Freud his paper, 'Psychic Conditioning and the Psychoanalytic Treatment of Organic Disorders' (Groddeck 1977: 109-31). 'It may interest you a little,' he writes, 'to see these fruits of your suggestions' (Groddeck 1977: 41). Suggestions, or *suggestion*? What he may be referring to is the strange piece of 'self-analysis' which opens the paper, and which he dates to early June (around the time of his second letter to Freud, which produced Freud's 'ultimatum'). Associations to the name 'Dora' and to an inflammation of the palate[2] become 'the instrument by which my conscious recognition of Freud's priority tried to penetrate into my inner unconscious mind'. Groddeck, in other words, concedes gracefully. Or does he? Is this 'penetration' intercourse or rape?

The two Its

'Priority', after all, was never the true issue, but rather what Freud calls 'originality', in its two senses of 'independent development' and 'real difference'. Groddeck does not refer to the first (Freud's imputation of cryptamnesia); and his text, as so often, blurs the second issue, which may be boiled down to the question: Is the It a synonym for the unconscious? Groddeck argues on both sides. He sets out his essentially non-Freudian notion of 'a personal It which lives man' (Groddeck 1977: 112), but then refers to 'a peculiarity of the human unconscious, of the It' (Groddeck 1977: 113). Later, in the same text, the I and the It are explicitly treated as a polar pair (Groddeck 1977: 131).

Freud is, of course, asking himself the same question and arrives at his own answer in *The Ego and the Id*, published nearly simultaneously with Groddeck's *Book of the It* (Groddeck 1961 [1923]). In this work Freud takes the very rare step of explicitly acknowledging his debt to someone else.[3]

> Now I think we shall gain a great deal by following the suggestion of a writer who, from personal motives, vainly asserts that he has nothing to do with the rigours of pure science. I am speaking of Georg Groddeck, who is never tired of insisting that what we call our I behaves essentially passively in life, and that, as he expresses it, we are 'lived' by unknown and uncontrollable forces. We have all had impressions of the same kind, even though they may not have overwhelmed us to the exclusion of all oth-

> ers... I propose to take [Groddeck's discovery]
> into account by calling the entity which starts
> out from the system *Pcpt* and begins by being
> *Pcs* the 'I', and by following Groddeck in call-
> ing the other part of the mind, into which this
> entity extends and which behaves as though
> it were *Ucs*, the 'It' . (Freud 1923: 362/23)

Here Freud seems incapable of making a simple, friendly gesture of acknowledgement without criticism, without hinting
that Groddeck has been 'overwhelmed' by this idea 'to the
exclusion of all others'. He even footnotes the passage with a
suggestion - true or false, it hardly matters - that Groddeck took
the concept or at least the term from Nietzsche, thus again rais-
ing the question of 'priority and originality' (Freud, ibid).

The most important point is that *Freud is wrong*. His own use
of the term 'It' is not cognate with Groddeck's. Freud's acknowledgement of debt is in fact an act of capture.

The most obvious formal difference between the two Its is
that Groddeck's is not opposed to the I, but prior to the splitting
of conscious and unconscious - or, indeed, of mind and body.

> I am by no means 'I', but a continually chang-
> ing form in which the It displays itself, and
> the 'I'-feeling is one of its tricks to lead man
> astray... to make of him life's pliant tool... The
> consciousness of the 'I', the manner in which
> we grownups make use of the idea 'I', is not
> inborn, but only gradually grows within
> man's mind... He has to learn it... I go so far as
> to believe that there is an individual con-
> sciousness even in the embryo... that every
> single separate cell has this consciousness of
> individuality, every tissue, every organic sys-
> tem... I must expressly emphasise one thing:
> the 'I' I claim for the cells, the organs etc. is
> not just the same thing as the It. Rather is this
> 'I' a mere product of the It, just as the ges-

> tures, the voice, the movements, the think-
> ing, building, walking upright, getting ill,
> dancing, are all products of the It.... Health,
> disease, talent, action and thought, but
> above all, perception and will and self-con-
> sciousness are only achievements of the It,
> expressions of life. About the It itself we
> know nothing whatever. (Groddeck 1961:
> 238-40)

As I have already indicated, Groddeck is quite intensely aware
that *The Ego and the Id* does not represent his own viewpoint.
He writes to his wife, after receiving Freud's book,

> *The Ego and the Id* is pretty, but quite uninter-
> esting for me. In reality it was written secret-
> ly to appropriate loans made by Stekel and
> me. And yet his It is only of limited use... He
> disregards the constructive aspects of my It,
> presumably to smuggle it in next time. Some
> of it is quite amusing. (Groddeck 1977: 13)

It's not surprising that by this point Groddeck is sensitive to
issues of priority in relation to Freud! But it is quite clear that
at the same time he draws a strong distinction between 'his It'
and 'my It'. The impact of Freud's book leads Groddeck to one
of his less ambiguous attempts at arguing the distinction of his
theory from Freud's:

> The only thing I can think of is a comparison
> which throws light on our relationship and
> our attitude to the world, but does not say
> anything about the book. [Or so Groddeck
> claims] ...In this comparison I appear to
> myself as a plough, and you as the peasant
> who uses the plough - or perhaps another
> one - for his purposes. The one thing we
> have in common is that we dig up the
> ground... Since the plough has no eyes, but

is afraid of stones, it occasionally sticks in order to make the farmer watch out... It [the plough] does not understand why the farmer insists on ploughing the stony ground first, the plough does not like going into the ground of the I where the distinction between psychological and physical is too pronounced for it... The plough, which has finally through hard experience come to the conclusion that it is not an I, tends to consider the concept of it [i.e. 'the concept of the I'] as an illusion produced by the It. The I, in its opinion, is apparently not even able to control the motility of voluntary muscles, much less that of the intestines, kidneys, heart or brain... It does not deny the I or the Over-I [Ego and Superego]. Yet they are merely tools for it, not existing entities... In other words, the plough considers the farmer a little obstinate. But then it has only the brains of a plough. (Groddeck 1977: 79-80)

This is mixed metaphor carried to extraordinary heights of subtlety! Explicitly, the ploughman/plough trope casts Groddeck as the unreflecting tool of Freud's higher strategy. Yet by making himself a non-human thing, an 'It', Groddeck identifies himself with that which for him is alone real. Freud, as the ploughman/Ego, is politely consigned to an illusory identity. Groddeck finally ventures a quite uncharacteristically precise criticism, which goes right to the heart of Freud's most privileged conceptualisations:

The investigation of castration can hardly bypass the act of birth, or of sucking and weaning, and I believe for the time being that this anxiety is centred as much in the mother as in the father, and that a third root can be found in [orgasmic] discharge. (Groddeck 1977: 80)

These are the issues that emerge in the 1920s as defining differences of psychoanalysis. To be within the analytic fold, one has to cleave to Oedipus: to recognise the primacy of the father (the 'father complex') and the centrality of castration. Groddeck, bringing in the mother, actually describes his own struggle to separate from and yet stay connected to Freud - as he says elsewhere:

> Man is the child of his childhood, and every-
> thing he lives is the long drawn-out fruitless
> attempt at growing up, at breaking away
> from his mother. (Groddeck 1977: 151)

He also, in the passage above, takes the same position as Reich (see Chapter Six), that orgasm anxiety is a central factor in neurosis.

With Groddeck, as with everyone else, Freud tries to elude the mother transference (and to stop Groddeck breaking away):

> Your categorising my person as a mother fig-
> ure, a role which I quite obviously do not fit,
> shows clearly that you are trying to evade
> the father transference. (Groddeck 1977: 75)

But Groddeck insists (in a letter dated only a few days after the 'plough and castration' letter quoted above):

> You do not in the least resemble my father
> but both you and your daughter Anna
> whom I did not want to recognise have my
> mother's eyes. And your name has lost the
> end bit, it should have an -e. [i.e. Freude,
> 'joy'].The death and castration wish is obvi-
> ous. (Groddeck 1977: 82)

If Groddeck's later work does cycle around restatements of the same theme, it may be because he cannot get what he needs from Freud, from his mother: permission to be separate but loved. A profound ambivalence reveals itself in Freud's attitude towards Groddeck. He is attracted, it seems, precisely by the sides of Groddeck's thinking and attitude with which he is unable to agree: Groddeck's 'mysticism', his emphasis on intuition and on the It's fundamental incomprehensibility - the sorts of qualities which are implied by Freud's phrase about the 'wild army' in fact. Several times Freud takes an apologetic tone towards Groddeck:

> I do not, of course, recognise my civilised, bourgeois, demystified It in your It. Yet you know that mine derives from yours. (Groddeck 1977: 93)

> I understand very well why the unconscious is not enough to make you consider the It dispensable. I feel the same. Yet I have a special talent for being satisfied with the fragmentary. For the unconscious is merely something phenomenal, a sign in place of a better acquaintanceship, as if I said: the gentleman in the havelock whose face I cannot see distinctly. What do I do if he appears without this piece of clothing? (Groddeck 1977: 58)

Similarly, he defends Groddeck from others - for example, Pfister:

> I energetically defend Groddeck against your respectability. What would you have said if you had been a contemporary of Rabelais? (Groddeck 1977: 6)

> I am not giving up my view of Groddeck either, I am usually not so taken in [sic] by anybody. But it doesn't matter. (Groddeck 1977: 7)

These and many other passages show us that the relationship

between Groddeck and Freud was unconsciously determined on both sides - powered, we might say, by the It or Id itself, by the energy of desire. Groddeck's It, though, as we have seen, is something other than Freud's, something vaster, more profound, yet less specific.

If Groddeck's It is not Freud's, then what is it? This is the one great question of Groddeck's career, and, he gives differing answers in different places - not unnaturally, since he explicitly sees the question as unanswerable. Anything one says about the It is just a finger pointing at the moon, a glass of water in the mirror: 'all concepts and names are inadequate and imprecise when applied to the It' (Groddeck 1977: 133). However, as he himself suggests, we may best grasp the concept by 'jump[ing] straight into the centre of things' (Groddeck 1977: 135): here again is one of his most uncompromising formulations, which I have already quoted at greater length.

> The It knows neither body nor soul since they are both manifestations of the same unknown entity... the It can be traced right back to the moment of fertilisation and even beyond this to the chain of parents and ancestors... life and death... are turned into arbitrary, artificial concepts as nobody can know when the It makes death or life... [I]t is fused with the environment... The differences of sex are blurred; male and female are one in the human It from time immemorial and are mixed anew in the act of fertilisation... (Groddeck 1977: 135)

It is clear from this that Groddeck cannot simply be enlisted as a 'pro-body' figure in psychoanalysis. His angle on things is altogether different: he is concerned with something that *precedes* - conceptually and historically - both body and mind. But neither is it my aim here to formulate a pro-body argument. I am simply trying to re-balance the picture and clear the ground for a reconceptualisation of the mind-body relationship which finally takes us out of 'the Cartesian theatre' (Dennett 1991: 107-8) altogether. This may be also what Groddeck is striving towards.

Reich: 'functional identity'

Discussing the difficulties of thinking about mind-body relations, Reich has this to say about Groddeck:

> Gradually a tendency became evident [in analytic theory] which some ten years later I criticised as the 'psychologisation of the physiological'... According to this conception, just about all physical illnesses resulted from unconscious desires or anxieties... The data were incontestable. Nonetheless, careful consideration rebelled against such a conclusion. How could an unconscious desire produce a carcinoma? ...Groddeck's *The Book of the It* abounds in such examples. It was metaphysics, but even mysticism is 'right in some way'.[4] And it was mystical only to the extent to which one could not say precisely when it was right, or when it was expressing correct data incorrectly. A 'desire' in the meaning of the word at that time could not conceivably bring about deep organic changes. *The act of desiring had to be grasped in a much deeper way* than analytic psychology was capable of doing. Everything pointed to deep biological processes, of which the 'unconscious desire' could only be an expression. (Reich 1973: 65-6, my italics)

This is certainly not a fair account of Groddeck, who says quite explicitly that:

> *There is no psychological cause for physical ill-*

> *ness.*[5]The unconscious [by which, for once, he means the It] is neither psyche nor physis. Personally I doubt whether the question can ever be put properly or that there will ever be an answer to it. (Groddeck 1977: 128, my italics)

However, Reich's passage contains a number of very important and interesting ideas. He is aiming - actually, like Groddeck - at achieving a *unitary* picture of 'mind' and 'body':

> It would be wrong to speak of the 'transfer' of physiological concepts to the psychic sphere, for what we have in mind is not an analogy but a real identity: the unity of psychic and somatic function. (Reich 1972: 340)

Reich begins with the fundamental link between *body* and *drive*.

> Freud said: We cannot consciously grasp what drive is. What we experience are merely derivatives of drive: sexual ideas and affects. Drive itself lies deep in the biological core of the organism; it becomes manifest as an affective urge for gratification. We sense the urge for relaxation but not the drive itself. This was a profound thought: it was understood neither by those sympathetic to nor those inimical towards psychoanalysis. It constituted a foundation of natural-scientific thinking upon which one could build with confidence. This is how I interpreted Freud: it is altogether logical that the drive itself cannot be conscious, for it is what rules and governs us. We are its object. (Reich 1973: 29-30)

Reich's sense of the implications of the Freudian unconscious is as profound and unswerving as Groddeck's.

> If Freud's theory of the unconscious was correct... then the inner psychic infinity had been grasped. One became an infinitesimal speck in the flux of one's own experiences. (Reich 1973: 39)

However, Reich is equally unswerving in his *concreteness*.

> *The Freudian 'unconscious' is present and concretely comprehensible in the form of vegetative organ sensations and impulses.* (Reich 1973: 63, original italics)

This is the 'much deeper grasp of desire' which Reich is seeking, the 'deep biological processes' of which desire is the 'expression'.

> Here, word language is not capable of explaining anything. The concepts which word language has formed about [sexuality] are themselves derivatives of the organ sensations which introduce, accompany and follow the superimposition. 'Longing', 'urge', 'copulation', 'conjugation', 'gratification', etc., are merely images of a natural process which words are not capable of making intelligible. (Reich 1972: 393)

Body ego

Equally, Reich anchors the concept of the ego in 'vegetative' processes - in the *voluntary musculature*. He gives a concrete and specific meaning to Freud's concept of the 'bodily ego' (Freud 1923: 364/25) - which he locates, not as Freud does in the *skin*, but in the *muscles*. Just as the ego binds unacceptable impulses in 'character armour', so the body binds the physical expression of those impulses in 'muscular armour', rigid muscles which concretely demonstrate inhibited action and affect.

> Character armorings were now seen to be
> functionally identical with muscular hyper-
> tonia... Muscular attitudes and character
> attitudes have the same function in the psy-
> chic mechanism: they can replace one anoth-
> er and be influenced by one another.
> Basically, they cannot be separated. They are
> identical in their function. (Reich 1972: 270-
> 1)

He provides a coherent 'biologically grounded' and *socially*
grounded account of repression, which presents the ego as the
totality of repressive processes.

> All our patients report that they went
> through periods in childhood in which, by
> means of certain practices in vegetative
> behaviour (holding the breath, tensing the
> abdominal muscular pressure, etc.), they
> learned to suppress their impulses of hate,
> anxiety, and love. Until now, analytic psy-
> chology has merely concerned itself with
> *what* the child suppresses and what the
> motives are which cause him to learn to con-
> trol his emotions. It did not enquire into the
> *way* in which children habitually fight
> against impulses. *It is precisely the physiologi-
> cal process of repression* that deserves our
> keenest attention... It can be said that *every
> muscular rigidity contains the history and mean-
> ing of its origin.* (Reich 1972: 300, original ital-
> ics)

This involves a complete break with Freud's view of both the
actual and the desirable body-mind relationship, in which
mental processes control the bodily, either inhibiting or precipitating energetic/emotional discharge.

> It is not that in certain circumstances a memory brings about an affect, but that *the concentration of a vegetative excitation and its breakthrough reproduce the remembrance*... Today we succeed in comprehending the unconscious not in its derivatives, but in its reality, by directly attacking the binding of vegetative energy. (Reich 1972: 315, original italics)

The notion of bound energy is very important here. Although he contradicts some aspects of Freud's thinking, Reich is giving concrete meaning to Freud's economic model - to the concept of the ego as *binding psychic energy*, which in the id is unbound. This is the picture which Freud creates in the *Project*, and returns to in *Beyond the Pleasure Principle*.

> The ego... is a mass of neurones which hold fast to their cathexis - are, that is, in a bound state... This bound state, which combines high cathexis with small current, would thus characterise processes of thought. (Freud 1950: 368)

> The impulses arising from the drives do not belong to the type of bound nervous processes, but of freely mobile processes which press towards discharge... It would be the task of the higher strata of the mental apparatus to bind the drive excitation reaching the primary process. (Freud 1920: 306-7/34-5)

Reich anchors the concepts of bound and unbound energy to the state of the musculature, and indeed of the autonomic nervous system (Reich 1972: 286-95).

Bringing the different aspects of psychical life together as facets of bodily life, Reich recasts some basic distinctions, reaching out for - although not really achieving - a *process* formulation.

> In short, the ego instincts are nothing other
> than the sum total of vegetative demands in
> their defensive function... The ego instinct is
> the id instinct directed either against itself or
> against another instinct... If the concept is
> correct which we have developed of the
> structure of the ego and the defense func-
> tion, then the systems, 'ego' and 'id', appear
> merely as different functions of the psychical
> apparatus and not as separate spheres of the
> psyche... That which is repressed and that
> which is warded off do not constitute two
> individual, topically separate spheres or
> forces; though antithetical, they constitute a
> functional unity. (Reich 1972: 302-3)

Reich believes that he has - in very Freudian style - *seen through*,
pierced through faulty representations to the bodily heart of
the matter. There is an uncomfortable triumphalism in all this,
reminiscent of Freud and Breuer's 'Preliminary
Communication'; perhaps it always seems so simple at the
start! But Reich's involvement with the body-as-psyche[6] is not
simple-minded - despite his *single*-minded approach. He continues to work verbally as well as bodily, combining the two
levels as appropriate:

> The vegetotherapeutic treatment of muscu-
> lar attitudes is interlaced in a very definite
> way with the work on character attitudes...
> Practical experience soon teaches us that it is
> just as inadmissible to exclude one form of
> work as it is to exclude the other. With one
> patient, work on the muscular attitude will
> predominate from the beginning, while with
> another, work on the character attitude will
> be emphasised. We also encounter a third
> type of patient with whom the work on the
> character and the work on the musculature

proceed simultaneously and partly alternat-
ingly. (Reich 1972`: 329-30)

Reassessing Reich

Since he was forced out of the IPA in 1934, Reich has been an
'unperson' within psychoanalysis. I use the expression 'forced
out' since the process was deeply secretive and manipulative.
Partly in order to appease the Nazis (Reich being at that time a
well-known communist), and partly because people like Jones
and Federn wanted rid of him, Reich was, without his knowledge, de-listed from the German Psychoanalytic Association
'because of the political situation'. When he found out, he was
asked to accede to this on the grounds that he would be a mem-
ber of the Norwegian Association as soon as it was accepted into
the IPA (Reich was living in Norway as a refugee from
Germany). However, the Norwegian Association was then told
that it could not be accepted unless Reich was excluded! (Sharaf
1983: 186-191) No public statement was ever made about Reich's
expulsion. (Jacoby 1986: 91-3)

Even when some of his ideas find their way back into the
mainstream, Reich himself is generally ignored. For example,
during my research for this book, I came across a paper by a
psychodynamically trained clinical social worker, arguing that
'verbal communications have dominated treatment theories'
but that 'breathing behaviors in treatment... may... convey a conscious or unconscious message which is possibly interpretable.
Breathing has meaning in the transference-countertransference
intersubjective world'. (Hunter 1993) Her bibliography lists
works by Freud, Alexander, Fenichel, Winnicott and many others - but nothing by Reich, who placed these issues at the centre
of his work.

Whether this is the result of ignorance (although it seems
highly unlikely, since she quotes from Lowen, who was treated
and trained by Reich and frequently refers to him) or of deliberate self-censorship, motivated by the knowledge that one
should not mention Reich in an analytically-oriented paper,
makes little difference to the point. There are many central and

significant analytic works - writings about transference, about resistance, even about character - where one might naturally expect reference to Reich, yet one finds only silence.

Insofar as there is a view on Reich's work, it is the sloppy and insupportable notion that he was 'psychotic' and therefore needs no consideration. (See Jacoby 1986: 82; Sharaf 1983: 193-4) Only one modern analytic article has seriously addressed Reich's work and sought to criticise it: Richard F Sterba's 'Clinical and Therapeutic Aspects of Character Resistance' (Sterba 1990 [1953]). I shall discuss what Sterba has to say in Chapter Eight, and try to demonstrate how he distorts Reich's position (which is at least preferable to ignoring it).

Although the 'disappearing' of Reich from analytic history[7] and theory is totalitarian and insupportable, there are clear and serious flaws in Reich's work. However, one can only properly criticise complex theories if one first takes them seriously. I want to identify two problematic areas in Reich's thinking: the first to do with the *style* of his analytic work, and the second with its *content*.

Reich's therapeutic approach is controlling in the extreme, with an emphasis on 'attacking' and 'smashing' defences. He speaks frequently in terms of a basic therapeutic task of 'breaking down of the character armor, or, to put it another way, specific destruction of the neurotic equilibrium' (Reich 1972: 292). This is a function of Reich's own overpowering character structure, and of his profound need for 'deep contact' which sought imperiously to sweep aside all obstacles. It is also related to his belief that he had privileged knowledge of what a person should be like, of what is 'normal' and 'natural', as we shall see in a moment.

It must be said, though, that there is ample evidence of a more sensitive and careful side to Reich's therapeutic style. The eminent American psychiatrist and analyst O. Spurgeon English was in a training analysis with Reich from 1929 to 1931 - one of a number of American candidates referred to Reich by Sandor Ferenczi - and later wrote a memoir of his experience. This portrays vividly and with dry humour Reich's interpretation of style as well as content.

> [H]e would frequently call attention to the
> monotony of my tone of voice as I free associ-
> ated. He would also call attention to my posi-
> tion on the couch, and I remember particular-
> ly that he confronted me with the fact that
> when I entered and left the office, I made no
> move to shake hands with him as was the
> custom in both Austria and Germany... I told
> him... that in New England, at least that part
> of New England I came from, we merely said
> hello and sometimes we didn't even do that.
> (English 1977: 241-2)

Spurgeon had two years of classical training analysis with
Reich - for part of that period this entailed seven sessions a
week! He is clear that 'I never regretted my choice of psychoanalyst in choosing Wilhelm Reich' (English 1977: 253). He relates
a story of one incident when Reich wanted to change a session
time in a way that was inconvenient for English, and questioned
English's unwillingness:

> I told him that I previously had kept his
> schedule from the beginning of analysis and
> that having made the appointment he should
> keep his, and that I further thought it was
> audacious and presumptuous of him to ques-
> tion whether my social engagements were
> more important than the analysis... When I
> had run down on all this, to which he had lis-
> tened patiently, he merely said 'You are per-
> fectly right'... I had the first and perhaps
> greatest lesson in my life of the fact that a
> human being may be self-assertive and be
> given a right to an opinion and not be criti-
> cized for it or have acknowledgement given
> grudgingly. (English 1977: 245)

My second criticism of Reich addresses his identification of deep vegetative impulses - the 'drives' - with genital sexuality, and his promotion of the latter as the answer to the human predicament. Perhaps paradoxically, I would argue that Reich's work is actually greatly strengthened if we discount what he himself regarded as its absolute core - his claim that 'orgastic potency' is a necessary and sufficient condition of human decency, productivity and happiness.

Reich seems to have no sense of the force of Freud's deconstruction of human sexuality, and little sense, one sometimes feels, of the subtleties, complexities and ambivalences of human desire in general. Although he talks of the need for 'a much deeper grasp of desire', his reduction of desire to genitality is *superficial*, and stems from an implicit essentialism of the body, a tendency to privilege unthinking physicality over and against the mental - what one might perhaps call 'somatic chauvinism'.

It is very probable that Reich's genitalism is itself a defensive response to his own experience of childhood sexual abuse - which Reich never admitted to be abuse, but portrayed rather as an exemplar of healthy childhood sexuality. He was one of many middle class children at this period to be drawn into sexual activity by their nursemaids and other servants, starting in Reich's case at the age of four (Reich 1990: 6). The result was that by the age of ten and a half Reich was in a condition he himself describes as 'sexual hyperesthesia' (Reich 1990: 21-2). At the age of eleven, Reich says, he began to have intercourse 'almost every day for years' with a cook. His way of dealing with these experiences was through a theoretical position which normalised them, by generalising from his own experiences. This is a natural and perhaps inevitable feature of any psychological theory, but if the theory is to prove useful it must deal with the issue of *differences* between people.

Of course, his theory could still be valid whatever its personal sources, but Reich's concept of genitality is simple in the extreme, and has various unfortunate consequences for his thinking. One is a naive naturalism which posits a somehow preordained developmental pattern through libidinal stages culminating in the formation of 'decent', 'healthy', 'genital characters' (Reich 1972: 181-2). A second is his total blind spot about any possibility of child sexual abuse - that children can be damaged by sexual *invasion* as well as by sexual *repression*. This is not to say that Reich ever or anywhere condones the sexual exploitation of children by adults (this sort of absurd projection has repeatedly been made onto him); but simply that he is not concerned with it, does not discuss it, ignores it. This is all the more surprising in the light of Reich's extreme sensitivity to other forms of childhood suffering, for example: around birth (Reich 1983: 3-4).

At the same time, another part of me resonates with Reich's argument that we resist his picture of sexual naturalness just because we know it is *true*.

> The fundamentally changed attitude... is sim-
> ple and natural... It is a secret ideal in all peo-
> ple, and it always means the same thing, even
> if it is called by a different name. (Reich 1973:
> 183.)

His detailed description of genital intercourse is powerful and beautiful. Maybe many of us have the sense that, if sex could always be like *this*, then our life would be changed utterly? Yet it is ridiculous to attach this sense of sexual epiphany, this 'fundamentally changed attitude', exclusively to a closely defined act of heterosexual penetrative intercourse. It is hard enough to find bliss anywhere; but when it does, rarely, appear, it comes in many, many forms and acts.

Reich's whole normative stance leads him to avoid any serious contestation of gender positions. Although there is little or nothing in Reich's work which depreciates women (the same is unfortunately not true as regards homosexuality) and although, long before Lacanian feminism, he introduced the term 'patriarchy' into analytic discussion (see for example Reich 1973: 7-8), he seems profoundly uninterested in anything other than a narrowly social egalitarianism of genders.

Despite his many shortcomings, though, the sheer range of Reich's work, his attempt to take a central position which communicates with the whole range of human and natural sciences, is enormously impressive; as is his great achievement of *bringing metapsychology back to the musculature*. This has created, at last, a proper place for energetics within analytic theory, making it possible for the 'information' and 'energy' models to be brought into coherent relation with each other. Reich makes sense of and finds a place for Freud's *economic* model of psychic processes; but, in doing so, he drastically undercuts the *topographical* model.

In the next chapter we shall explore how Reich and post-Reichian psychotherapists have attempted to use these ideas about the body as part of a therapeutic practice.

> It is essential to know towards what [the ana-
> lyst's] attention is directed; and, as all our
> labours show, it is certainly not directed
> towards an object beyond the subject's speech
> in the way it is for certain analysts who make
> it a strict rule never to lose sight of that object.
> If this were to be the way of analysis, then it
> would surely have recourse to other means -
> otherwise it would be the only example of a
> method that forbade itself the means neces-
> sary to its own ends. (Lacan 1977: 45)

> There seems to be a certain relationship
> between the capacity in general for the relax-
> ation of the musculature and for free associa-
> tion. (Ferenczi 1988a: 282n)

Breath

Without direct experience, it may be hard to see how 'bodywork' - that is, the therapist focusing upon the client's bodily
process, through touch or otherwise - can have anything to do
with psychoanalysis. Certainly there are problems in bringing
the two together, as we shall see. But firstly I want to give a very
brief outline of the basic arguments against dismissing the idea
out of hand.

In Reich's mature conception of therapy, breathing plays a
role closely analogous to that of free association. Free association, the 'fundamental rule', is a demand with which no one can
fully comply. As Ferenczi first pointed out in 1927, it 'represents
an ideal which... can only be fulfilled after the analysis has
ended' (1988a: 210). In other words, as Adam Phillips puts it,
'the patient is not cured by free-associating, he is cured *when he
can free-associate*' (199:, 102). It is not actually evident that *anyone*
can free associate; or, rather, that whilst free associating, anyone

can remain 'themselves' in the sense of maintaining an experience of consistent, continuous and bounded identity. It could be
argued that one purpose of free association is to educate us in
how to do without such an identity.

In a very similar way, no one can actually breathe! To put it
less dramatically, when one tries to allow the breath to happen
freely *while at the same time attending to it consciously*, sooner or
later consciousness and spontaneity begin to interfere with each
other. Resistance begins to emerge, resistance which corresponds to repression and which is embodied in the breath.
Breathing is on the interface between voluntary and autonomic
function: any attempt to 'control ourselves' - which is in large
part what repression is - will emerge in the breath. This seems
to be at least part of the reason why many schools of meditation
are centred on attention to the breath.

'Imagine,' Reich says,

> that you have been frightened or that you
> anticipate great danger. You will involuntari-
> ly suck in your breath and hold it... You will
> soon breathe out again, but the respiration
> will not be complete. It will be shallow... It is
> by holding their breath that children are in
> the habit of fighting against continual and
> tormenting conditions of anxiety which they
> sense in the upper abdomen. They do the
> same thing when they sense pleasurable sen-
> sations in the abdomen or in the genitals, and
> are afraid of these sensations... The way in
> which our children achieve this 'shutting-off
> feeling in the stomach', with the help of res-
> piration and abdominal pressure, is typical;
> and universal... In reduced respiration, less
> oxygen is introduced... With less energy in
> the organism, the vegetative excitations are
> less intense and, therefore, easier to control.
> (Reich 1973: 306-9)

In other words, control of breath is a major weapon in children's battles to become the person whom they are told they should be: someone well-behaved, self-controlled, and impervious to impulses of excitement, grief or anger.[1] It is through breath that we create and maintain what I have elsewhere called 'the spastic I' (Totton and Edmondson 1988: 17) - the ego that is based upon body *tension* rather than upon body *awareness*.

> It was clear now that as the physiological mechanism for the suppression and repression of affects, the inhibition of respiration was the basic mechanism of neurosis in general. (Reich 1973: 308)

The central focus of Reichian bodywork, then, is on re-establishing a fuller and more spontaneous breath - *not* as an effort of will, like a form of yoga, but by gradually letting go of our need to protect ourselves from feeling by not breathing. By working systematically through all the levels of resistance to spontaneous breath - to 'being breathed' - the therapist and client will encounter the familiar repetition compulsion, transference neurosis and other phenomena which appear through systematic work using free association, or indeed any other sustained encouragement to let things happen spontaneously and without censorship. As Ferenczi says of his 'relaxation technique':

> But with this, as with every novelty, we soon find that it contains something very, very old - I had almost said, something commonplace. Are not both these principles [relaxation and frustration] inherent in the method of free association? (Ferenczi 1988b: 115)

The demands which interfere with each other are not in fact consciousness and spontaneity, as I suggested above, but *consistency* and spontaneity. The 'spastic ego' has learned to regard consciousness as a matter of self-consistency, continuous self-commentary which saves appearances. Like free association, attention to breathing reveals the impossibility of maintaining both consistency and spontaneity. Or, from a slightly different angle, it reveals that we cannot *deliberately* be consistent or spontaneous - because we can never be anything else.

Michael Eigen is, to my knowledge, the only 'mainstream' analyst to write about breathing (Eigen 1993: 43-7).[2] His ideas are developed from work with the post-Reichian bodywork therapist Stanley Keleman (Eigen 1993: xviii; e.g. Keleman 1975). He describes well how reconnecting with the spontaneous breath can have a profound therapeutic effect, parallel to that achieved through traditional analytic approaches.

> As the ego gradually allows itself to participate deeply, at least, periodically, in the flow of breathing *qua* experienced breathing, it more securely grasps its own basic ambiguity of being both without and within the body: 'I am but am not my body.' *The experience of breathing provides the most continuous lived bodily form for the ego's fundamental experience of itself...* As one patient reported: 'When I feel my breathing fully, I feel as though I've come into the clear.' (Eigen 1993: 44-5, my italics)

I would go even further, and suggest that through attention to the breath, through watching its appearance and disappearance, the ego grasps its own basic ambiguity of *existing and not existing*. We shall look at this theme in the next chapter.

As I have said, the goals of bodywork are basically consistent with those of verbal work - whatever these may be! One verbal or body-centred practitioner may see their work as being about freeing spontaneity, whilst another may focus on facilitating their client's adaptation to conventional social demands. The account that I am giving here of both bodywork and verbal work is biased strongly towards the former, in line with Reich himself who, of course, combined his bodywork techniques with verbal work. He proposed, however, that - at least for some kinds of client, at some points in the therapy - working *directly* on the bodily level, on the muscular 'binding of vegetative energy' (Reich 1973: 315) - and not only on its psychical derivatives - is more productive. This matches my own experience and that of many other therapists who work on both levels.

To speak of my own experience for a moment, my initial training in Reichian therapy assumed that bodywork was generally appropriate for all clients. This is what we were being trained to do. Certainly, there was verbal interaction alongside the bodywork, with some attention to transference and countertransference, but bodywork was regarded very much as a complete and self-sufficient approach to psychotherapy - with, to be honest, a certain amount of condescension towards the toilers in the fields of language.

This is the understandable end result of Reich's expulsion from the psychoanalytic movement - an initial reaction, like Timon of Athens, of 'I banish *you*', which for subsequent generations has set up a separate world of 'orgonomy', or 'Reichian therapy', cut off from any sense of Reich's own history. However, this approach does not represent Reich's mature work, where verbal and body-oriented work alternate and interact with each other in a very sensitive and fluid way. (It is also untrue that bodywork is the best or, indeed, even a suitable approach for all clients, as we will see later.)

The Fish and the Ape

Either verbally or bodily, Reich's approach to therapy is characteristically active, perhaps to the point of potential invasiveness. He thinks always in terms of '*breaking down*... the character armour, or, put another way, specific *destruction* of the neurotic equilibrium' (Reich 1973: 292, my italics). This is a matter of Reich's personal style, for better or worse, and not intrinsic to his methods. Bodywork, as much as verbal work, is often conducted slowly, gently, and (at least comparatively) non-actively. Nor does it necessarily involve touch. For several years, Reich worked simply with a version of Ferenczi's 'relaxation technique', patiently and repeatedly encouraging clients just to breathe and to let go to any spontaneous bodily phenomena -

trembling, jerking, or whatever manifested itself.

Reich offers a detailed account of such an analysis in *The Function of the Orgasm* (Reich 1973: 309-29) which also demonstrates that, alongside his confrontative approach, he worked with considerable care and sensitivity.[3] He describes how, over six and a half months of daily sessions (which means at least six, perhaps seven days a week),[4] he encouraged his analysand to 'give in to every impulse' .The man in question presented with two striking features: what Reich calls his 'psychic reserve', his extreme superficiality, politeness, and inability to express aggression; and his 'very striking facial expression', a small tight mouth which 'hardly moved in the act of speaking'.

Reich decides to focus on the latter, and points it out to the patient. '[F]ollowing the consistent description of the rigid attitude of his mouth, a clonic twitching of his lips set in, weak at first but growing gradually stronger. He was surprised by the involuntary nature of this twitching and defended himself against it.' Reich encourages the client to give in to the twitching, and

> his lips began to protrude and retract rhythmically and to hold the protruded position for several seconds... In the course of these movements, his face took on the unmistakable expression of an infant... The various manifestations in his face... gradually aroused the patient's interest. This must have some special meaning, he said. (Reich 1973: 311)

Pulling gently on this thread, Reich and his patient gradually unravel the whole structure of his defences. For a long while the facial manifestations, even when they quite plainly portray grief or anger, are not accompanied by any felt emotion. Reich realises that the muscle tensions in the face represent 'not only the warded-off affect but also the defence': that is, in line with Reich's general theory, the muscle spasticity is structured like a symptom, 'containing' both the unconscious impulse and its repression. 'Several weeks passed' - in effect, twenty or more sessions of patient, repetitive work with the facial twitch - before the crying and anger began to express themselves more fully, still without emotional involvement, but with the patient having

> an immediate grasp of the meaning of his action, without any explanation on my part. He knew that he was expressing an over-whelming anger which he had kept locked up in himself for decades. The emotional detachment subsided when an attack pro-duced the remembrance of his older brother, who had very much dominated and mistreat-ed him as a child. (Reich 1973: 314)

As the work continues, we see it move flexibly between bodily and verbal work, with Reich in effect following the patient's emotional charge as it shifts from bodily to psychic focus and back again.

> It is not customary in character-analytic work to deal with a subject, no matter how topical, unless the patient enters upon it of his own accord in a fully affective way. (Reich 1973: 317)

So while the patient *speaks* detachedly of his experience, his *body* reacts emotionally, and Reich chooses to stay with the body expression until the emotion comes into the words.

The spasms and twitchings spread gradually into the chest and belly, and then jump to the legs. 'Quite involuntarily, I was reminded of epileptic clonisms... There were times in the treat-ment of this patient when I was uncertain whether or not I was confronted with a true epileptic.' The 'gap between his muscu-lar actions and the patient's perception of them... remained unchanged'. (Reich 1973: 317-318) In other words, there was still no emotional *experience* even in these dramatic bodily expres-sions.

To progress further Reich has to step back, as it were, and consider the client's character.

> We both knew that he was very cautious...
> This 'caution' was also contained in his mus-
> cular activity... I began to deal with his cau-
> tion, not from the psychic side, as I am usual-
> ly in the habit of doing in character analysis,
> but from the somatic side. For instance, I
> pointed out again and again that, while it was
> true he revealed his anger in his muscular
> actions, he never followed through, never
> really struck with his raised and clenched
> fist... After consistently working on the
> defense against the muscular action for a
> number of sessions, the following episode
> from his fifth year of life suddenly occurred
> to him... (Reich 1973: 319)

The patient describes a betrayal by his mother, and connects it with both 'his defensive attitude towards women' and his general character trait of caution. However, the holding-back continues. One day, the patient begins to talk about his enthusiasm for trout fishing, and describes in detail the process of casting the line and so on.

> In the act of telling and demonstrating this to
> me, he had an enormously greedy, almost
> sadistic expression on his face. It struck me
> that... he omitted one detail, namely the
> moment at which the trout bites into the
> hook. (Reich 1973: 320)

However,

> roughly four weeks elapsed before the fol-
> lowing took place: ...strange twitchings
> appeared in the abdomen... The upper part of
> his body jerked forward, the middle of his

abdomen remained still, and the lower part of his body jerked towards the upper part. The entire response was an organic unitary movement. There were sessions in which this movement was repeated continuously... In one such attack, his face had the unmistakable expression of a fish. Without any prompting on my part, before I had drawn his attention to it, the patient said 'I feel like a primordial animal,' and shortly afterward, 'I feel like a fish'. (Reich 1973: 320)

'His caution became understandable now,' Reich says: 'he did not trust anyone. He did not want to be caught.' And now real change occurs:

In the process of working through this connection, his personality underwent a conspicuous change. His superficiality disappeared; he became serious. The seriousness appeared very suddenly during one of the sessions. The patient said literally: 'I don't understand; everything has become so deadly serious all of a sudden.' (Reich 1973: 321)

Through this image thrust forward by the body, Reich and his patient discover the relationship with the mother. Later in the work, through a similar image of a gorilla, they discover the relationship with the father.

The patient experienced a severe attack of anxiety. He jumped up, his mouth contorted with pain; beads of perspiration covered his forehead; his musculature was stiff as a board. He hallucinated an animal, an ape. In doing so, his hand had the bent attitude of an ape's paw, and he uttered sounds from the depth of his chest, 'as if without vocal cords,' he himself said afterward. It was as if some-

> one had come very close to him and threat-
> ened him. Then, trance-like, he cried out,
> 'Don't be angry, I only want to suck.' (Reich
> 1973: 325-6)

The 'fish' betrayed by the mother, the 'ape' threatened by the
father. Once these two primordial figures have emerged from
the body armouring, the work can be concluded, as the patient
realises he believes - his body believes - that:

> 'a man is hard and unyielding; any form of
> surrender is feminine'... Immediately follow-
> ing this realisation, his infantile conflict with
> his father was resolved. On the one hand, he
> felt sheltered and protected by his father... At
> the same time, he strove to stand on his own
> feet and be independent of his father... When
> he finally experienced surrender in the
> reflex,[5] he was deeply baffled by it. 'I would
> never have thought,' he said, 'that a man can
> surrender too.' (Reich 1973: 327-8)

Touch

In this case history, Reich does not use touch. In fact, it seems to
date from early in his exploration of bodywork, and to be one of
the founding cases of his new method. Later on, though, in the
late 1930s, Reich began to intervene directly with his hands,
using massage-like techniques to overload tense muscles to the
point of release, and to 'irritate' pressure points so as to stimu-
late emotional expression. Although he never refers to it, Reich
is in some ways repeating the explorations of Georg Groddeck,[6]
the 'special kind of massage' (Groddeck 1977: 21) through
which

> the patient's changing expressions reveal hid-
> den secrets of his [sic] soul that in no other
> way could come to the knowledge of his doc-

tor. Unconscious impulses and deeply buried traits of character betray themselves in his involuntary movements... (Groddeck 1977: 236)

Unlike Groddeck, so far as we know, Reich's project was not only to *understand* through the use of bodily pressure, but also to *release* repressed affect and create the conditions for therapeutic change. Although some schools of post-Reichian work have stayed with his earlier methods, others have taken up and extended the use of this sort of physical intervention:

> The chronic contraction of the skeletal muscles can be worked on directly... To mobilize a chronically contracted muscle one must first increase the contraction to a point which cannot be maintained. The muscle thus overstrained must relax. This is done by direct pressure on the muscle with the thumb, by irritating or stimulating it, such as by tickling or pinching. Direct pressure is the usual and most effective means. One will find near the insertion of the muscle a very sensitive spot where contraction is greatest and it is here that the muscle responds best to stimulus... Of course the muscle will only contract back down again unless the emotion (and ideas) that is being held back is released. For this reason groups of muscles that form a functional unit in holding back emotions are worked on together... Where muscles cannot be reached by the hands other methods must be used, such as gagging [i.e. retching] (Baker 1980 : 47)

Other techniques include asking the client to make various movements and expressions, including hitting out, kicking, squeezing and so on, as well as encouraging the use of the voice in shouting, growling, screaming and other emotional expressions.

Clearly, this sort of work shades into non-psychotherapeutic bodywork styles such as Rolfing, where the intention is to release muscle and fascial tension so as to improve posture and bodily functioning. In fact, the shading works both ways: it would be hard today to find a method of deep body massage which shows no awareness of the concept of emotional holding and release. Even practitioners whose work is primarily contextualised as 'complementary or alternative medicine' have been influenced by a trickle-down from Reichian views. As one example, *The Endless Web* by Schultz and Feitis is a book on Rolfing, a method of deep massage aimed at freeing the connective tissue of the body. Although the whole focus of the method is physical and proto-medical, looking at how people 'use their structures inefficiently' and seeking to 'free the soft tissues so that the body can move freely by balancing through planes that are horizontal and vertical' (Schultz and Feitis 1996: 45), the book is studded with Reichian concepts:

> Most holding patterns are related to emotional fear, lack of trust... Movement patterns express personality patterns... Holding the breath is a way of stopping that physical flow [of emotional discharge]. Perhaps we do this because we don't want to experience the sensation or the emotion... Holding the breath is a pattern most of us use to ward off unwanted feelings. To some extent, we are taught to hide emotion. (Schultz and Feitis 1996: 46-8)

However, it is the *context* of Reichian therapy which makes the work clearly psychotherapeutic in intention - the realisation that 'the muscle will only contract back down again unless the emotion (and ideas) that is being held back is released' (Baker, loc. cit.), and that for this to happen involves more than poking and yelling. As we saw very clearly in Reich's case history, focusing on the involuntary aspect of the body acts as a 'royal road' to eliciting recognisably psychoanalytic material, which is then worked through in familiar ways. Bodywork of this kind, however, is a great deal more than simply a way to gather material: in combination with interactive verbal work, it is also a way to *change* the individual's psychosomatic structure.

Transference in bodywork

In the 'Fish and Ape' case history, unlike several others, Reich does not specifically discuss the transference relationship. It is undoubtedly true, though, that even this sort of continual focus on the body, let alone direct touch, will 'heat up' the transference. This will not necessarily be in a directly sexual sense, but will depend upon the client's material and character structure: a hysterical character will certainly be having sexual fantasies about what is going on - often quite consciously - but other characters will apprehend bodywork in a variety of different ways, as being about nurturing, mastery, or whatever are their primary issues.

Intimate physical contact, in our culture, generally implies one or more of the following: a sexual relationship, an adult-child relationship, a 'making better' relationship (doctor, nurse, dentist, etc.). This can be enormously confusing for both parties, especially if the therapist is not able to bring awareness to these implications. Without proper training, a mutual trance can be established where both people are fantasising about their relationship in one or more of the three ways outlined above, and not owning those fantasies. (This is, of course, also true of verbal therapy, especially - but not exclusively - when the client lies on the couch.)

The greatest difficulty will often arise around the 'making better' scenario: because bodywork does tend to carry with it a sense that 'making better' is at least part of what is going on - as it quite appropriately is with an osteopath, a masseur, etc. My experience is that there are real and persistent difficulties with the countertransference position around bodywork, for this reason: therapists either enjoy the sense of power and effectiveness that this identification offers, or use it as a protective cloak - a protective white coat, in fact - against more frightening feelings in themselves and their clients. However, many analysts have the same countertransference problem (often without seeing it as a problem) in purely verbal therapy, where the medical metaphor of cure dominates their work.

Despite Freud's own well-known opposition, there has always been a powerful tendency within psychoanalysis to see it as a 'special branch of medicine' (Freud 1926b: 166/229). In fact the only issue on which Freud was defeated in the International Psychoanalytic Association was the restriction of entry into the American analytic profession to medical doctors. Freud voted against the restriction. Certainly, there were issues of status and income involved here; but also, one may insist, issues of countertransference - of how analysts choose to *position* themselves in relation to their analysands.

As it turned out, Reich himself was a 'conservative' on this issue. In the debate of 1927 (Reich, 1927: 252), he was in favour of restricting training to medics (in opposition to figures whom one might think of as much more 'conservative', such as Sachs - 1927: 200 and Freud himself - 1926b). This is a view that Reich never changed, even after his expulsion from the IPA and the many radical vicissitudes of his work. It is as if he maintained the 'medical model' as a guarantor of scientific respectability, along with a corresponding inhibition of the full use of transference and countertransference. Reich situates the analytic encounter, with or without bodywork, as a transaction between *adults*; his work never really addresses the regressive dimension of analysis, and often tends to approach neurosis, character structure, body armour, as 'foreign bodies' to be dismantled and stripped away by medical-style treatment.

In a sense it is extraordinary that Reich maintained this view, in the face of his own work and the profound insight it gives into how deeply character structure is bound up with the whole formation of the ego. Reading Reich's work, one can see two unintegrated aspects - almost, 'two Reichs': one who sees himself as a medic of the mind, 'smashing' and 'dissolving' defenses and 'releasing' healthy genitality; and another who works patiently and carefully to uncover defences, to *meet* them with acceptance and understanding and to celebrate them as largely successful strategies for dealing with intolerable stress.

In any case, succeeding generations of bodyworkers have taken a very different position. As Babette Rothschild says:

> Many schools of body work (and some of psychotherapy) deny or discount the existence and/or significance of transference and counter-transference. Classic to body work of the 60's and 70's was an expectation that the work was for personal growth and that all participants were adults and expected to maintain mature feelings towards their facilitator/therapist/teacher. (Rothschild, 1994: 25)

In this context, transference-countertransference feelings were seen as 'unequal' and suspect. An accurate criticism of some analytic attitudes of superiority to the client - themselves bound up with the medical model - was generalised into a rejection of all relationships between client and practitioner that were not perfectly symmetrical in structure. This leads to the curious fact that bodywork tends to be *intra*-personal rather than *inter*-personal in its model of therapy. (This is explicitly the position of, for example, the Hakomi Method - see Kurtz 1990).

These two streams, then - the medical model, and humanistic reluctance to explore asymmetric relationships - came together to obscure understanding of the transference and counter-transference. In many forms of therapeutic bodywork little or no attention is paid to the transference. The results of this are unlikely to be helpful, and may easily range from the unfortunate to the disastrous. However, it is just as possible - and important - to attend to and interpret transference and counter-transference phenomena in this modality as in a purely verbal one.

What, then, are the *extra* transferential issues in body-centred therapy as opposed to purely verbal work? As I have said, transference is likely to be 'hotter' when the fact of there being two bodies in the room is explicit rather than implicit. The feelings will not be different, nor even stronger, but they are likely to be rather more in the here-and-now, rather more accessible to consciousness. This has a lot to do with the use by many body-centred therapists of the damping-down effect of the medical model - wrapping themselves, if not literally then metaphorically, in a white coat. And yet, of course, the medical relationship is itself an intensely transferential one, including directly sexual transference ('playing doctors and nurses'); it is only on a superficial level that the 'white coat attitude' sobers things up.

The more I consider transference in bodywork, the more it seems to me to produce much the same issues as in verbal work. For example, we have the same choice about what to follow in bodywork: unconscious desire, or the transference resistance. In other words, we must choose between supporting the 'deepest' impulse that we perceive in the client - generally, the ego's impulse to surrender in one way or another to an unconscious desire - or supporting the impulse to resist, to fight back, to understand the situation as an interpersonal one. This is exactly the question which Reich answered in *Character Analysis*, coming down decisively in favour of working 'from the outside inwards', interpreting the resistance rather than the 'id-impulses'.

> Interpretations involving deeper probing
> have to be avoided as long as the first front of
> cardinal resistances has not become manifest
> and been eliminated... Faced with the choice
> of interpreting unconscious contents or taking
> up evident resistances, the analyst will
> choose the latter. Our principle is: No interpretation
> of meaning when a resistance interpretation
> is still to come. (Reich 1972: 29)

The same principle applies in body psychotherapy: to follow whatever path in bodywork has the strongest charge of transference for the client - to work with the body issue or body area that expresses the relationship with the therapist, and in particular the *resistance* to the therapist. That is, as therapist I will focus on whatever part of their body wants to do something in relation to *me*: to hold me, push me away, be touched by me, fend me off, hit me, turn away from me...

Often a very small amount of actual bodywork will produce enough material for one or more whole sessions of discussion. In fact, even when bodywork is explicitly on the agenda, we may never get that far; feelings *about* bodywork, or about the therapist, may become obvious before we do anything else. For example, as the client starts to lie down it may be clear to one or both of us that there is an unwillingness to proceed, or equally a striking eagerness, and we may spend the session exploring that.

Working in this way leads to a redefinition of Reichian work as centred on *breathing and relationship,* as an exploration of the odd-sounding but fundamental question: *how can I breathe and relate to someone at the same time?* As Reich pointed out, whenever we have difficult feelings in relation to someone else, we restrict our breathing in order to keep those feelings down (often quite unconsciously). Alternatively, in order to keep *breathing*, we cut off *relating*, for example by turning away or closing our eyes. Doing both at once, staying open internally and externally, is very demanding; yet a very valuable 'active technique' through which to explore core therapeutic issues. It immediately brings the focus to transference issues - and to countertransference, because this sort of intense face-to-face relating, combined with attention to the breath, is highly demanding for the therapist as well.

Having started out in practice as a 'pure' bodyworker I find, after fifteen years, that I 'do' a lot less bodywork - certainly of a hands-on kind. But although I do less, by keeping relationship at the centre of the therapy, the bodywork I do is much more focused and useful. Also, it integrates much more fluidly with talking, rather than maintaining the rather abrupt and awkward boundary between speech and bodywork that many bodywork practitioners experience. I do less hands-on bodywork now because I have a wider range of skills, which allows me to use bodywork when, and only when, it is the best tool for the situation.

Many of the difficulties in integrating bodywork into psy-

chotherapy - and many of the transference issues it brings up -
are essentially cultural problems around bodies and touch. Just
as in the early days of psychoanalysis, body-centred therapy
rubs against some of society's sorest spots (see Berman 1990,
Efron 1985). This is not necessarily a bad thing, but it makes the
work peculiarly sensitive.

Some indications and contraindications for bodywork

As I have already mentioned, I came out of my initial training
under the impression that one could pretty much always usefully employ bodywork with a client. This has turned out not to
be the case. The simple fact of compliance - even of enthusiastic
demand - in no way establishes that bodywork will be helpful
in accessing core issues.

To give three common examples: abuse survivors may con-
sent to bodywork as a means of *repeating*, rather than remembering and working through, the experience of abuse. Schizoid
characters (whether or not abused) may be sufficiently out of
contact with their own feelings and sensations that they just
don't *know* that they find bodywork terrifying: they go along
with the process while what they experience as their self is, in
effect, floating up to the ceiling and observing from a safe dis-
tance. Masochistic characters may demand to be pummelled
and poked, seeking a fantasised 'release' while in actuality they
absorb the pressure into their defensive structure - and make the
therapist sweat![7]

Of course, as many therapists will recognise, all of these
strategies can be used without bodywork as a vehicle. But in
each case I would say that bodywork hinders rather than helps
any mutual clarity, by inserting an apparent mechanism for
'cure' *in between* client and practitioner; and may even do damage, through re-stimulating both trauma and defence against
trauma.

As I indicated in Chapter One, bodywork is primarily useful
when it can offer a *bridge* between 'somatic' and 'psychic' modes
of experience. It is most appropriate for clients who either need
to be met in the register of their own predominant mode of

experience, before being encouraged to explore other registers like the verbal and intellectual, or, having been met in the verbal and intellectual registers, need to explore the unknown territory of the body.[8]

For many of us in Western advanced-capitalist culture, the body is indeed unknown territory. And one of the aims of the following three chapters will be to explore some of the deeper reasons why, and the ways in which, this has come about. Why it is that, in Freud's crucial perception, the ego tends to experience the body as its enemy?

Chapter Six - Body as Death

Lacan's body

Lacan has little to say about the body. As far as he is concerned, the unconscious certainly is not an expression of 'deep biological processes', of 'vegetative organ sensations and impulses' (Reich 1973: 63 and 66). On the contrary, it is an intellectual phenomenon, 'structured like a language' (Lacan 1977: 234). He explicitly scorns Reich for 'seeking the ineffable organic expression beyond speech... in order to deliver it from its armour' (Lacan 1977: 101), not because it isn't *there*, as what Lacan calls the Real, but because it is not, by its nature, expressible. One can hardly exaggerate, says Lacan, 'the little physiology that is of interest to the unconscious' (Lacan 1977: 302) or, indeed, the little physiology that is of interest to Lacan.

There is a rather complex point here. Lacan would of course agree that physiology as a signifying system in the symbolic order is as interesting to the unconscious as any other signifying system. This is sufficiently demonstrated by Freud's physiological and anatomical dreams in *The Interpretation of Dreams*. What he is criticising is the idea that the *object* of physiology - the real of the body - is 'of interest to the unconscious'. For Lacan, the unconscious is of the symbolic order, the order of language.

As he says on the same page:

> of course, psychoanalysis involves [as well as its most central concern, the symbolic order] the real of the body and the imaginary of its mental schema. But... we must first perceive that the more or less departmented integrations that appear to order [development], function in it above all like heraldic elements, like the body's coat-of-arms. (Lacan 1977: 302)

It is precisely these two categories - 'the real of the body and the imaginary of its mental schema' - which Lacan accuses Reich of mixing up in a confused attempt to express the inexpressible, to symbolise the real: 'Reich's error... caused him to take armorial bearings for an armour' (Lacan 1977: 109).

'Armorial bearings', heraldic devices, are one of Lacan's images for the 'mental schema of the body', the ways in which the body is organised by libidinal investments. Lacan argues that Reich has mistaken this imaginary system - the erogenous zones and their armourings - for something actual, bodily; and has further conflated the actual with the Real. The Real, in Lacan's terms, is that which stands outside symbolisation. We can say nothing about it. Reich, attending to the orders of the Imaginary and the Real, is talking about everything except that which it is possible to talk about.

'Outside the sphere of human language'

Reich's views on language are utterly incompatible with Lacan's.

> The ideas of orthodox psychology and depth psychology [i.e. psychoanalysis] are chained to word formations. However, the living organism functions beyond all verbal ideas and concepts. Human speech, a biological form of expression at an advanced stage of development, is not a specific attribute of the living organism, which functions long before language and verbal representations exist. (Reich 1972: 358-9)

The happy coincidence of Reich's use of the word 'chained' heightens the contrast. For Reich, it is *psychoanalysis*, rather than - as for Lacan - the human subject, which is bound by chains of signifiers. Reich steams ahead, blithely ignoring the subtleties of the philosophers:

> Evidently, language derives from the sensa-
> tions perceived by body organs... Expressive

movement is an inherent characteristic of the protoplasm. It distinguishes the living organism from all non-living systems. The word *literally* implies - and we have to take it literally - that something in the living sphere 'presses itself out' and, therefore, 'moves'... Literally, 'emotion' means 'moving outward'; at the same time, it is an 'expressive movement'. The physiological process of the plasmatic emotion or expressive movement is inseparably linked to an immediately comprehensible meaning which we are wont to call the 'emotional expression'. (Reich 1972: 358-9)

How can we get from the expressive plasmatic movement to language? Quite easily, Reich argues:

We are not playing with words. Language is clearly derived from the perception of inner movements and organ sensations, and the words that describe emotional conditions directly reflect the corresponding expressive movement of the living organism. (Reich 1972: 359, original italics)

However,

the beginnings of living functioning lie much *deeper* than and *beyond* language. *Over and above this, the living organism has its own modes of expressing movement which simply cannot be comprehended with words.* (Reich 1972: 359, original italics)

He goes on to draw an analogy with music:

Every musically inclined person is familiar with the emotional state evoked by great

music. However, if one attempts to translate
these emotional experiences into words,
one's musical perception rebels. *Music is
wordless and wants to remain that way.* Yet
music gives expression to the inner movement of the living organism. (Reich 1972: 359,
my italics)

In Chapter Seven we shall look at some more recent work
that gives us an approach to Reich's insistence on non-verbal
modalities of meaning. He moves straight from this passage
about music to draw radical conclusions for psychoanalytic
technique.

If the analyst allows the patient to speak at
random, he [*sic*] finds that the patient tends
to *circumvent* his afflictions, i.e., to *conceal*
them in one way or another. If the analyst
wants to arrive at a correct appraisal of his
patient, he must begin by asking the patient
not to speak. This measure proves very fruitful, for as soon as the patient ceases to speak,
the emotional expressions of his body are
brought into much sharper focus... If the
patient appeared to laugh in a friendly way
while he spoke, his laughter might modulate
into an empty grin during his silence... If the
patient appeared to speak about his life with
reserved seriousness, an expression of suppressed anger might easily appear in the chin
and neck during his silence. (Reich 1972: 360)

Reich's tactic here is in a sense an amplification of what orthodox analysis achieves by withholding the conventions of polite
conversation, by putting silence and space around the
analysand's words until their unconscious content is 'brought
into much sharper focus'. So, with apparent casualness, Reich
dustbins the whole central technique of free association, of ask-

ing the analysand to *speak*: really, he says, it's better if they don't. We can sense in the background Ferenczi's active technique of prohibition, also aimed at bringing out the 'emotional expressions of [the] body'.

Reich appears to be rediscovering, a bit naively, a key axiom of psychoanalysis: that 'human language... often functions as a defense' (Reich 1972: 360). Psychoanalysis is enormously familiar with this fact, and employs it in resistance analysis on both macro- and micro-scales - as Reich knows very well. But he says something more than this:

> In many cases the function of speech has deteriorated to such a degree that the words express nothing whatever and merely represent a continuous, hollow activity on the part of the musculature of the neck and the organs of speech... It is my opinion that in many psychoanalyses which have gone on for years the treatment has become stuck in this pathological use of language. (Reich 1972: 360-1)

Lacan and Reich coincide in their withering contempt for such timeserving analytic hackwork.

Reich, however, develops a form of therapy which

> lies essentially outside the sphere of human language. Naturally, we too make use of the spoken word, but the words we use do not conform to everyday concepts but to organ sensations. There would be no point whatever in making the patient understand his condition in physiological terminology... It is not at all necessary for us to be able to point out exactly which individual muscles are contracted... We work with the language of facial and bodily expression. Only when we have sensed the patient's facial expression

are we in a position to comprehend it. (Reich
1972: 361-2, my italics)

Reich's vocabulary here is quite misleading. In talking about
the 'language' of bodily expression, he appears to align himself
with the common Lacanian response to any mention of non-verbal behaviours - that these are really all just more signifiers.
However, the bodily phenomena with which Reich is concerned
here are not signifiers; they have no communicative *purpose* at
all. They lack the arbitrary quality which is central to the
Saussurian notion of signification. Reich is exploring bodily
impulses before the point at which they start to become anything we can properly call communicative - they are still essentially discharge phenomena.

The implicit analogy is with animal calls: an alarm call is a
discharge of anxiety, which becomes a stereotyped cue for other
animals through a process of reflex association.[1] Reich specifically says that we understand 'body language' through *an intuitive response in our own bodies*, which is nothing like language:

> The patient's expressive movements
> involuntarily bring about an imitation in our
> own organism. By imitating these move-
> ments, we 'sense' and understand the expres-
> sion in ourselves and, consequently, in the
> patient. Since every movement is expressive
> of a biological condition, i.e., reveals an emo-
> tional condition of the protoplasm, the lan-
> guage of facial and bodily expressions
> becomes an essential means of communicat-
> ing with the patient's emotions. (Reich 1972:
> 362)

This passage makes it much clearer that by 'expression' and
'communication', Reich means rather 'demonstration' and 'connection'.[2] Unlike language or other systems of signification,
where that to which any particular element refers is essentially
arbitrary (for instance, 'cat' could serve just as well as the name

for dogs), there is instead an *intrinsic* correspondence between these 'expressive movements' and what they 'express'.

There can be no argument that Reich's vision of therapy, the alternative he proposes to analytic hackwork, is diametrically opposed to Lacan's. Rather than an analysis which devotes itself wholly and minutely to language, he suggests one which 'lies essentially outside the sphere of human language': a psychoanalysis of the Real.

Vile bodies

There is plainly detectable in Lacan's references to bodily matters an unease, a discomfort, even at times a revulsion. In his discussion of the 'Irma's Injection' dream, for example, he says that

> what [Freud] sees in there, these turbinate bones covered with a whitish membrane, is a horrendous sight... There's a horrendous discovery there, that of its form in itself is something which provokes anxiety, the foundation of things, the other side of the head, of the face, the secretory glands par excellence, the flesh from which everything exudes, at the very heart of the mystery, the flesh in as much as it is suffering, is formless, in as much as its form in itself is something which provokes anxiety. (Lacan 1988b: 154)

This seems an oddly self-revelatory passage.[3] What is so 'horrendous' about the image in question that, for Lacan, it might be expected to make Freud (who was after all a doctor and an anatomist) wake up in shock (Lacan 1988b: 155)? I am reminded of my daughter, who at the age of seven or eight hated to hear words like 'ribs' or 'lungs' because they reminded her that her body has insides. Certainly, this reaction is a common feature of growing up, and remains as a flavour in our lifelong experience of ourselves. It seems, though, that for Lacan this revulsion at 'the flesh one never sees' (note the role of *sight*, Lacan's privileged modality) has become a component of his personality, and his personality in turn has left its imprint on his theory.[4]

This will, of course, always be the case for any theory. I am surely not alone if my own interest in theory has to do with its capacity to illuminate my *experience*, which is profoundly conditioned by (in a relationship of mutual causation with) my character structure. But to illuminate is not simply to *support*; an important role of theory is to enter into *dialogue* with my experience, to problematise and criticise it. In this area, for once, Lacan seems not to have noticed that there is anything problematic. He apparently takes it for granted that the body is terrifying and *unheimlich* - that, to use Kristeva's terms, *the entire body* is an 'abject' (Kristeva 1982: 2-6).

> I spit *myself* out, I abject *myself* within the same motion through which 'I' claim to establish myself. (Kristeva 1982: 3, original italics)

In her theory of abjection, Kristeva argues that our revulsion against various bodily substances and fluids is because we use them, so to speak, to push ourselves off from the unconscious: to define ourselves as clean and proper ('*propre*': in French, both 'clean' and 'mine') over against these essentially undefinable and identity-blurring elements of our existence. In this passage, Lacan seems to be treating the whole interior of the body in this fashion, the flesh which in 'its form in itself is something which provokes anxiety'.

This possibly personal quirk of Lacan, however, enables him to emphasise an important point in psychoanalytic theory. The body partakes, in Lacanian terms, of the Real, and the Real of the body is unknown to the ego. Yet the body is not only unknown, it is inherently traumatic.[5] As Paul Verhaeghe puts it,

> [Freud] had discovered the erotic impulses of childhood. Obviously, these impulses devel-

> op themselves along the lines of the eroto-
> genic zones. The moment they emerge, they
> are strange, even 'alien', to the psyche... The
> Real is apparently traumatic *in itself* and
> inaugurates a primal anxiety as a basic
> affect. (Verhaeghe 1996: 28, original italics)

Like Ferenczi, and like Laplanche, this line of Lacanian thinking confronts an apparent paradox in Freud's theory: that the
infant is innately sexual, and *yet* this sexuality is somehow
wounding and fills us with anxiety. Ferenczi's answer is 'the
confusion of tongues' - the traumatic aspect derives from an
abusive misapprehension of the child's tender sexuality by the
adult, taking it up into a passionate context. This finally led
Ferenczi to retract the whole notion of infantile *sexuality* as
such. (See Ferenczi 1988b: 156) Laplanche's answer is 'primal
seduction' - that the infant's sexuality is in fact a foreign body,
originating in a projection from the mother which irretrievably
colours the infant's experience of contact and nurturing. (See,
for example, Laplanche 1995.) Both these positions, I think,
deny that the embodiment of the human infant is founded
upon an *inherent* trauma.

   Lacan's position (at least in Verhaeghe's gloss) is that this
innate sexuality *is* innately traumatic, and that the human condition is fundamentally one of splitting (*Spaltung*) and turning
against ones own being.

> There is something originally, inaugurally,
> profoundly wounded in the human relation
> to the world. (Lacan 1988b: 167)

It does not take Jacques Derrida to show us that notions of the
'original' and 'inaugural' must always be treated with suspicion: they constitute points of purchase by which a particular
political goal tries to present itself as something always-already
achieved. Is this 'original, inaugural and profound' wound any
more than an instantiation of late Romantic angst? Why does
Lacan *want* us to be wounded? He himself says elsewhere:

The unconscious is neither primordial nor
instinctual; what it knows about the elemen-
tary is no more than the elements of the signifier. (Bowie 1991: 72)

And generally, Lacan is as scathing about notions of 'origin' as
he is concerning the 'natural'. Malcolm Bowie puts it well:

Like all dynamicists of the mind, [Lacan]
needs something to make things move. But
he adamantly denies himself the support of
nature as a source of propellant energy: the
instincts are accorded no explanatory power
in the discussion of human desire, and 'natural' analogies between the human and non-
human worlds are continually devalued.
'The Other' propels where nature, instinct
and nervous excitation do not. (Bowie 1991:
83)

Unless I am mistaken, the argument that infantile sexuality
is inherently traumatic reinstates the drives as a motive force in
'the discussion of human desire' - and quite rightly. In what follows, however, I shall try to explain why I believe that the theory of inherent sexual trauma is *not* right.

Body, Ego, Orgasm, Death

It might be wondered why I bother to examine Lacan and Reich
together. They are, quite blatantly, at opposite ends of the analytic spectrum. Their thought is, as I have suggested, often not
only opposed but incommensurable, holding no useful terms in
common. Large portions of Lacan's 'Field and function of
speech and language' (Lacan 1977: 30-113) can appropriately be
read as a biting critique of the sort of work Reich proposes. But
although Reich and Lacan are at opposite poles from one another in so many ways and on so many levels, from theory to personality structure,[6] it is not often noticed that they agree on a
very important point. In all of analytic theory, they, along with

Groddeck,[7] are *the thinkers who most clearly problematise the ego.*
For Lacan, this is famously the case. (See, for example, Lacan
1977: 5, 15, 41-2, 126-8) The ego is an illusion, a false identification which takes place in the 'mirror stage', a sustained attempt
on the part of each human subject to be something they are not.
It is important to note that the illusion in the mirror is a *bodily*
one: a conjuror's substitution of body image for bodily *experience.*

> The original notion of the totality of the body
> as ineffable, as lived, the initial outburst of
> appetite and desire comes about in the
> human subject via the mediation of a form
> which he [*sic*] at first sees projected, external
> to himself, and at first, in his own reflection...
> Man knows that he is a body - although he
> never perceives it in a complete fashion,
> since he is inside it, but he lives it. This
> image is the ring, the bottle-neck, through
> which the confused bundle of desires and
> needs must pass in order to be him, that is to
> say in order to accede to his imaginary struc-
> ture. (Lacan 1988a: 176)

Reich might well agree with this image of 'the ring, the bot-
tle-neck'. He would certainly agree, though not quite in Lacan's
sense, that the ego is an 'imaginary' structure. But (like Lacan,
I think) he locates the imagining of the ego in the first instance
not *within* the child, but in the adults *around* it. Consistently,
Reich denies that inner conflict is primary, and stresses instead
conflict between the inner and outer worlds.

> The psychic process reveals itself as the
> result of the conflict between drive demand
> and the external frustration of this demand.
> Only secondarily does an internal conflict
> between desire and self-denial result from
> this initial opposition... There are social,

more correctly, economic interests that cause
such suppressions and repressions... (Reich
1972: 287)

The ego is identified with this imaginary "inner morality"
(Reich 1972: 287), the sense of oneself as a *good* boy/girl which
'originates in the muscular pushing back and holding back of
faeces' - 'the prototype for repression in general' (Reich 1972:
342). Repression is *identical with* chronic muscular tension, particularly in the erogenous zones:

> In the oral zone, repression is manifested as a
> tightening of the musculature of the mouth
> and a spasm in the musculature of the larynx,
> throat and breast; in the genital zone, it is
> manifested as a continual tension in the
> pelvic musculature. (Reich 1972: 342)

And this tension/repression originates in the *socially-conditioned*
project of *pretending not to have the feelings and desires one has.*

> All our patients report that they went
> through periods in childhood in which, by
> means of certain practices in vegetative
> behaviour (holding the breath, tensing the
> abdominal muscular pressure, etc.), they
> learned to suppress their impulses of hate,
> anxiety, and love. (Reich 1973: 300)

This suppression of affect-laden muscular impulses, Reich
argues, is the process which creates the neurotic ego, the illusory sense of self which is functionally identical with the muscular control of body impulses, in particular of sphincters ('the
ring, the bottle neck'). Where Reich differs crucially from Lacan
is that he portrays the possibility of a 'genital character', a
healthy, non-rigid ego which is in effect an emergent property of
the unified representation of the body in the central nervous
system (Reich 1972: 180-5). Since the ego and the id are 'merely... different functions of the psychic apparatus [changed in a

later footnote to 'biopsychic apparatus'] and not... separate spheres of the psyche' (Reich 1972: 303), they are not *inherently* in conflict. Therefore, the ego can, at least in the ideal case, tolerate the overwhelming impulses of the id - *if* external reality supports it in doing so.[8]

Whatever the ideal case, though, the practical reality, as Reich certainly in the long run accepted, is that the human ego is a neurotic structure. His description of the 'genital character' (Reich 1972: 176-85) is more a manifesto or a visionary aspiration than an account of any sort of existent reality.[9] A key aspect of the ego's neurosis is that it experiences the drive impulses as carrying the threat of *death*. For the remainder of this chapter, I want to explore the very different ways in which Reich, Lacan and Freud express this central point of agreement between them.

For Reich, it is very important to contest the Freudian theory of the death drive, as

> an attempt to use a metaphysical formula to explain phenomena which... cannot yet be explained. Like every metaphysical view, the hypothesis of the death drive probably contains a rational core, but getting at this... is difficult because its mysticism has created erroneous trains of thought. (Reich 1972: 332)

What Reich means by a 'rational core' is a *biologically grounded* account which does not imply inherent conflict (since, as we have seen, Reich does not regard intrapsychic conflict as fundamental, but as contingent). He attempts to provide this account of the death drive by drawing upon his clinical experience that even though he encountered in his patients

> strivings after disintegration, unconsciousness, non-being, dissolution, and similar longings... psychic material which seemed to confirm the existence of an actual original

striving after death... [this] is predominantly
manifested at the end of the treatment, at a
time, in other words, when the patient is
faced with the task of overcoming his [*sic*]
orgasm anxiety. (Reich 1972: 333-4)

Why, Reich asks, should patients 'on the verge of recovery' lack-
ing masochistic tendencies and negative therapeutic reactions,
nevertheless exhibit the effects of the so-called 'death drive'?
(Reich 1972: 334). His answer is that death represents *orgasm*.

The striving after non-existence, nirvana,
death, is identical with the striving after
orgastic release. (Reich 1972: 336)

As he puts it elsewhere:

The patient's fear of death could always be
traced back to a fear of catastrophes and this
fear, in turn, could be traced back to genital
anxiety. Moreover analysts who accepted the
theory of the death drive frequently confused
anxiety and drive. It was not until eight years
later that the matter became clear to me: *fear
of death and dying is identical with unconscious
orgasm anxiety, and the alleged death drive, the
longing for disintegration, for nothingness, is the
unconscious longing for the orgastic resolution of
tension.* (Reich 1973: 155, original italics)

For what, after all, 'dies' in orgasm? Nothing but the ego, the
impression of continuous self-monitoring awareness, which (if
we are fortunate) temporarily disappears. For Reich, the ego is
in effect structured like a symptom, in that it carries within itself
the profound desire for its own dissolution, for the resolution of
the state of tension which constitutes its being. At the same
time, of course, the ego profoundly *fears* its own 'death'. Unlike
Lacan, Reich radically separates from these ambivalent attitudes to death the whole question of *aggression*, which he sees

as a natural human function, 'the life expression of the musculature, of the system of movement' (Reich 1973: 156). However,
it seems very likely that Reich would have acknowledged that
aggression in practice can be used in the service of
death/orgasm anxiety, in the sort of ways Lacan describes.

This account claims to be a major clarification of Freud's theory of the death drive. From Reich's perspective, the death
drive is one case where Freud's genius for synthesis let him
down. Freud merely yoked together several phenomena which
are actually quite disparate - the desire for annihilation of tension; aggression; the 'negative therapeutic reaction'; the repetition compulsion; and masochism *per se*, which Reich also
explains - in a bodily way - as a desire to *burst* (Reich 1972: 329-
31). Bringing all these phenomena together under the aegis of a
cellular drive to 'restore an earlier state of things' (Freud 1920:
308/36) is, from a Reichian viewpoint, a brilliant exercise in
mystification.

Reich also strenuously objects to Freud's revised theory of
anxiety, which understands it no longer as a direct transformation of repressed sexual libido, but rather as a 'signal' of the
(perceived) danger which leads to repression - essentially, the
threat of castration. The details of the issue, and Freud's reasons for revising his views, are rather recondite (see Freud
1926a: 230-6/78-86) but, for Reich, constitute yet another abandonment of the 'actual neurosis' which remains central to his
thinking, the direct relationship between sexual frustration and
emotional disturbance. For Reich, there is 'a functional antithe-
sis between sexuality and anxiety' (Reich 1973: 263) - the same
bodily energy turns from one to the other. Freud's revision of
this view meant that 'there is no longer any psychoanalytic theory of anxiety that satisfies the clinical needs' (Reich 1973: 137).

Freud's view of the 'nirvana principle' facet of the 'death
drive' is, however, close to Reich's position. In *The Ego and the
Id*, Freud sandwiches between two pieces of quasi-biological
speculation the crucial point of '*the likeness of the condition that
follows complete sexual satisfaction to dying*' (Freud 1923: 388/47,
my italics). Freud regards this as 'explained' by 'the ejection of
the sexual substances in the sexual act', corresponding 'in a

sense to the separation of soma and germ plasm' (Freud 1923: 388/47). A more cogent explanation, perhaps, can be found in the *loss of muscular tension and of conscious awareness and thought* which orgasm hopefully brings - that which Reich calls the 'ultimate surrender to the involuntary', his yardstick of 'orgastic potency' (Reich 1973: 108).

Without bodily and psychic tension - without *binding* - the perspective which we call the ego cannot exist. This is the sense in which we can understand Freud's point that 'the pleasure principle seems actually to serve the death drives' (Freud 1920: 338/63); it is the pleasure of orgasm which melts the ego into its *'petite mort'*. ('Melt' is one of Reich's favourite words.) The concept of binding, which Freud develops in the *Project for a Scientific Psychology* (Freud 1950: 308) and returns to in *Beyond the Pleasure Principle*, underlies a good deal of Reich's thinking, and supports his image of the almost literal binding of repressed impulses into muscular armouring - perhaps as one might bind strips of leather to form physical armour.[10]

There are a number of passages in Lacan's work which seem parallel to this account of the ego from his own language-oriented viewpoint. These are most clear in the early papers on the mirror stage and 'Aggressivity in psychoanalysis'. In the first of these, Lacan portrays the ego (the 'I') as

> that apparatus for which every instinctual thrust constitutes a danger, even though it should correspond to a natural maturation - the very normalisation of this maturation being henceforth dependent, in man, on a cultural mediation, as exemplified, in the case of the sexual object, by the Oedipus complex... This conception... throws light on the dynamic opposition between [primary narcissism] and sexual libido, which the first analysts tried to define when they invoked destructive and, indeed, death instincts...
> (Lacan 1977: 5-6)

If we unpack this condensed but really very clear passage, Lacan is saying that the interpolation of culture (later the symbolic order) between human beings and nature transforms the process of development and maturation from a natural unfolding into a series of invasions by alien forces. The ego is precisely that part of our being which, identifying with culture, feels it has something to protect, and therefore experiences nature - the drives, 'instinctual thrusts' - in this way. Lacan argues that Freud's 'death drive' is a name for this opposition between ego and drive. Like Reich, Lacan is reinstalling the early analytic opposition between libido and ego drives.

Interestingly, Jean Laplanche, in his article 'A Metapsychology Put to the Test of Anxiety', puts forward a reinterpretation of the death drive which seems to me extremely close to Reich's position.

> My basic idea is then as follows: the death-drive is not a discovery but a reaffirmation, a deepening of the original and fundamental affirmation of psychoanalysis: sexuality; *it is nothing other than the extreme of sexuality, in its least civilized aspect, working according to the principle of free energy and the primary process.* (Laplanche 1981: 85, my italics)

Not only does Laplanche echo Reich's view that the death drive represents the ego's experience of sexuality, he also echoes his derivation of anxiety from this experience.

> Anxiety is the impact of destructuration produced on the ego and its objects by the drive-attack. Or, to put this in another way, it is the irreconcilable (*unverträglich*) ego-dystonic residue of sexual desire. (Laplanche 1981: 88)

The major difference between Laplanche and Reich seems to be that the former regards *Beyond the Pleasure Principle* as making a great - though misunderstood -advance, while Reich sees it as basically retrogressive.

Lacan, to return to him, seems to portray aggressive and destructive impulses, especially those aimed at one's own body - 'images of castration, mutilation, dismemberment, dislocation, evisceration, devouring, bursting open of the body... *imagos of the fragmented body*' (Lacan 1977: 11) - as attempts by the unconscious to undo the imaginary identification of the ego, to unbind its energies. (Reich would probably consider them to be alienated representations of orgasmic surrender - which is, I am arguing, the same thing.) Lacan refers to the death drive theory as 'the most profound attempt so far made to formulate an experience of man [*sic*] in the register of biology' (Lacan 1977: 8) and speaks, in an oddly 'Reichian' way, of

> the lure of spatial identification, the succession of phantasies that extends from a fragmented body-image to a form of its totality that I shall call orthopaedic - and, lastly, to the assumption of the *armour* of an alienating identity, which will mark with its rigid structure the subject's entire mental development.
> (Lacan 1977: 4, my italics)

Richard Boothby, in *Death and Desire*, claims to offer a Lacanian account of the death drive which uncannily (and evidently unknown to Boothby) matches Reich's position, though in a more intellectual register. Working from passages like the above, he argues that - to go back to the original terms of the *Project*, as discussed in Chapter Two - 'mind' *cannot* represent 'body' completely, or even sufficiently. Death is, in a sense, the ultimate proof of this. The mind cannot recognise or understand physical death, which is part of the Real, but neither can it escape it. In a closely parallel way, the ego is constantly faced with its inability to comprehend and encompass the drives, the inherent impulses of the organism:

> Almost the whole of the life of the organism escapes it [the ego], not only in so far as that life is the most commonly misrecognised by

> the ego, but in that for the most part it does-
> n't have to be known by the ego. (Lacan
> 1966: 179-80, quoted in Boothby 1991: 57)

The ego experiences the 'life of the organism' ('the flesh one never sees') as the threat of death, what Freud describes as the ego's 'fear of being overwhelmed or annihilated' by both 'external and... libidinal danger' (Freud 1923: 399).

> The 'death' at stake is not the demise of the
> physical organism but rather the mutative
> effects on psychical structure exerted by
> energies that remain foreign to its organiza-
> tion. (Boothby 1991: 224)

Though both powerful and convincing, I don't think that Boothby's account really corresponds with Lacan's later viewpoint. However, Boothby's work does take up a strong theme in Lacan's earlier writings which is transcended rather than contradicted in the later theory; Boothby accurately captures Lacan's vision of the ego as - rather like the Soviet Russian system - monolithically despotic yet, simultaneously, desperately fragile.

Whether or not Boothby is putting forward a Lacanian position, he is certainly (unwittingly) putting forward a Reichian one.

> The crucial polarity becomes not that
> between the organic and the inorganic,
> between biological life and death, but rather
> that between the organic and the properly
> psychological, between the force of unbound
> instinctual energies and the bound structure
> of the ego. (Boothby 1991: 83)

Boothby puts the project of the *Project* - what I have called 'the human psychic apparatus as a representation of the human somatic apparatus' - at the centre of human existence, yet maintains that it is unachievable.

If the essential labour of psychic life consists in representing the forces that animate the body, Lacan shows ever more strikingly the impossibility of completing that task. What is at issue is the impossibility of complete coincidence between the psychic and the somatic. It is precisely this impossibility that is signified by the submission of the psychological individual to 'death'. *The doctrine of the death drive implies the profound inadequacy of every self-image of the human being.* (Boothby 1991: 224-5, my italics)

If this position is at all correct, then we seem to have come right back to an inherent opposition between mind and body. Is there really no way forward out of this for psychoanalysis?

Chapter Seven - Bodymind

> Mind is probably not conceivable without some sort of *embodiment*. (Damasio 1996: 234, italics in original)

Reformulating the question

Along with virtually every other analytic thinker, Boothby is arguing within the terms of the Western philosophy of mind and body, terms which, as we saw in Chapter One, are quite fundamentally flawed, incoherent, and inadequate. If we posit a basic Cartesian split between 'mind' and 'body', then we are inexorably led to confront a 'mystery' in their relationship, which is otherwise so blatantly apparent - a 'puzzling leap from the mental to the physical', as Freud puts it (Freud 1916-17: 297/258).

This phrase, in a different translation, was taken up by Felix Deutsch and a group of American analysts as the title for an entire book on the theory of conversion, *On the Mysterious Leap from the Mind to the Body*. In this volume, one contributor after another argues that 'there is no separation between psyche and soma; therefore there can be no leap' (Deutsch 1959: 11); that 'all mental and physical phenomena' are 'different aspects of a single process of biological adaptation' (Deutsch 1959: 16); and that 'man's view of himself as composed of two separate parts, "mind" and "body", is essentially an ambivalent fantasy' (Deutsch 1959: 19).

Unfortunately, these writers - like many others who have instinctively sought the same position - lacked an adequate intellectual framework within which these ideas could be formulated. Within traditional Western philosophy, they can appear only as essentially mystical. As Groddeck put it, 'the route that I have taken leads clearly to the sentence: All things are one' (Groddeck 1977: 136).

Groddeck is not vastly unhappy to be led in this direction. Wild horses will not drag Reich there. Yet he does very much want to reach the 'rational core' of these ideas, the 'some way' in which 'even mysticism is "right"' (Reich 1973: 65). He develops his method of 'orgonomic functionalism' to this end (Reich 1960: 17-26), and is led into the investigation of bioelectrical phenomena (Reich 1973: 368-79), and ultimately into the theory of 'life energy' (Reich 1973: 382-86). Whether or not there is any validity in these researches (and personally I think there is a great deal), we might now argue that they are not a *necessary* response to the problem of the body-mind relationship, which can more coherently - and much more conveniently - be handled by information theory.[1]

Information theory draws a sharp distinction, which would have saved Freud enormous pains, between *energy* and *information*. As Bateson shows us information, definable epigrammatically as 'any difference which makes a difference' (Bateson 1980: 242) is the crucial currency of mind. Information requires 'collateral energy' as its *carrier*, its mode of incarnation, so to speak; but it is *not* that energy, and any other form of energy could in principle incarnate the same information, in just the same way that four apples and four elephants can both embody 'four'.

> The ON position of the switch is a pathway for the passage of energy which originates elsewhere. When I turn the faucet, my work in turning the faucet does not push or pull the flow of water. That work is done by pumps or gravity whose force is set free by my opening the faucet. (Bateson 1980: 113)

Thus, 'mental processes are triggered by difference... and that difference is *not* energy and usually contains no energy' (Bateson 1980: 112). It was the lack of this distinction, and the consequent empty concept of 'mental energy', which hamstrung Freud's work on the biological underpinnings of mind. As we have seen, Reich's concept of body armour shows a way to make sense of 'mental energy' by reformulating it as bodily (biochemical) energy under mental control. Now we can take a step further.

Bateson points out with great force that 'mental process is always a sequence of interactions between parts', and that 'the *explanation* of mental phenomena must always reside in the organisation and interaction of multiple parts' (Bateson 1980: 103). These parts are not restricted to a particular organ or organism. Western thought has been enormously confused by what Freud calls the 'irrefutable proof that mental activity is bound up with the function of the brain as it is with no other organ.' As he then admits, and as is still essentially the case eighty years later (see Solms and Saling 1986),

> every attempt to go on from there to discover a localisation of mental processes, every endeavour to think of ideas as stored up in nerve-cells and of excitations as migrating along nerve fibres, has miscarried completely. (Freud 1915a: 176-7/175)

Information theory, particularly in Bateson's hands, offers a *materialist* account of why this is so - and thus renders unnecessary Freud's invention of a specifically *non*-material topography of the psyche. 'Mind' is a phenomenon consisting of *differences* manifest (in the case of human beings) in the *interaction* of brain, body and environment.[2] Reich's work, properly viewed, makes a crucial contribution towards understanding this interactive system, the energy of which is provided in large part by the *musculature*.

We can now see a fruitful approach to the 'mental energy' problem. Critics inside and outside psychoanalysis have queued up to point out that Freud's central concept of psychic energy is badly flawed, and that nothing happens in neural processes which can sensibly be thought of as 'energetic'. A suitably robust statement of this position is Swanson's:

> Psychic-energy, libido, and related concepts in Freud's drive-discharge theory are either impossible, useless, or mistaken. (Swanson 1977: 629)

Many have suggested that the energetic model should simply be scrapped - replaced, for example, with an information model. Others have equally vehemently argued in support of psychic energy, and yet others have argued that no metapsychological theory of any sort is required.[3]

All this indicates, however, an insufficient understanding of information theory. Although information itself is not energy and does no work, it cannot exist without being 'incarnated' as a difference *in something* - in some form or other of energetic system. And that incarnation is not a passive but an active process, an 'interaction between parts', as Bateson puts it. Freud realised that energy is a part of mind, but he did not fully see why: because *we need our bodies to think with*.

This is, then, I believe, the solution to the question of 'psychic energy' which has taken up so many pages of analytic theory.[4] 'Psychic energy' is quite simply *bodily*, metabolic energy, as that energy involves itself in psychological processes. And 'drive' is that energy as perceived by, represented in, an alienated psyche. If Body is a part of Mind, as Bateson shows, then the drives are the marks of that partaking.

What Bateson also points out is that mental systems operate on *feedback* - both negative (homeostatic - like a thermostat, which works to minimise deviation from a central point), and positive (amplifying - like the howl set up between an electric guitar and a loudspeaker, where deviation is maximised rather than minimised). It should be possible on this basis to conceptualise the ego as a runaway feedback phenomenon which *pits muscular energy against itself* - using muscular tension to inhibit muscular impulse. Perhaps the ego is 'designed' evolutionarily as a homeostatic governing device, a means of stabilising the flow of energy (drive) in the human system. Given paradoxical information, which resets its threshold, it goes into negative escalation and shuts down energy flow below the organismically healthy point.

This sort of idea would take us right back to the *Project*, to Freud's presentation of the conscious mind as a neural monitoring system, a reflexive device for 'keeping off quantity' (Freud 1950: 309), for minimising internal and external stimulus.

> It would seem as though the characteristic of quality (that is, conscious sensation) comes about only where quantities are as far as possible excluded. (Freud 1950: 309)

This sense of the psyche as *trying to stop things happening* stayed with Freud all his life. Perhaps the germ of truth in it is that psyche - in particular the conscious mind and the ego as body representation - *does* perform a homeostatic function, not to *minimise* excitation but, instead, to control its *variation*.

However, Bateson generalises this function from the purely organismic level, through his conception of paradox:

> The truth of the matter is that every circuit of causation in the whole of biology, in our physiology, in our thinking, our neural process, in our homeostasis, and in the ecological and cultural systems of which we are parts - every such circuit conceals or proposes these paradoxes and confusions that accompany errors and distortions of logical typing. (Bateson 1980: 121; see also Wilden 1987: Ch 3)

Bateson argues that the solution to any paradox always lies in the introduction of logical hierarchy - the distinction between *levels* which avoids endless *loops*. It seems worth remarking here on how self-consciousness appears to involve both 'levels' and 'loops', and on how 'double-binds' (or 'contradictory injunctions' - another of Bateson's concerns (Bateson 1973: 173-98) damage the ability of consciousness to handle paradox constructively.

Thinking with the body

Bateson developed his ideas largely on philosophical grounds in the 1960s and 70s. Much more recently, neuroscience has - partly independently, and partly by drawing on information theory - arrived at an extremely similar understanding. In his

Descartes' Error: Emotion, Reason and the Human Brain, Antonio R Damasio suggests that:

> the mind arises from activity in neural cir-
> cuits, to be sure, but many of these circuits
> were shaped in evolution by functional requi-
> sites of the organism, and that *a normal mind
> will happen only if those circuits contain basic
> representations of the organism*, and if they con-
> tinue monitoring the states of the organism in
> action. In brief, neural circuits represent the
> organism continuously, as it is perturbed by
> stimuli from the physical and sociocultural
> environments, and as it acts on those envi-
> ronments. If the basic topic of these represen-
> tations were not an organism anchored in the
> body, we might have some form of mind, but
> I doubt that it would be the mind we do have.
> (Damasio 1996: 226, my italics)

Damasio, a distinguished neuroscientist, whose ideas on affect we have already encountered, argues forcefully that the brain-body relationship is two-way:

> [T]he representations your brain constructs to
> describe a situation, and the movements for-
> mulated as response to a situation, depend on
> *mutual brain-body interactions*. (Damasio 1996:
> 228, my italics)

Indeed, these 'interactions' are so fundamental that the two can-not meaningfully be separated. Just as Bateson says, the envi-ronment is also drawn into an interactive circuit with the brain-body dyad:

> Perceiving the environment, then, is not just a
> matter of having the brain receive direct sig-
> nals from a given stimulus... The organism
> actively modifies itself so that the interfacing

can take place as well as possible. The body proper is not passive. Perhaps no less important, the reason why most of the interactions with the environment ever take place is that the organism requires their occurrence in order to maintain homeostasis, the state of functional balance... Perceiving is as much about acting on the environment as it is about receiving signals from it. (Damasio 1996: 225)

Damasio also has a great deal to say about the organism's internal *representations* of itself and its environment - ideas which parallel Freud's formulations on the 'body ego'.

To ensure body survival as effectively as possible, nature, I suggest, stumbled on a highly effective solution: *representing the outside world in terms of the modifications it causes in the body proper*, that is, representing the environment by modifying the primordial representations of the body proper whenever an interaction between organism and environment takes place. (Damasio 1996: 230, original italics)

Damasio suggests that this 'primordial representation' encompasses biochemical states of brain structures; the viscera, 'including... the muscular mass and the skin, which functions as an organ and constitutes the boundary of the organism'; and the musculoskeletal frame.

These representations... must be coordinated by neural connections, I suspect that the *representation of the skin and musculoskeletal frame* may play an important part in securing this coordination. (Damasio 1996: 230, my italics)

Damasio argues that the image of the skin and musculature

as a boundary gives a schema fundamental to the bodymind's orientation of its data. He goes on to suggest that these primordial representations of the body 'provide a core for the neural representation of self'. This offers striking support for Freud's intuition that

> the ego is ultimately derived from bodily sensations, chiefly from those springing from the surface of the body. It may thus be regarded as a mental projection of the surface of the body... (Freud 1923: 364-5n/26n)

In line with what we were saying earlier, the ego can be represented as *both* homeostatic regulator *and* body-schema representation - from the different perspectives of the efferent and afferent nervous systems respectively. We have come back round to Freud's double portrayal of consciousness in the *Project* - as representation and as regulator of quantity.

Damasio's ideas about the inseparability of 'body' and 'mind' find support from a number of contemporary thinkers on infant development and perception. For example, Fogel suggests that 'the self is the dialogic relationship between the point of observation, the rest of the body and the perceptual flow field in which the body is immersed' (Fogel 1993: 143). Gibson generalises the concept of proprioception, generally understood as the perception of one's own body state, as:

> ego reception, as sensitivity to the self, not as one special channel of sensation or as several of them. I maintain that all the perceptual systems are propriosensitive as well as exterosensitive... (Gibson 1979: 115)

Building on this, he argues that:

> awareness of the persisting and changing environment (perception) is concurrent with the persisting and changing self (proprioception in my extended use of the term). This

> includes the body and its parts and all its
> activities from locomotion to thought, with-
> out any distinction between the activities
> called 'mental' and those called 'physical'.
> Oneself and one's body exist along with the
> environment, they are co-perceived. (Gibson
> 1987: 418)

We need to be careful with all this: words like 'ego' and 'self' have very different meanings for analysts, for psychologists, and for philosophers. But certainly we are building up a picture of the ego which combines *embodiment* with *relatedness*. If it is true that right from the beginning, the infant builds its sense of self through embodied relationship, then it begins to be clear how disturbances in the surrounding adults and their ways of caring can be 'built in' to the developing infant in a very fundamental way - and can create a 'spastic ego' which is damaged in functionally equivalent ways along the two dimensions of embodiment and relationship.

Another input comes from Taylor's re-formulation of psychosomatics in terms of 'self-regulation'. It may be by coincidence that he uses Reich's term 'self-regulation', but it seems a highly appropriate coincidence. Taylor brings together work in a number of fields - 'developmental psychology, developmental biology, personality psychology, psychoanalysis, and several of the biomedical sciences' (Taylor 1992: 479). He paints a picture of health and illness which is very much equivalent to a modern formulation of Reich's ideas, suggesting how 'variables in the early social environment... can influence the maturation of self-regulatory capacities and thereby increase an individual's resilience or vulnerability to illness and disease' (Taylor 1992: 478). Taylor identifies alexithymia - 'deficits in affect representation and regulation' - as risk factors in illness and disease; in other words, a poor capacity to know what you are feeling and to express it can make you ill. Relationship damage is functionally equivalent to embodiment damage.[5]

Bodymind

As we consider information theory, it becomes apparent that this is what Freud is describing in the *Project*. His imaginary neurology, although based on what now seems utterly insufficient information, in fact goes straight to the heart of the matter. From his 'paths', 'contact-barriers' and 'excitations', he constructs what Bateson calls 'circuits of causation', or what are now generally known as 'logic circuits'. These are the basic building blocks of information theory, diagrams reminiscent of electric circuitry, which represent relationships such as: IF, AND, OR and so on (for a 'psychoanalysis-friendly' account, see Peterfreund 1980.)

As I have suggested (Chapter Two), Freud lacked a conceptual base from which to understand his own ideas, so to speak. Since he could not establish them as biology, he recast them as metaphor. Ironically enough, biology, since the 1960s, has been recasting itself as a theory of information processing in complex systems! (See Prigogine and Stengers 1985: 153-76; Coveney and Highfield 1995). Freud said in 1920 that

> the uncertainty of our speculation has been
> greatly increased by the necessity for borrow-
> ing from the science of biology... [The]
> answers it will return in a few dozen years to
> the questions we have put to it... may be of a
> kind which will blow away the whole of our
> artificial structure of hypotheses. (Freud 1920:
> 334)

He was both right and wrong in curiously ironic ways: the 'answers' returned by biology offer a new theory of information which can ground both biology and psychoanalysis.[6]

I want here - at last - to offer the outlines of a model. I propose to give (relatively) rigorous form to the popular notion of the 'bodymind', through a model (based on Bateson's and Damasio's work and that of other researchers in the fields of development and perception) of mind as *necessarily manifest in and through body,* and to suggest that the concept and experience of mind as disembodied, actually or potentially, is in fact dysfunctional.[7]

What follows from the inherent embodiment of mind is a correspondingly inherent 'mentalisation' of the body. Psychic processes are in fact widely *distributed* through the bodybrain system, because of the very nature of neurological activity.[8] Among other things, the body *remembers*; in particular, it remembers trauma. What also follows from this is that *subjectivity is a bodily function*, not primarily a linguistic one. Subjectivity is also a *relational* function, but relating occurs first of all through the body.

The unpacking of these two paragraphs will take up the rest of the chapter. I will draw on work from a number of areas to justify my position: some analytically-based work (Winnicott, Stern, Kristeva), and some from more empirical traditions (Van der Kolk, Perry, Stern again). But I want to stress again at this point that it seems to me that Freud, Reich, Groddeck, and Ferenczi - indeed, even Lacan - were each, in very different styles, groping for these sorts of ideas, and producing them in more or less confused and incomplete forms. For Freud, Ferenczi and Reich, this is the significance of the search for a *biological* grounding of psychology; they needed, but couldn't find, a way of understanding bodymind identity. Lacan's fascination with linguistics can be situated in relation to the notion of digital *difference* upon which language rests (see Wilden 1972: Ch I), and his concern with knots in relation to the quality of *recursiveness*, which Bateson sees as central to mental systems (Bateson 1980: 217).

Reich also approaches the idea of recursiveness in his diagrams of neurotic structure (e.g. Reich 1973: 146), and he succeeds in grasping the crucial point of the body's role as *a component of mind*, which is so confusing for both Freud and Lacan (though Reich hardly sees the point with full clarity):

> [T]he processes in the organism demonstrat-
> ed that the quality of a psychic attitude is
> dependent upon the amount of somatic exci-

tation from which it is derived... It was vague,
elusive. It was merely clear that biological
energy governs the psychic as well as the
somatic. A functional unity prevails. (Reich
1973: 265)

Groddeck's It, which 'knows neither body nor soul since they
are both manifestations of the same unknown entity' (Groddeck
1977, 135), is in some ways also Bateson's Mind, as is Ferenczi's
'semisubstance' with its quality of 'being both body and mind
simultaneously' (Ferenczi 1988: 7).

The neurobiology of trauma

Ferenczi's 'semisubstance' can be understood as describing the
laying down of neurological styles of perception and reaction, as
suggested in the following passage from a more recent neuro-
biological work:

> The brain develops... from less complex
> (brainstem) to most complex (limbic, cortical
> areas). These different areas develop, orga-
> nize and become fully functional at different
> times during childhood... This means that
> there are different times during which differ-
> ent areas of the CNS... either require (critical
> periods) or are most sensitive to (sensitive
> periods) organizing experiences (and the
> neurotrophic cues related to these experi-
> ences). Disruptions of experience-dependent
> neurochemical signals during these periods
> may lead to major abnormalities or deficits in
> neurodevelopment - some of which may not
> be reversible... Disruption of critical cues can
> result from 1) lack of sensory experience dur-
> ing critical periods or, more commonly, 2)
> atypical or abnormal patterns of neuronal
> activation due to extremes of experience (e.g.,
> child maltreatment). (Perry *et al*, 1995: 276)

The authors go on to elaborate on these 'disruptions' (the material is important enough to quote at length):

> If a child faced with threat responds with a hyperarousal response, there will be a dramatic increase in... release of norepinephrine [which] regulates the total body response to the threat. The brain regions involved in the threat-induced hyperarousal response play a critical role in regulating arousal, vigilance, affect, behavioral irritability, locomotion, attention, the response to stress, sleep, and the startle response... Initially following the acute fear response, these systems in the brain will be reactivated when the child is exposed to a specific reminder of the traumatic event (e.g., gunshots, the presence of a past perpetrator). Furthermore, these parts of the brain may be reactivated when the child simply thinks about or dreams about the event. Over time, these specific reminders may generalize (e.g., gunshots to loud noises, a specific perpetrator to any strange male...) This use-dependent activation of these areas leads to sensitization, and sensitization of catecholamin... systems leads to a cascade of associated functional changes in brain-related functions... This sensitization of the brain stem and midbrain neurotransmitter systems also means the other critical physiological, cognitive, emotional and behavioral functions which are mediated by these systems will become sensitized.... A traumatized child may, over time, exhibit motor hyperactivity, anxiety, behavioral impulsivity, sleep problems, tachycardia, hypertension and a variety of neuroendocrine abnormalities... This also

means, of course, that these components of
the fear response, themselves, become sensitized. Everyday stressors which previously
may not have elicited any response now elic-
it an exaggerated reactivity - these children
are hyperreactive and overly sensitive. This is
due to the fact that, simply stated, the child is
in a persisting fear state (which is now a
'trait'). Furthermore, this means that the child
will very easily be moved from being mildly
anxious to feeling threatened to being terror-
ized. In the long run, what is observed in
these children is a set of maladaptive emotional, behavioral and cognitive problems
which are rooted in the original adaptive
response to a traumatic event. (Perry *et al*,
1995: 278)

Neuroscience also addresses the central psychoanalytic
theme of *traumatic memory*, in terms which illuminate, for example, Ferenczi's experience of his patients' hysterical trance with
subsequent amnesia:

Memories (somatic or symbolic) related to the
trauma are elicited by heightened arousal.
Information acquired in an aroused, or otherwise altered state of mind is retrieved more
readily when people are brought back to that
particular state of mind. State dependent
memory retrieval may also be involved in
dissociative phenomena in which traumatized persons may be wholly or partially
amnestic for memories or behaviors enacted
while in altered states of mind. (Van der Kolk
1994)

It is not only impossible to say here whether we are describing
a 'psychic' phenomenon or a 'somatic' one, it is actually mean-

ingless. When neuroscience attends in sufficient detail to a sufficiently complex process, it reveals that a neurological description is - in Reich's terminology - 'functionally equivalent' to a psychological one - so long as it includes, as above, the environmental and relational context. Which is primary? Which is a 'representation' of the other? The question has no content; the only basis for choice between descriptions is in terms of which is most relevant or economical or what one wants to do - the level on which one wishes to intervene, for example.[9] There is no reason why intervention at the level of symbolisation through psychotherapy should not effect neurological change - neurological change occurs every time we have a new thought or feeling. Neurology is - finally - offering Freud the tools he needed to accomplish the *Project*.

What I am saying here is very close to Holt's argument in 'The Death and Transfiguration of Metapsychology':

> Very briefly, the idea is as follows: we begin by treating the human person as a psychobiological system, a natural unity in which it is possible to discern and abstract out a psychological subsystem and a biological subsystem... General systems theory is an attempt, not terribly successful so far, to develop a model of the nature and functioning of all systems, or somewhat more narrowly, of living systems... What makes systems theory look worth exploring is that it does have some properties of both contemporary psychoanalytic and neuroscientific theories. Despite its own considerable deficiencies... I believe that it can serve as a starting point for attempts to construct just such a bridging model as I have described... But whether that turns out to be a fruitful lead or a false one, there is no reason in principle that such an intermediary or Janusian model might not be found, with one face turned

> towards biology, one towards psychology...
> [T]he model should not itself be either neuro-
> physiology or psychoanalysis; it can serve a
> valuable function for both disciplines by giv-
> ing them a common language and a common
> set of propositions... (Holt 1981: 139-40)

Following on from this, I want to look at some analytic thinking which converges with the sorts of ideas we have just been
discovering in neuroscience. Apart from Reich, Groddeck and
Ferenczi, I am aware of three analytic thinkers who particularly
strive to bridge the supposed 'mysterious leap' between mind
and body. They are an extremely mixed group: D W Winnicott,
Julia Kristeva, and Daniel Stern.

Winnicott: soma, psyche and mind

D. W. Winnicott speaks of the 'psyche-soma', a unified bodymind in which:

> the psyche and the soma are not to be distin-
> guished except according to the direction
> from which one is looking. One can look at
> the developing body or at the developing
> psyche. I suppose the word psyche here
> means the *imaginative elaboration of somatic
> parts, feelings, and functions,* that is, of physical
> aliveness. (Winnicott 1987: 244, original ital-
> ics)

'Psyche', in other words, is as much a bodily function as 'soma'.
Winnicott uses 'mind' in a rather different sense from the way
we have looked at it so far, to indicate *alienated* mind, suggesting that it

> has a root, perhaps its most important root, in
> the need of the individual, at the core of the
> self, for a perfect environment. (Winnicott
> 1987: 246)

Through fantasy elaboration of its experience, the infant with a 'good enough mother' will cope with negative but bearable experiences, until it:

> turns a good-enough environment into a perfect environment, that is to say, turns a relative failure of adaptation into adaptive success. What releases the mother from her need to be near-perfect is the infant's understanding. (Winnicott 1987: 245)

Winnicott makes clear that the failure of perfection is a necessary condition for growing up:

> it is a characteristic maternal function to provide *graduated failure of adaptation*, according to the growing ability of the individual infant to allow for relative failure by mental activity, or by understanding. (Winnicott 1987: 246, original italics)

However, under certain circumstances (in reality, more or less universally) a 'mind' - a sense of oneself-as-thinking, we might say - can develop which is experienced as separate from and in opposition to the body.

> Certain kinds of failure on the part of the mother, especially erratic behaviour, produce over-activity of the mental functioning. Here... we see that there can develop an opposition between the mind and the psyche-soma, since in reaction to this abnormal environmental state the thinking of the individual begins to take over and organise the caring for the psyche-soma, whereas in health it is the function of the environment to do this. In health, the mind does not usurp the environment's function, but makes possible an understanding and eventually a

making use of its relative failure. (Winnicott
1987: 246)

If the mind comes under increasing strain as it tries to make up
for environmental failure, for a lack of good holding, then:

> we find *mental functioning becoming a thing in
> itself*, practically replacing the good mother and
> making her unnecessary... The psyche of the
> individual gets 'seduced' away into this mind
> from the intimate relationship which the psyche
> originally had with the soma. The result is a
> mind-psyche, which is pathological. (Winnicott
> 1987: 246-7)

Winnicott thus develops a distinction between the embodied and
relational mind, as we have described it earlier in this chapter, and
the disembodied mind which manifests damage in the way it
relates:

> For instance, one can observe a tendency for
> easy identification with the environmental
> aspect of all relationships that involve depen-
> dence, and a difficulty in identification with the
> dependent individual. (Winnicott 1987: 247)

This is what has been called a 'compulsive caring' pattern. From
a psyche-soma where the *whole body* thinks, and 'the psyche-soma
is not... felt by the individual... to be localized anywhere', we move
to a '*mind*-psyche' which 'is localized by the individual, and is
placed either inside the head or outside it in some special relationship to the head' (Winnicott 1987: 247).
One of the aims of psychosomatic illness, Winnicott argues,

> is to draw the psyche from the mind back to the
> original intimate association with the soma...
> One has... to be able to see the positive value of
> the somatic disturbance in its work of counter-
> acting a 'seduction' of the psyche into the mind.
> (Winnicott 1987: 254)

We can compare this with Taylor's work outlined above. Winnicott explicitly goes on from this to argue for the value of bodywork ('physiotherapists and relaxationists'):

> In one example of the application of these principles, if one tries to teach a pregnant woman how to do all the right things one... feeds the tendency of the psyche to lodge in the mental processes. *Per contra*, the relaxation methods at their best enable the mother to become body-conscious, and... help her to a continuity of being... (Winnicott 1987: 254)

Kristeva: the semiotic

Julia Kristeva is among those who explicitly limit the analytic situation to one of *speech*:

> There is a couch on which one person lies down and speaks, and an armchair in which another person sits and listens; the motor faculties are thus blocked, and the displacement of instinctual energies into speech is thus facilitated. (Kristeva 1988: 4)

'Instinctual (i.e. *triebhaft*, drive) energies' are expressed in a particular *form* of speech.

> Analytic language works with signs that encompass representations of at least three types: representations of words, ...representations of things, ...and representations of affects (labile psychic traces subject to the primary processes of displacement and condensation, which I have called *semiotic* as opposed to the *symbolic* representations inherent in, or derivative of, the system of language). (Kristeva 1988: 4 original italics)

The semiotic component or aspect of language is *the speech of the body*, the direct imprint of the unconscious upon our language, expressed in rhythm and quasi-rhythmic features like onomatopoeia, assonance, alliteration, etc. (Kristeva 1984: 26-7) The semiotic is the direct record of the developmental processes which create the subject:

> Discrete quantities of energy move through the body of the subject who is not yet constituted as such and, in the course of his [sic] development, they are arranged according to the various constraints imposed upon this body - always already involved in a semiotic process - by family and social structures. In this way the drives, which are 'energy' charges as well as 'psychical' marks, articulate what we call a *chora*: a nonexpressive totality formed by the drives and their stases in a motility that is as full of movement as it is regulated.[10] (Kristeva 1984: 25)

The 'semiotic *chora*' is thus (again) structured like a symptom: it embodies - and this is the precise word - both the primal energies of the body, and the repressive processes which constrain those energies, and in doing so *forms the subject and her body*. It relates to:

> a preverbal functional state that governs the connections between the body (in the process of constituting itself as a body proper) and the protagonists of family structure... The kinetic functional stage of the semiotic precedes the establishment of the sign... (Kristeva 1984: 27)

Kristeva emphasises the profound ambivalence of the semiotic, as the point of coincidence of those forces which constitute the speaking individual, and those forces which subvert it:

> The semiotic chora is no more than the place
> where the subject is both generated and
> negated, the place where his [sic] unity suc-
> cumbs before the process of charges and
> stases which produce him. (Kristeva 1984:
> 28)

The semiotic chora, it becomes clear, can be represented in
terms of the neurological/developmental process of body
schema representation which we have described, the dual
structure of embodiment and relationship which gives rise to
mind. It can also be related to the notion of the ego as an
expression of 'the connections between the body (in the process
of constituting itself as a body proper) and the protagonists of
family structure.' For Kristeva, the chora is inseparable from *the
mother's body* - a sort of 'transitional object' in the individuation
of infant from mother (Kristeva 1984: 27-8). We shall return
briefly to the implications of this in Chapter Nine.

From this brief outline we can see that the concept of the
semiotic is a powerful tool for several kinds of investigation,
and a potential bridging concept between the artificially sun-
dered 'body' and 'mind'. This is explicitly part of Kristeva's
intention:

> A stratified concept of significance enables
> us to understand how logical language, bol-
> stered by infralinguistic (semiotic) represen-
> tations, can find physical expression. We
> thus develop a powerful model of the
> human in which language is not divorced
> from the body; 'word' and 'flesh' can meet at
> any moment, for better or worse. (Kristeva
> 1988: 6)

But although Kristeva's theory takes us some way towards
a non-dichotomous analytic model, it does not go far enough.
She still privileges the linguistic as constitutive of the human -
that is, language finds 'physical expression' rather than the

body finding linguistic expression - and she portrays this process as, at the same time, inherently splitting:

> As speaking beings... we have always been divided, separated from nature. (Kristeva 1988: 8)

If 'language is not divorced from the body' for Kristeva, then lawyers have certainly been consulted. We still seem to be stuck within (a revised, language-oriented, and possibly slightly romantic version of) the dualistic 'Cartesian theatre' (Dennett 1991, 39 and passim). It is useful at this point to come back to material of a quite different kind, some 'third-person' rather than 'first-person' information about how this infantile 'presubject' becomes a subject, as gathered and presented in a coherent theory by Daniel Stern in *The Interpersonal World of the Infant*.

Stern: body as subject

Paradoxically, what makes Stern's book particularly valuable is that, educated as a Mahlerian experimentalist, he appears to know little or nothing about the theories we are discussing. So the enormous points of contact between his ideas and those of Reich, Lacan, Ferenczi, Kristeva and, of course, the early Freud, have a special force. But I want to begin with a major point of disagreement between Stern's empirically-based theory, and the view of Lacan and most other analytic theorists that the pre-verbal infant is not a unified subject.

For Stern, subjective identity begins within months of birth.

> Recent findings about infants... are more in accord with the impression of a changed infant, capable of having - in fact, likely to have - an integrated sense of self and others. These new findings support the view that the infant's first order of business... is to form the sense of a core self and core others. The evidence also supports the notion that *this task is largely accomplished during the period between*

> *two and seven months.* Further, it suggests that
> the capacity to have merger- or fusion-like
> experiences as described in psychoanalysis
> is secondary to and depending upon an
> already existing sense of self and other.
> (Stern 1985: 70, my italics)

Part of the support for this position is of course provided by the developmental researchers whom we have already quoted - Meltzer, Butterworth, and others. Stern demonstrates in some detail how this sense of self (which is of course a *sense,* and not a concept or understanding) develops out of repeated experiences of 'self-invariants' which '[do] not change in the face of all the things that do change' (Stern 1985: 71-2). He focuses on four such factors: 'self-agency', 'self-coherence', 'self-affectivity', and 'self-history', showing how all four are available to infants in the early months of life.[11]

> During this period the infant has the capaci-
> ties to recognise those events that will iden-
> tify a self and an other. The social interactive
> situation offers multiple opportunities to
> capture those events. And the integrative
> processes are present to organise these sub-
> jective events. (Stern 1985: 99)

In a sense, what Stern is describing here is the equivalent of Kristeva's 'semiotic *chora*', but without its ambivalence. Stern portrays an idealised process of unequivocal gain, and does not focus on the disturbances and interruptions of these 'integrative processes' - disturbances which Kristeva would see as not merely contingent but inherent in socialisation. He describes the development of subjectivity in terms of rhythmic, multisensory processes of interaction between infant and environment, particularly the mother - just as Kristeva does.

For Stern, a key element in the development of a unified subjectivity is the infant's

> innate general capacity... to take information
> received in one sensory modality and some-
> how translate it into another sensory modali-
> ty... It involves an encoding into a still myste-
> rious amodal representation, which can then
> be recognised in any of the sensory modes.
> (Stern 1985: 51)

In other words, a baby has an innate capacity to know from an
object's *feel* what it will *look* like, and vice versa (Stern 1985: 47-
8).

> It is clear that the capacity is present in the
> first weeks of life. Infants are pre-designed to
> be able to perform a cross-modal transfer of
> information that permits them to recognise a
> correspondence across touch and vision... No
> learning is needed initially, and subsequent
> learnings about relations across modalities
> can be built upon this innate base. (Stern
> 1985: 48)

This capacity exists across *all* modes of perception, including
time, intensity, hearing, proprioception, and affect. It means
that:

> Infants do not need repeated experience to
> begin to form some of the pieces of an emer-
> gent self and other. They are predesigned to
> forge certain integrations. (Stern 1985: 52)

Meltzoff and Moore (1995) give a similar description of infants'
'supramodal representation of human acts', which is:

> something like an act space or primitive body
> scheme that allows the infant to unify the
> visual and motor/proprioceptive informa-
> tion into one common 'supramodal' net-
> work... The representation of the other's body

> is separate from the representation of one's
> own body. Although both representations
> use the supramodal language, they are not
> confused... There is a primordial connection
> between self and other. The actions of other
> humans are seen as like the acts that can be
> done at birth. (Meltzoff and Moore 1995: 53)

The underlying qualities of the infant's integrated experience will be some sort of rhythm and intensity. This emerges especially clearly in relation to *affect*, where Stern introduces the concept of 'vitality affects' (Stern 1985: 53-60). Distinct from the traditional 'category affects' of fear, rage, grief, joy and so on, vitality affects are captured by dynamic, kinetic terms such as 'surging', 'fading away', 'fleeting', 'explosive', 'crescendo', 'decrescendo', 'bursting', 'drawn out' and so on.

> A 'rush' of anger or of joy, a perceived flood-
> ing of light, an accelerating sequence of
> thoughts, an unmeasurable wave of feeling
> evoked by music, and a shot of narcotics can
> all feel like 'rushes' .They all share similar
> envelopes of neural firings, although in dif-
> ferent parts of the nervous system...
> Expressiveness of this kind is... inherent in
> all behaviour. (Stern 1985: 54-6)

Stern argues that this sort of quality is primary in the infant's organisation of experience.

> The infant is far more likely to perceive
> directly and begin to categorise acts in terms
> of the vitality affects they express. Like
> dance for the adult, the social world experi-
> enced by the infant is primarily one of vital-
> ity affects before it is a world of formal acts.
> It is also analogous to the physical world of
> amodal perceptions, which is primarily one
> of abstractable qualities of shape, number,
> intensity level and so on. (Stern 1985: 57)

As this passage indicates, vitality affects are a particular kind of 'amodal representation', or 'activation contour' (Stern 1985: 57-9). The *pattern* of 'surging', 'bursting', 'explosion' and so on is not tied to any particular sensory mode; it is wholly abstractable, and thus dovetails with the innate capacity for abstraction which Stern has described, as one of the fundamental building blocks of infant experience.

Looked at in this light, Reich seems to be seeking over and over again to describe vitality affects, to which he clearly had a particular sensitivity - as, presumably, do body psychotherapists and dance and movement therapists in general.

> The rhythmicity of one's movements, the alternation of muscular tension and relaxation in movement, go together with the capacity for linguistic modulation and general musicality. The sweetness of children who have not been subject to any severe repressions... has the same basis. On the other hands, people who are physically stiff, awkward, without rhythm, give us the feeling that they are also psychically stiff... They speak in a monotone and are seldom musical. (Reich 1972: 345-6)

Vitality affects provide an empirical foundation for the sense shared by Reich and Kristeva (among many others) that there is a constitutive *bodily* layer of human identity. Reich states:

> I already knew that the 'how', i.e. the form of the behaviour and the communications, was far more important than what the patient told the analyst. Words can lie. The expression never lies. Although most people are unaware of it, it is the immediate manifestation of character. (Reich 1973: 171)

The typically rhythmic quality of vitality affects is also described by Kristeva:

> Neither model nor copy, the *chora* precedes
> and underlies figuration and thus speculari-
> sation and is analogous only to vocal or
> kinetic rhythm. We must restore this motili-
> ty's gestural and vocal play... on the level of
> the socialised body... (Kristeva 1984: 26)

Indeed, Stern shows the crucial role of affect in general in
the development of core identity, because of the stable feedback
that emotional expression gives the infant:

> the constellation of three different kinds of
> feedback: from the infant's face [i.e. proprio-
> ceptive sensation], from the activation pro-
> file, and from the quality of subjective feel-
> ing. (Stern 1985: 90)

In other words, the 'hardwired', biologically defined, cross-cul-
turally stable correspondence of particular internal experience
to particular physiognomic expressions,[12] helps the infant
build up a felt sense of 'this is me'.

Stern goes on to outline the caretaking adult's role in supporting the development of coherent self/other awareness in
the infant, through what he calls 'affect attunement' (Stern
1985: 138-61). Basically, this entails frequently-repeated interactions in which the baby acts in one modality, and the adult
responds in a different modality *with the same rhythm or activation profile* (Stern 1985: 140-2). For example, the baby bangs
rhythmically and the parent matches with a rhythmic sound; or
a ten-month-old girl finally puts a piece in the correct part of a
jigsaw puzzle.

> She looks towards her mother, throws her
> head up in the air, and with a forceful arm
> flap raises herself partly off the ground in a
> flurry of exuberance. The mother says, 'YES,
> that girl.' The 'YES' is intoned with much
> stress. It has an explosive rise that echoes the

girl's fling of gesture and posture. (Stern
1985: 141)

As this example suggests, 'most attunements seem to occur
with the vitality affects' (Stern 1985: 156). Affect attunement - a
process of which parents are largely unaware (Stern 1985: 149) -
is an interpersonal extension of the fundamental knitting-
together of the world which we have already described.

> The capacities for identifying cross-modal
> equivalences that make for a perceptually
> unified world are the same capacities that
> permit the mother and infant to engage in
> affect attunement to achieve affective inter-
> subjectivity. (Stern 1985: 156)

Affect attunement, of course, also offers endless opportuni-
ties for what we can call 'affect discordance', or for more subtly
effective 'semiotic' communications to the forming baby from
the adults who care for it.

> Discrete quantities of energy move through
> the body of the subject who is not yet consti-
> tuted as such and, in the course of his devel-
> opment, they are arranged according to the
> various constraints imposed upon this body -
> always already involved in a semiotic process
> - by family and social structures. (Kristeva,
> 1984: 25)

Language and body

> No language matches another, no language
> models the world. But almost, almost... And
> between the dropped and the caught stitches
> of that immaterial, impossible weaving some-
> how: the meaning comes. (Jones 1992: 310)

What are the implications of all this? There are many, both

metapsychological and clinical (for some of the latter, see Stern 1985 Chapters 10 and 11). Most importantly, for our purpose, Stern argues with great force and much supporting material that subjectivity in most usual senses of the word is *not* dependent upon language acquisition. On the contrary, it is a *bodily* phenomenon, bound up intrinsically with other bodily phenomena like affect and expressiveness, and with the sort of rhythmic and cross-sensory grounding which Kristeva, Reich, and Damasio, in very different styles, have all suggested.

In fact, Stern goes as far as to suggest that language, for all its clear advantages, involves a definite *loss* or distancing of subjective experience.

> Some global experiences at the level of core- and intersubjective relatedness such as the very sense of a core self do not permit language sufficient entry to separate out a piece for linguistic transformation. Such experiences then simply continue underground, nonverbalised, to lead an unannounced (and, to that extent only, unknown) but nonetheless very real existence... Language can... fracture amodal global experience [by anchoring experience to] a single modality of sensation... The forms of slippage between personal world knowledge and official or socialised world knowledge as encoded in language... is one of the main ways in which reality and fantasy can begin to diverge. (Stern 1985: 176-8)

Although this position is over-simplified, setting up a straight opposition between 'language' and 'experience' which cannot be sustained, and ignoring the whole realm of poetic, 'semiotic' language use, it refers to a 'slippage' which we *do* experience, and anchors it in certain features of language. Stern gives an experimental example of the 'divergence between world knowledge and words' (Stern 1985: 175) which would have delighted Reich. Shown the same piece of clay first rolled out long and thin, then as a lump, a child will *say* that the lump is heavier; but when handed first one piece then the other, high-speed film shows that the child's muscles do not 'believe' this, but anticipate an equal weight. Only the child's *words* are Piagetian - her[13] body, as Reich would say, does not lie!

Stern also points out that affect is particularly hard to ver-balise in a rich and detailed way (Stern 1985: 178-9), and that language is suited to pulling out the common element in repeat-ed experiences but tends to lose the unique and unrepeatable specificities of experience (Stern 1985: 177).

> Infants' initial interpersonal knowledge is mainly unsharable, amodal, instance-specific, and attuned to non-verbal behaviours in which no one channel of communication has privileged status with regard to accountabili-ty or ownership. Language changes all of that... Language forces a space between inter-personal experience as lived and as repre-sented. And it is precisely across this space that the connections and associations that constitute neurotic behaviour may form. (Stern 1985: 182)

Here we are back to Kristeva's position,[14] which itself echoes Lacan:

> As speaking beings... we have always been divided, separated from nature. This split has left within us traces of the pre- or translin-guistic semiotic processes that are our only access to the species memory or the bioener-getic neuronal maps. These semiotic process-es (archaic traces of the links between our erogenous zones and those of the other, stored as sonorous, visual, tactile, olfactory or rhythmic traces) diachronically constitute a *presubject* (the *infans*). (Kristeva 1988: 8)

This is in fact extraordinarily close to Stern's 'Anglo-Saxon' formulation, *except for the crucial last phrase.* Stern does not see the non-speaking 'infans' as a presubject; for him, subjectivity is constituted in *prelinguistic* bodymind interactions with the world and others. This is also clearly Reich's position, and the one which I have argued in this book. It allows for a fundamentally different formulation of the intrinsic tension between linguistic and non-linguistic experience. It is different because it is non-paradoxical: language, which undermines some aspects of our subjective reality, is *not* at the same time *constitutive* of that reality, however deeply it influences all our internal and external representations. At least potentially, language can be shifted from the role of bad master to that of good servant. Like intellectuality in general, it can be seen properly as 'itself... a vegetative activity' (Reich 1972: 306), a natural function of the human bodymind which is potentially capable of modelling, with greater or lesser success, *any* aspect of experience, including the non-linguistic.

There may be a false metaphor at the heart of the problem: *language as container*, the sense that it is something which has an inside, an outside and a membrane between the two, so that things are either 'inside language' or 'outside language' - or, as some argue, there is *no* thing (knowable) outside language. Of course, the 'inside' of language consists only of words and their formal relationships; the 'outside' of language is everything else... But this is to consider the logical set of that-which-is-language (even then 'inside' and 'outside' are only metaphors), which is not the real issue. We tend to use a much cloudier metaphor of language as a container, a basket, a net which catches and holds experience. This is a metaphor which powerfully 'captures' some of our experience of language use, but the trouble is that if we look in the net - so to speak - we don't find anything there except language!

What might be a more helpful metaphor? The other image which constantly recurs in thinking about the subject is of a *map*. A map is a sort of 'container' but what it contains, quite clearly, is an *image* of the territory in question. This image shares some but not all of the arbitrariness of language: it is symbolic, but it is also analogistic (analog as well as digital - Wilden 1972). There is a 'mapping' of the *relationship* between the elements which is not arbitrary in the Saussurian sense. This is, in fact, what the term 'mapping' means. Language-as-map has the merit of avoiding the 'inside-outside' metaphor - we put things *on* the map, but at the same time those things remain *in* the world. The map, like language, is a representation; it is also a transformation, but a non-arbitrary one. (A mirror is a form of mapping.) Unlike language, the map saves relationships.[15]

The truth seems to be that the incapacity of language to represent the Real applies globally, but not locally. *As a whole*, language is incommensurate with reality - the map can never fully represent the territory, can never be laid over it in a one-to-one, point-by-point correspondence, not least because reality does not seem to be made up of 'points'. Yet, *at any particular moment*, we can speak of whatever we choose.

The always arbitrary relationship of sign and signifier can be applied to any aspect of experience. A trivial example makes the point: there is a minor literary form, represented most recently by Douglas Adams' and John Lloyd's *The Meaning of Liff* , which consists in coining names for phenomena which have previously escaped representation. For example: '*Aberystwyth*: A nostalgic yearning which is itself more pleasurable than the thing being yearned for'(Adams and Lloyd 1983: 7). There will *always* be infinitely many quanta of reality, and combinations of quanta, which are unrepresented in language - 'unannounced (and, to that extent only, unknown)' (Stern 1985: 176). But also, each and any of these is *always* potentially subject to representation. Naming the most ineffably subtle of emotions is no more or less arbitrary or accurate than naming a chair. The ambiguity of reality, its capacity to be divided up in many different ways, is a problem of *perception*, not specifically of language.

Psychoanalysis and empirical research

Work like that of Stern has also been attacked from the other side, so to speak, by those who want to keep the truth status of psychoanalysis - rather as with mathematics or philosophy (or theology) - wholly independent of empirical data.

> The psychological theories that emerge from such evidence [i.e. infant research] differ so fundamentally from Freud's perspective on the human condition that their links to psychoanalysis appear irretrievably broken. The etiology of the psychoneuroses has been shifted from inherent and irreconcilable conflicts between personal desire and civilization, to empirical assumptions about the long-term effects of real experience and of the quality of nonverbal communications between infant and mother, amplified and exacerbated by later similar disturbances of social interaction. (Wolff 1996: 387)

There are many levels on which one could take issue with this - including the idea that one can oppose 'conflicts between personal desire and civilization', on the one hand, and 'disturbances of social interaction' on the other. The latter may precisely embody the former, and this indeed seems a necessary part of any Freudian theory, for how else is the infant to *find out about* its conflicts with civilisation?

But also contained in arguments like Wolff's, it seems to me, is a sense that psychoanalysis is on an altogether different level from other forms of knowledge, in particular from experimental science. Rather like Marxism, psychoanalysis is taken to be a unique Science with a capital 'S', one which does not have to justify its axioms in the actual world, or, even more importantly, *to articulate its discourse with other discourses*. Psychoanalysis is portrayed as a closed system, in much the way that it is often parodied by critics: 'unless you believe it you cannot assess it'.

A difficult balance is required here. We need to maintain analytic theory as essentially *open* to other discourses, as all living systems must be open to their environment (Wilden 1972 passim). At the same time, we need to maintain its relatively privileged status in relation to certain *aspects* of knowledge: that psychoanalysis can 'see through' some sorts of false or incomplete knowledge that are essentially opaque to other systems. In other words, psychoanalysis can study the *unconscious* aspects of other forms of knowledge. One particularly relevant issue here is that of 'observation'. Experimental science, including the study of infants, relies on a fairly naive notion of 'objective observation', which is open to critique from analysis (as also from other approaches which throw into question notions of 'objectivity' and 'fact'). Psychoanalysis, in fact, has developed its own methodology for studying infants - Infant Observation (Harris and Bick 1987, Miller *et al* 1989) - which gives a very different meaning to the term 'observation', treating as central data the phenomena of projection and projective identification which are ignored by psychology.

There is a potentially fruitful project of bringing together Infant Observation and infant observation, so to speak: of developing an approach which combines attention to quantifiable data with attention to subjectivity and unconscious processes - to *both* how the parent and the observer feel, *and* what the parent and the infant do. Daniel Stern's work would form a powerful hypothesis on which to base such a project.

Chapter Eight - Body As Character

> Observation teaches us that individual
> human beings realise the general picture of
> humanity in an almost infinite variety of
> ways. If we yield to the legitimate need to
> distinguish particular types in this multiplic-
> ity, we shall, at the start, have the choice as
> to what characteristics and what points of
> view we shall take as the basis of our differ-
> entiation. For that purpose physical qualities
> will doubtless serve no less well than mental
> ones; the most valuable distinctions will be
> those which promise to present a regular
> combination of physical and mental charac-
> teristics. (Freud 1931: 361/217)

> In general a human being cannot bear oppo-
> site extremes in juxtaposition, be they in his
> personality or in his reactions. It is this
> endeavour for unification that we call char-
> acter. (Freud, in Jones 1955: 263)

Character in psychoanalysis

What Boothby in Chapter Six calls 'mind', what Verhaeghe
calls 'psyche', both are, more accurately, descriptions of the *ego*.
This misrepresentation is not that of Boothby or Verhaeghe, but
rather that of the ego itself. As Lacan, Reich, Freud, Winnicott
and others all recognise in their different ways, what is initially a 'body ego' tends powerfully *to identify itself with the mental*,
and to identify the mental with itself. The corollary of this is
that bodily excitations are then experienced as a threat to mental stability, interrupting the continuity of the presentation of
self to self.

   Clarifying the philosophical weaknesses of this position is
not really enough. More than a theory, this is an *experience*: a

positioning of the subject as mental rather than bodily, which needs to be understood analytically, as an overdetermined choice. The 'mental ego' is clearly a common experience in our culture but, equally clearly, not a universal, permanent and total experience (or we could hardly observe it). What sorts of coordinate systems are available to map these positionings?

One such system is provided by the analytic theory of character, or rather, by that theory as taken up and developed by Reich and other body-oriented therapists. Character theory is important for two reasons. Firstly, it offers us a way of contextualising the 'mind-body' arguments and differences. Secondly, it demonstrates what can be achieved through bodymind-centred analytic theory. I want to work my way into this topic through a summary of the historical development of character theory in analytic thought.

As things stand at the moment, after

> close on a century of analytic thought about
> character... there is not an agreed upon defin-
> ition, not even an agreement about the locus
> of description. (Liebert 1988: 58)

With character, as with so many other psychoanalytic ideas, the *history* of the concept has been lost, become opaque to most of those who talk about it. If we investigate that history, things take on a very different appearance. Among other discoveries we find that here, again, it is trauma which has led to amnesia - in this case, the trauma of Reich's expulsion and the accompanying *Totschweigen* ('deathly silence'; Kurzweil 1993: 8) about his ideas.

The first character structure to be explored - and we shall see how this is important and non-accidental - is the 'anal'. Freud's 1908 paper 'Character and Anal Eroticism' was greeted, as Strachey says (Freud 1908: 207/168), with 'astonishment and indignation' for its introduction of the notion that respectable and praiseworthy character traits like parsimony and orderliness could have their sources in such dirty business. Freud never wrote a great deal about character, but the idea that vicissitudes of development through developmental stages and erogenous zones could give rise to permanent structures of adult behaviour and experience was taken up by Abraham, Jones, and later by Reich.

Three approaches to character

Psychoanalysis recognises three varieties of character. The first, which we can call 'structural', is defined by Fenichel as 'the ego's habitual modes of adjustment to the external world, the id, and the superego' (Fenichel 1989: 467; see Kernberg 1970). The structural interpretation of character derives mainly from the ego psychology of Anna Freud (Freud, A. 1986). It is the primary form of character theory which has developed within the psychoanalytic world since the expulsion of Reich. In the 1931 paper quoted above, Freud actually suggested a sketch of a system of 'libidinal types', based upon the individual's primary allegiance to id, ego, superego or a blend of two of these. In a general sense, the structural description of character is a development of this paper, although not along the lines specifically proposed by Freud.

The second, which we can call 'descriptive', is based directly on psychopathology - e.g. the obsessive, hysteric, phobic etc. A 'phobic character' is one likely - under appropriate circumstances - to experience phobias, and so on. This is basically a nosological system, a way of organising data, inherited from Kraepelinian psychiatry; in itself it implies no theory of the origins or development of character structure. As with any nosological system, it is easy to lose sight of the fact that *only* such a theory of origins can establish whether meaningful - rather than factitious - entities are in fact being discussed.

The third approach, which we can call 'dynamic', derives character from the fate of the drives as the individual traverses different erogenous zones in the course of developmental experience - e.g. the oral, anal, phallic, etc. This is in fact Freud's first theory, and the one which was taken up and developed first by Abraham and later by Reich. Freud himself later moved on to the structural approach, executing a sweeping change in emphasis - from character as derivative of libidinal drives to character as derivative of identifications with the parents in the form of structured ego representations.(Liebert 1988: 50)

Now, as Freud indicates in the epigraph to this chapter, there are clearly an infinite number of ways to classify different sorts of human beings. Some are more useful than others, however. It's like sorting buttons - you can put all the red ones together, or all the wooden ones, or all the ones with four holes - it depends entirely on what you are planning to do with them! The descriptive approach to character is focused on the goal of differential diagnosis - it is what we might call a DSM approach.[1] The structural approach has the goal of systematising the ways in which the ego deals with *internal* conflicts; though in some ways powerful, is also basically abstract and formal in its systematisation. It offers little in the way of an historical account of how and why a specific character type comes into being, ultimately depending on the old analytic fallback of 'constitution'. Neither of these two approaches addresses body typology.

The dynamic system of character based on developmental phases, especially as elaborated by Reich and subsequent bodywork therapists, seems to me a particularly powerful approach because it brings together three parameters: the *historical* (developmental), the *attitudinal*, and the *bodily*. In fact it achieves exactly what Freud calls for, 'a regular combination of physical and mental characteristics'. It is firmly anchored to an explanatory model which suggests in some detail how each individual character structure originates in situations of childhood repression and deprivation.

As we have seen in Chapter Four, Reich defines character as *'an armouring of the ego* against the dangers of the outside world and the repressed drive demands of the id' (Reich 1972: 155). This armouring will be encountered in therapy as a *style of defence*, as the form rather than the content of what the analysand produces.

> Character resistance is expressed not in
> terms of content but formally, in the way one
> typically behaves, in the manner in which
> one speaks, walks and gestures; and in one's
> characteristic habits (how one smiles or
> sneers, whether one speaks coherently or
> incoherently, *how* one is polite and *how* one is
> aggressive). (Reich 1972: 51-2, original ital-
> ics)

However:

> The character resistance which is manifested
> in terms of form is just as capable of being
> resolved with respect to its content, and of
> being traced back to infantile experiences
> and drive interests as the neurotic symptom
> is. (Reich 1972: 52)

Character, for Reich, originates in our fundamental experiences
of relationship.

> At the basis of all reactions exists not the
> antithesis between love and hate, and cer-
> tainly not the antithesis between eros and
> the death drive, but the antithesis between
> ego (*'person'; id = pleasure ego*)[2] *and outer
> world*. On an elementary level, there is but
> one desire which issues from the biopsychic
> unity of the person, namely the desire to dis-
> charge inner tensions... This is impossible
> without contact with the outer world.
> Hence, the *first* impulse of *every* creature
> must be the desire to establish contact with
> the outer world. (Reich 1972: 271, original
> italics)

Our experience of frustration of this desire sets up a character structure which, like a symptom, both conceals and pre-

sents, expresses and protects our desire. Its form will depend upon the libidinal phase at which traumatic frustration is experienced. (Reich 1972: 175).

> The entire world of past experience was *embodied* in the present in the form of character attitudes. A person's character is the functional sum total of all past experiences. (Reich 1973: 145, my italics)

> A person's character conserves and at the same time wards off the function of certain childhood situations. (Reich 1973: 305)

Character in the clinic

Only one modern analytic paper has seriously addressed Reich's theory of character and sought to criticise it: Richard F Sterba's 'Clinical and Therapeutic Aspects of Character Resistance'. The author

> undertake[s] to demonstrate... that the concept of 'character resistance', as Reich formulated it, has to be discarded as an artefact which owed its existence to the peculiarities of Wilhelm Reich's theory and technique of psychoanalytic therapy. (Sterba 1990 [1953]: 274)

In an intelligent analysis, Sterba isolates what he calls several 'basic errors' in Reich's approach. These are: 'that he denies the genuine character of positive transference, especially in the beginning of analysis'; that he 'ignores the phenomenon of ambivalence'; that he imposes a 'rigid concept of mental stratification' in his concept of layers of resistance; and that he exaggerates the importance of neglecting an initial 'secret' resistance. All of these could - and probably should, at least partially - be granted without damaging Reich's general thesis.

Sterba finally raises his 'main objection': that Reich's concept of character itself is 'far too limited'. He objects to Reich's central emphasis on *resistance* as the essential quality of character, and substitutes Anna Freud's 'much broader' concept of character as:

> approximately the whole set of attitudes habitually adopted by an individual ego for the solution of the never-ending series of inner conflicts. (Sterba 1990 [1953]: 284)

This concept - what I have described as the 'structural' approach to character - is indeed much broader, yet it is also much weaker. It reduces character to a fair approximation of 'personality', and does so by quietly eliminating Reich's emphasis on crucial interpersonal experiences, and substituting 'never-ending... *inner* conflicts'.

In *The Ego and the Mechanisms of Defence*, Anna Freud directly criticises what she sees as Reich's view of character, and makes a travesty of it in the process:

> When in analysis we succeed in tracing these residues [i.e. character armour] to their historical source, they recover their mobility and cease to block by their fixation our access to the defensive operations upon which the ego is at the moment actively engaged. Since these modes of defence have become permanent, we cannot now bring their emergence and disappearance into relation with the emergence and disappearance of instinctual demands and affects from within... Hence their analysis is a peculiarly laborious process. I am sure that we are justified in placing them in the foreground only when we can detect no trace at all of a present conflict between ego, instincts and affect. And I am equally sure that there is no

justification for restricting the term 'analysis
of resistance' to the analysis of these particular phenomena, for it should apply to that of
all resistances. (Freud, A. 1986: 33)

Reich, of course, does not make this artificial distinction
between a person's habitual and current 'modes of defence', but
recognises that the two are likely to be the same - most particularly in analysis. He meets these sorts of criticisms very directly
in *Character Analysis*:[3]

> This principle ['that the repressed material is
> never loosened and made conscious from the
> perspective of the drive but always... from the
> perspective of the defence'] was miscon-
> strued by my critics... to mean that, for me,
> character and defence were identical; that,
> therefore, I unjustifiably limited the concept
> of character. If this were so, I would immedi-
> ately have to correct it. But... I stated that *the
> most important and most conspicuous character
> trait becomes, in analysis, the most crucial resis-
> tance for the purpose of defense...* The fact that,
> over and above this, it has different, chiefly
> sex-economic functions, that it serves to
> maintain the relationship to the outside
> world and to preserve the psychic equilibri-
> um, is thoroughly described and elaborated
> in Part I of the present volume. (Reich 1972:
> 296n, original italics)

Here Reich encapsulates his view of character: that it 'serves to
maintain the relationship to the outside world and to preserve
the psychic equilibrium'. This is a profound formulation, and
one which anticipates much modern (mostly non-analytic) work
that stresses the *creative and protective* aspects of character structure. Like a neurotic symptom, character is a means of survival:
it constitutes resistance not only in the therapeutic sense, but

also in a sense approaching that suggested by the term 'the French Resistance' - an organised, covert system which obstructs and sabotages oppressive forces. (In fact I think this *is* the therapeutic sense - that therapeutic resistance originates in resistance to oppression). As many countries around the world have found out, dismantling resistance forces when the war for liberation is over can be a major problem, even if one grants that analysis is not in actuality an invasion force!

There is a very large issue here,[4] which goes back to Ferenczi's profound criticism of psychoanalysis in works like 'Confusion of Tongues' (Ferenczi 1994b), where he both identifies *and agrees with* many analysands' unconscious sense that the analyst is not genuinely 'on their side'. From a very different angle, similar points about resistance are forcefully made in the anthology *Women, Girls and Psychotherapy: Reframing Resistance*, which argues that psychotherapy, particularly of girls, needs to find out how to support the movement

> from a psychological resistance which takes
> the form of not knowing and covers a series
> of disconnections, to a political resistance
> which exposes false relationships and brings
> relational violations out into the open, to a
> healthy resistance to disconnection which
> grants immunity to psychological illness -
> the resistance which is rooted in wanting
> and having honest relationships. (Gilligan *et al.*, 1991: 27)

Character and society

Reich's position on character implies a view of human development which stresses *both* the biologically-based drives, *and* object relations, together with their social context:

> The first psychoanalytic views were based
> on the conflict between drive and outer
> world. The complete disregard of this basic

concept by present-day theories has no effect on its validity. It is the most pregnant formulation of all analytic psychology... The psychic process reveals itself as the result of the conflict between drive demand and the external frustration of this demand. Only secondarily does an inner conflict between desire and self-denial result from this initial opposition... The question of why society demands the suppression and repression of drives can no longer be answered psychologically. There are social, more correctly, economic interests that cause such suppressions and repressions in certain eras. (Reich 1972: 287)

It is this understanding of character which leads Reich to the formulation that *'the character structure is the congealed sociological process of a given epoch'* (Reich 1972: xxvi), and that 'every social organisation produces those character structures which it needs to exist' (Reich 1972: xxii). These views are of course developed at length in *The Mass Psychology of Fascism* where Reich tries to show, in formulations reminiscent of Althusser (1971), how the needs of the hegemonic class are mediated through the family, in order to create a pliable and obedient individual character structure:

Authoritarian society's fight against the sexuality of children and adolescents, and the consequent struggle in one's own ego, takes place within the framework of the authoritarian family, which has thus far proven to be the best institution to carry out this fight successfully. Sexual desires naturally urge a person to enter into all kinds of relations with the world, to enter into close contact with it in a vast variety of forms... Sexual inhibition is the basis of the familial encapsulation of the individual, as well as the basis of individual self-consciousness. (Reich 1975: 90, my italics)

The anal character is the quintessentially *armoured* and *repressed* character - which is why it was the first character to be identified and described. Anality, organised around sphincter tension, could be seen as the prototype of the 'spastic ego' (Totton and Edmondson 1988: 17), the binding of energy into defence and alienation from one's own impulses and needs - the model, in a sense, for all character structures.[5] 'The muscular pushing back and holding back of faeces,' Reich says, is 'the prototype for repression in general' (Reich 1972: 342). Indeed, from the beginning, analytic theory has aligned anality with capitalism.[6]   Reich argues that while 'normal' authoritarian culture depends upon the family instilling a rigid, inhibited and repressed character structure, fascism itself appeals to the impulses which are held *below* that tight armour of musculature and character attitudes, and which curdle into hate and destruction.

> The surface layer of social co-operation is not in contact with the deep biological core of one's selfhood; it is borne by a second, an intermediate character layer, which consists exclusively of cruel, sadistic, lascivious, rapacious and envious impulses... If one penetrates through this second layer of perversion, deeper into the biological substratum of the human animal, one always discovers the third, deepest layer... In this core, under favourable conditions, man is an essentially honest, industrious, cooperative, loving, and, if motivated, rationally hating animal... [But] drop the mask of cultivation, and it is not natural sociality that prevails at first, but only the perverse, sadistic character layer. (Reich 1975: 13-14)

This is one of Reich's deepest disagreements with orthodox Freudian analysis: his insistence that, by nature, human beings are *essentially* loving, cooperative and rational. Although this position is clearly and explicitly 'essentialist', it is in this respect no different from its polar opposite, Freud's (and Lacan's) belief that human beings are *essentially* split and conflictual. One could restate Reich's position as a claim that there is a realistic possibility both of individual happiness, and of social arrangements which are not fundamentally oppressive. However, Reich founds this position on the project of dissolving neurotic character structure and attaining 'genitality'. As we shall see below, it is possible to revalue character more positively, and to think in terms of integration rather than dissolution.

Modern character theory

The expulsion of Reich from the psychoanalytic world has meant that 'dynamic' character theory has been developed largely in non-analytic circles. This is because Reich and his followers themselves worked outside psychoanalysis, but also, no doubt, because the association of character theory with Reich had made it unpopular within analysis. I would argue that this is much to the loss of psychoanalysis, and in what follows, I hope to show the great value of later work done in non-psychoanalytic circles.

I can only give a general outline here of how, through various contributions,[7] the subject of character has been greatly fleshed out. Work has been done on the origins and functions of character, its clinical role, how to recognise it, its expression in body types, and its corresponding metabolic, perceptual, cognitive and neurological types. It has been considered from the point of view of British object relations (e.g. Boadella and Smith 1986, Southgate 1980), ego psychology (e.g. Johnson 1985), classical analysis (e.g. Lowen 1985, Baker 1980), humanistic psychotherapy (e.g. Kurtz 1990, Totton and Edmondson 1988), orgonomy (e.g. Boadella 1987, Baker 1980), and therapeutic bodywork (e.g. Keleman 1975, Painter1982)[8]. The number of identified character structures has been increased: it is now widely agreed among theorists that there are six basic characters, although these are given different names by different authors. In addition to the familiar oral, anal, and phallic characters of classical theory, there are the hysteric, the ocular (or schizoid), and the psychopathic, all understood as normal developmental stages rather than simply - as the names might seem to imply - pathological structures.[9]

Embodied character

Clearly, a theory of character as response to the impact of trauma on the erogenous zones is a *body-centred* theory. The Reichian and post-Reichian conception of character anchors each particular structure in the relational events of developmental life. As we have seen, Reich takes the leap from a 'one-body' to a 'two-body' perspective (Rickman 1950), and argues that libido theory itself, and the erogenous zones in particular, demand that 'the *first* impulse of *every* creature must be the desire to establish contact with the outer world' (Reich 1972: 271). But the hammer-blows of rejection or aggression that permanently shape our libidinal structure hit us initially in a specific erogenous zone. To have this effect, the blow must have fallen when that zone was at the centre of our developmental agenda - during its activation phase, so to speak.

This brings us back to the neurologically-based theories of trauma examined in the last chapter, which are wholly consistent with Reich's approach to character, and with more modern work which identifies for each character structure different patterns of arousal, perception and metabolism (see Kurtz 1990: 51 and Ch 16):

> A very narrow window - a critical period - exists during which specific sensory experience was required for optimal organization and development of the part of the brain mediating a specific function. While these phenomena have been examined in great detail for the primary sensory modalities in animals, similar use dependent neurodevelopment occurs in all parts of the human central nervous system. Abnormal micro-envi-

ronmental cues and atypical patterns of neural activity during critical and sensitive periods, then, can result in malorganization and
compromised function in brain mediated
functions such as humor, empathy, attachment and affect regulation. Some of the most
powerful clinical examples of this phenomenon are related to lack of attachment experiences early in life. (Perry *et al* 1995: 276)

This sort of data and interpretation offers a potential bridge
towards a unification of attachment theory and post-Reichian
character theory - which is very centrally concerned with 'functions such as humor, empathy, attachment and affect regulation'. The emphasis on the brain in the passage just quoted is
really best seen as a choice of interpretative level. As I have
argued at length in Chapter Seven, and as the passage above in
fact acknowledges, the brain is *mediator* rather than central
source and location of the kinds of changes we are considering.
The brain is meta-processor, but character (or traumatic adaptation) occurs in the bodymind as a whole.

Here we are concerned with what we might call *non-cata-
strophic* trauma - *relatively* tolerable, marginally traumatic interactions with carers which nonetheless demand less than optimal
adaptation of function. This is reminiscent of Winnicott. We
might think of character as the result of what he calls 'impinge-
ments' - that is, less than wholly adequate elements of caring
which demand from the infant or child a response, an effort of
adaptation (Winnicott, 1949). As he makes very clear, without
this effort of adaptation there is no *person* - yet, at the same time,
each demand for effort reduces the range and freedom of the
personality. This inevitable compromise between expression
and protection defines character.

As libidinal charge traverses the body in the early years of
life, then, it is transected by a series of more or less successful
encounters with the outside world, in the shape of our primary
carers. These encounters not only shape our psychic structure;
they also, for Reich and his followers, shape our *physical* struc-

ture. Character can be recognised in the body, before the analysand even speaks. Overall body shape, distribution of muscle and fat, breathing, skin colour and texture, posture, movement style - character is literally *embodied* in all these.

Reich's case histories are remarkable for their vivid sense of his analysands' embodiment; he moves from precise descriptions of individuality to correlate general bodily traits with character structure. Always he moves between the quality of *embodiment* and the quality of psychic *presence* - of what Stern calls 'vitality affect':

> Others frequently ward off their repressed aggression by 'insinuating' - as one such patient once put it - themselves into the favour of any person capable of rousing their aggression. They become as 'slippery' as eels, evade every straightforward reaction, can never be held fast. Usually, this 'slipperiness' is also expressed in the intonation of their voice; they speak in a soft, modulated, cautious, and flattering way. In taking over anal interests for the purpose of warding off the aggressive impulses, the ego itself becomes 'greasy' and 'slimy' and conceives of itself in this way. (Reich 1972: 175)

Eventually, Reich becomes confident enough to sketch out systematically the bodily concomitants of particular character structures. For example:

> [T]he facial expression and the gait of the hysterical character are never severe and heavy, as they are in the compulsive character; never arrogant and self-confident, as they are in the phallic-narcissistic character. The movements of the archetype have a kind of lilting quality (not to be confused with elastic), are supple and sexually provocative. (Reich 1972: 205)

These sorts of analyses have been greatly developed by later Reichians and post-Reichians, and carried well beyond the descriptive level. Here, for example, Alexander Lowen analyses the typical oral structure:

> This structure is frequently associated with low blood pressure and a low normal basal metabolism... The chest is generally deflated, the belly is without turgor and feels soft and empty to palpitation... Movements of reaching out with the arms are generally experienced unpleasurably... The legs are never experienced as stable supports for the body. The feeling of weakness in the legs can be shown to be based upon a true perception of their function... The oral character tends to compensate the weakness of the legs by locking the knees while standing. This gives the legs a feeling of rigidity... Above all the muscular system of the oral character structure is underdeveloped as compared with the frame of the body. (Lowen 1958: 173-5)

These excerpts from a much longer description are paralleled for each of the other characters. It is notable how Lowen moves easily between subjective and objective descriptions, and meaningfully connects the two. The whole burden of this style of thinking about character is that the body accurately portrays the psychic structure. But the relationship is not passive and one-way, as the word 'portrays' might imply: we could better say, again, that the body *embodies* the psychic structure. The psyche is not simply 'in' the body in a passive sense; the psychic and the somatic aspects of our experience profoundly condition and shape each other at every point.

There are several ways in which we can seek to understand this connection between character and the body - several *levels* of interpretation are available. We could start out from the musculature, and consider the very specific effects of traumatic interaction on the quality of voluntary control over particular muscles and muscle groups. For example, the anal sphincter is not under voluntary control in a human infant. It is actually physiologically *impossible* to prevent defecation by tightening the sphincter until the age of several months; pressure from carers to be 'clean' before that age can only be met by tensing the whole gross musculature of the pelvic floor, buttocks, thighs etc. Clearly the *quality* of control in the anal sphincter itself, once achieved, is going to be different depending on the different social experience around toilet training; the sort of gross tension I have just described is likely to disturb the development of fine, precise voluntary control. We may well consider that the habitual use of pelvic and associated musculature can be expected to affect the general state of this part of the body, through its indirect effect on functions like blood flow, oxygenation of tissue, elimination of toxins via the lymph system, and so on.

Our voluntary musculature has a differential development rate in general - we spend several years gradually attaining control of our movements, and in each muscle group gross and fine motor control also occur differentially (Rothwell 1994). This provides the possibility of a detailed mapping of voluntary muscle control onto developmental sequence, so that traumatic interaction will appear as a disturbance in specific body areas and affect the final shape and movement and postural style of the adult body. Elements of such a mapping have already been accomplished (Bernhardt, Bentzen and Isaacs 1996, Bentzen and Bernhardt 1992).

But this level of interpretation is not the only one available. Indeed, it is arguable whether in itself it fully explains the manifestation of character in the body. What we so often experience is an *expressive* quality - the impression that the body *mimes* and *performs* characterological themes, so that - for example - an oral body may give a powerful impression of a plant which has bolted towards an inadequate light source, or an anal body may appear literally 'squashed' and 'held in'. Experiences like this pull us in several different explanatory directions. For instance, they raise again the question of 'somatisation' of the 'fundamental hysteria' that may be considered to be at the root of every character structure, so that the 'auto-plastic' function of the body inscribes it with meaning. On the other hand, we might think in terms of a *two-way* interaction between Damasio's body-schema and the body, mediated not only through musculature but directly through the multifold homeo-static autonomic functions of the brain.

On a very different explanatory level, we could return to Julia Kristeva and the semiotic, as:

> a preverbal functional state that governs the connections between the body (in the process of constituting itself as a body proper) and the protagonists of family structure... The kinetic functional stage of the semiotic pre-cedes the establishment of the sign...
> (Kristeva 1984: 27)

Kristeva emphasises the profound ambivalence of the semiotic, as the point of coincidence of those forces which constitute the speaking individual, and those forces which subvert it. Again, like character, the semiotic is structured like a symptom:

> The semiotic chora is no more than the place where the subject is both generated and negated, the place where his unity succumbs before the process of charges and stases which produce him. (Kristeva 1984: 28)

Each of these explanatory levels may be useful in an appro-priate context. The overall point is that character is specifically a *quality of embodiment*, an expression of the individual's experi-ence of bodily impulse and its satisfaction or denial. As Reich says,

> economically, the character in everyday life and the character resistance in the analysis serve as a means of avoiding what is unpleas-ant (*Unlust*), of establishing and preserving a

> psychic (even if neurotic) balance, and final-
> ly of consuming repressed quantities of
> drive energy and/or quantities which have
> eluded repression. The binding of free-float-
> ing anxiety... is one of the cardinal functions
> of the character. (Reich 1972: 52-3)

Character as creative

I have described the structural, Anna Freudian approach to
character as weaker and blander than the dynamic approach,
reducing character to personality. The kernel of truth in that
approach, though, is its realisation that character is not ultimately a matter of pathology, but a matter of existence as a
human being. Each character position defines a *theme*, so to
speak - almost in the musical sense. The theme may be existence, nurturing, validation, self-regulation, achievement, or
meta-communication. There is nothing pathological about
these themes; all of them will play themselves out in every life.
What determines how harmoniously and creatively they perform, so to speak, is the degree and kind of trauma we
encounter in our initial attempts to *express* each theme, and the
strategies we therefore adopt to *preserve* each theme, even at the
cost of concealing it.

John Conger offers a balanced view of character in human
life:

> Character provides a meeting place for psy-
> che and soma. Character as a defensive
> structure gathers us when we are scattered
> and organises us into an identifiable pattern
> of rigidity and energetic withdrawal, bind-
> ing our anxiety, rage, sadness and longing.
> Character is what keeps us separate, exempt
> and special, and what hold us back from sur-
> render to our energetic nature. Character
> represents a practice of self-cure, an ongo-
> ing, hasty, rigid solution imposed over our

instability to maintain an intact sense of self.
Daily our anxiety persuades us not to relin-
quish our protections... Character is the shell
that energy leaves behind, and as such it provides a house; but the shell, as we grow,
becomes too small. (Conger 1994: 95-6)

At a remarkably early date it was Ernest Jones - often a specialist in the positive - who was the first to point out, in a brilliant paper entitled 'Anal-Erotic Character Traits', that both
advantageous and disadvantageous qualities derive from 'the
interrelations of the different anal-erotic components with one
another and with other constituents of the whole character.'
Among the negative anal character traits he lists

the incapacity for happiness, the irritability
and bad temper, the hypochondria, the
miserliness, meanness and pettiness, the
slow-mindedness and proneness to bore, the
bent for dictating and tyrannising, and the
obstinacy... (Jones 1977: 437)

But, among the positive,

may be reckoned especially the individual-
ism, the determination and persistence, the
love of order and power of organization, the
competency, reliability and thoroughness, the
generosity, the bent towards art and good
taste, the capacity for unusual tenderness,
and the general ability to deal with concrete
objects of the material world. (Jones 1977:
436-7)

I find these lists exceptionally interesting and subtle.
Immediately noticeable is that while 'generosity' appears in the
positive list, 'meanness' features in the negative: an accurate
reflection of the way in which a given character position will
manifest as either *a* or anti-*a*; either a particular trait or, by nega-

tion, its opposite. This relates to the distinction later drawn by Fenichel between 'reactive' and 'sublimatory' character traits: those which say 'I don't want', or those which disguise and make acceptable what I do want. (Fenichel1989: 174-5)

In this case, it is the 'sublimatory' trait - meanness, disguising anal retentiveness - which is seen as negative, and the 'reactive' trait - generosity - as positive (although generosity may also sublimate the use of faeces as gifts - the distinction between reaction and sublimation is not simple). But it is important that there is no straightforward pattern to this: for example, the 'sublimatory' traits of 'determination and persistence, the love of order', and so on, all appear in the positive list.

Jones recognises, in fact, that the *fundamental quality* of each character position[10] can express itself either usefully or damagingly. In other words, each character position reflects a developmental stage which we all go through - which we all *need* to go through - in order to attain adult competence and creativity. We all need to be able to 'deal with concrete objects of the material world,' as Jones puts it. Equally, we all need to be able to think and imagine (ocular stage), to take in nourishment and stand on our own feet (oral stage), to use play and fantasy to manage our internal and external objects ('psychopathic' stage), to push ourselves forward and conquer reality (phallic stage), and to play, flirt and meta-communicate ('hysteric' stage).[11]

Character and theory

> James told of how, when walking on a summer evening in the park alone, watching the couples make love, he suddenly began to feel a tremendous oneness with the whole world, with the skies and trees and flowers and grass - with the lovers too. He ran home in panic and immersed himself in his books.
> (Laing 1965: 91)

This passage from Laing's *The Divided Self* is very 'Reichian' in tone. Generally, it reminds us of numerous passages in which Reich describes the reappearance in neurotic individuals of deep contact with the world:

> the feeling of 'a peculiar contact with the world' intensified. He assured me that there was a complete identity between the emotional seriousness which overcame him now and the sensations which he had experienced as a small child... He described it as follows: 'It is as if I were at one with the world... It is incredible how I now sense the depth of the world.' (Reich 1973: 325)

More specifically, the passage from Laing encapsulates what Reichians, following Elsworth Baker, have called the 'ocular character structure' (Baker 1980: 141-152) or - in more widespread terminology - the 'schizoid character'. [12] As Lowen puts it (1958: 348), the schizoid character shows a 'basic antipathy to material reality and the tendency to complete instinctual defusion.' Contact easily becomes intolerable to the ocular character, overwhelming their weakly defined ego and drowning the ability to discriminate in a flood of emotion and sensation.[11] The libidinal impulse here is to do with deep contact and merging. As the 'first' character structure, in the sense of the structure associated with the earliest experiences, the ocular is in some sense also the *primary* character structure, the prototype of the general tendency of drive to disestablish the ego. To the extent that an ocular character cannot tolerate this, they often defend ego identity through *thought*, identifying the two as I have described.

This fear of ego-loss and thought-loss often leads to and is concealed by *a choice of thought as the primary mode of experience*: 'he ran home in panic and immersed himself in his books'. Ocular characters may avoid flooding by staying in the 'ivory tower' of mentalised existence - sometimes of an eccentric and delusionary nature, but often creating very valuable and profound conceptual systems - 'rising above' everyday appearance to grasp the deep structure of reality. As we have seen, each character position has vast creative aspects, and those of the ocular character include both rationality and inspiration - two different styles of 'head-centred' experience.

As we have also seen, though, each character position, carried to extremes and separated off from the others, becomes limiting and restrictive. In the case of the ocular character this can manifest in part as a rejection and devaluing of bodily and affective experience, a belief that everything should ideally be rational and mental - a sort of 'Mr Spock' (from Star Trek) approach to the world.

I want - gently - to suggest that psychoanalysis tends to exhibit features of both the creative and the restrictive aspects of the ocular character structure. As we have examined, psychoanalysis tends to seek to turn both emotion and muscular impulse into *thoughts*. The idea that this is the right way to go is an almost unexamined axiom. Analysts themselves, even if they do a lot of feeling, as many do, tend to see the central activity of their work as *thinking*, processing their analysands' intellectual and emotional material through their own mental activity. Freud himself certainly had some of the traits of an ocular character - for example in his famous unwillingness to look at analysands and be looked at in turn by them.

So, when Freud writes

> What I am asserting is that this technique is the only one suited to my individuality; I do not venture to deny that a physician quite differently constituted might find himself driven to adopt a different attitude to his patients and to the task before him... (Freud 1912: 111)

then I want to take him quite seriously, and to suggest that what he refers to as his 'individuality' has a lot to do with his character structure, one which was quite obviously excellently suited to do psychoanalysis - but undoubtedly not the only character structure suitable for the job.

Unsurprisingly, however, Freud's character has stamped itself upon his creation, psychoanalysis, which now itself has something of an ocular character. As Reich says, 'every social organisation produces those character structures which it needs to exist' (Reich 1972: xxii) and psychoanalysis, as a social organisation, has done just that. This gives it some of its great strengths - for example its carefulness with boundaries, the amount of space that it tends to provide for clients to find out for themselves, its sensitivity to subtle nuance, and its simple *intelligence* - all of which Ernest Jones would call 'advantageous' aspects of the ocular structure.

But Reich points out the direct limitation of the ocular position:

> It is commonly assumed that human intellect has a solely objective function and that it is directed towards the world... Two things are overlooked here: 1) the intellectual function itself is a vegetative [i.e. bodily] activity; and 2) the intellectual function may have an affective charge whose intensity is no less than any purely affective impulse... Intellectual activity can be structured and directed in such a way that it looks like a most cunningly operating apparatus whose purpose is precisely to avoid cognition... (Reich 1972: 305-6)

What he describes in the last sentence, the defensive function of 'intellectualisation', analysis obviously knows all about. But might there be subtle layers of intellectual defence built into the structure of analysis itself - namely: defence against the full acknowledgement of affect and, in particular, against the full valuation of bodily experience? Winnicott's description of 'mind' over and *against* 'psyche-soma' (Winnicott 1949: 246-7) is a delineation of aspects of the ocular character. It also delineates aspects of psychoanalysis itself.

Chapter Nine - Sexed and Gendered Body

> With little girls, so we have supposed, things
> must be similar, though in some way or
> other they must nevertheless be different.
> (Freud 1925b: 332-3/249)

Dividing by two leaves an odd number

Certain questions are perhaps only askable when the answers
no longer *matter* - when, for instance, they can no longer be
used to justify systems of oppression. One example is the question of differences between 'races' (if races can be said to exist
[Kohn 1996]). Another is that of differences between 'sexes' or
'genders' (if, again, either or both of these categories can usefully be said to exist [Butler 1990, Riley 1988]). A third is that of
differences between 'sexualities' (if... [Foucault 1979]). In other
words, an adequate theorisation of gender and sex[1] may have
to wait upon the social rearrangements which are so urgently
required - and probably (historically speaking) imminent.
These may, in time, provide us with a psychic space in which to
think rationally and creatively about female and male, feminine and masculine - or, indeed, to supplement these dualities
with further options. In the meantime, confusion may be the
best we can hope for; certainty of any kind would be dangerous.

Theory may have a role to play in maintaining that useful
confusion, levering open that psychic/social space - a sort of
guerrilla-theorisation.[2] It would in any case be ludicrous to
ignore the topic in a book which is largely about the body in
psychoanalysis. A body's sex, for analytic thought, has always
figured as a crucial defining feature of 'its' subject's subjectivity; a male/female dividing line is assumed to be inscribed
through conscious and unconscious alike. Psychoanalysis, in
other words, has always been concerned with 'Some Psychical
Consequences of the Anatomical Distinction Between the
Sexes' (Freud 1925b).

The anatomical distinction in question - 'the' rather than 'an', we notice - is famously defined by Freud as the self-evident superiority of the penis to the clitoris.

> They [little girls] notice the penis of a brother or playmate, strikingly visible and of large proportions, at once recognise it as the superior counterpart of their own small and inconspicuous organ, and from that time forward fall a victim to envy for the penis.
> (Freud 1925b: 335/252)

If we did not know that this was Freud's own work, how easily it could be read as a parody! I don't intend to labour the absurdity, the partiality (in every sense), of Freud's argument. However, we need to recognise that any formulations of our own are certain to be equally partial, equally locked into invisible co-ordinates of time and place. So long as the 'consequences' - not simply 'psychic' but social, cultural, political - of the 'anatomical distinction' in question are so extreme - so 'strikingly visible and of large proportions', one might say - this will remain the case. 'Distinction', in fact, must be read as a verbal noun, as an ongoing process: it is the *making* of the distinction, of precisely *this* distinction - of visibility and size, as the marks of 'superiority' - which have the 'consequences' indicated. The distinction *is* the consequences, the consequences *are* the distinction.[3]

I said, though, that I did not intend to labour the point; hoping that it has been sufficiently made. (But what *is* sufficient? How visible and of what proportions? On this topic, all understandings are double, *doubles entendres*.) Let us simply acknowledge that in passages such as this, Freud - having given us precisely the tools we need in order to know better - aligns himself definitively with the trend in psychoanalysis which maintains that, if subjects are only interrogated with sufficient rigor, kept awake for long enough under the harsh lights of analytic technique, they will *all* eventually confess to gender, break down, and acknowledge that, yes, they are male or female, anatomi-

cally distinct and liable to the consequences. (And, of course, to
deny is, precisely, to affirm...)

This is of course not the only point of view in psychoanalysis. Contemporary Lacanians, or some of them at least, believe
that certainty about one's sex is equivalent to psychosis.
Neurotics and normal neurotics alike, they maintain, in conse-
quence of the castration complex, precisely *do not know* whether
they are male or female, and construct a masculinity or femininity as a shelter against this radical doubt - gender as a con-
sequence of sexual uncertainty. Putting it in this way, though, I
am implying an equivalence, a symmetry, between male and
female, masculine and feminine, which is emphatically denied
in Lacanian thought: 'The Woman does not exist'. As Malcolm
Bowie puts it, Lacan displays 'a monomaniacal refusal to grant
signifying power to the female body' (Bowie 1991: 147). Writers
like Verhaeghe and Fink, though, suggest that this is a mis-
reading of Lacan's position, that he is trying simply to describe
what *is*, rather than what should or could be. This seems a surprisingly unsophisticated project - is it, in fact, possible to
describe what *is* without a theory of what *could be*?

Either way, even if the subject does not know which sex or
gender it belongs to, there is still only a choice of two possibilities, the famous two doors marked 'Gentlemen' and 'Ladies'
(Lacan 1977: 151). This brilliant trope of Lacan, though, is still
open to qualification. What, for example, of the third door we
quite often see nowadays marked 'Disabled'? Even more point-
edly, what of the third door that used to be seen in the Southern
United States marked 'Coloured'? Each is a third, diminished
position, degendered but placed alongside gender - like, in fact,
the category of 'Children', as in 'men, women and children'.
Each subverts, through debasement, the two-value logic of
male/female, masculine/feminine.

It is initially in reaction to Lacan that Luce Irigaray takes her
stand, which could be summarised as a refusal (monomaniacal
or not) to *deny* signifying power to the female body. However
open some of her work may be to non-essentialist interpretation (Schor 1994), in recent writings Irigaray seems to put her
cards on the table, and to move from her earlier project of open-

ing up the options, to one of closure.

> The natural... is at least *two*: male and female.
> This division is not secondary, nor unique to
> human kind... Without sexual difference
> there would be no life on earth.[4] It is the man-
> ifestation of and the condition for the produc-
> tion and reproduction of life. Air and sexual
> difference may be the two dimensions vital
> for life. Not taking them into account would
> be a deadly business. (Irigaray 1996: 37, orig-
> inal italics)

And if there is still any ambiguity in the above:

> It is evident that male and female corporeal
> morphology are not the same and *it therefore*
> *follows* that their way of experiencing the sen-
> sible and of constructing the spiritual is not
> the same. (Irigaray 1996: 38, my italics)

In that extraordinary 'it therefore follows', Irigaray reaches what
one might call the rock-bottom of biologism: biology is definitive of human possibility, - is, after all, in the famous Freudian
quotation, *destiny*.

Every point in Irigaray's argument is and has been bitterly
contested by other feminists. There are (at least) two ways of
considering the argument: firstly, as a philosophical debate
about theory, and secondly as a political debate about strategy,
about how feminists can most successfully pick apart the thick-
ly woven fabric of patriarchal thought, and demolish the stage
on which women simply *cannot appear*, except as men in drag.
(See Riviere 1929, Irigaray 1985a, etc.)

Ranged mutely or articulately against all these positions are
those individuals of uncertain, ambiguous or intentionally non-
dualistic sex and/or gender, including transsexuals (all), trans-
vestites (some), 'hermaphrodites' and the genitally unusual,
and those deliberately assuming the (or a) 'third gender'. All of

these categories, as Foucault argues (1979, final chapter; 1980, introduction), demonstrate that it is in fact *not* the case that *all* humans partake of one of two available sexes or genders.

What seems to some a matter of *fact* - an inescapable biological reality - is nothing of the kind, either empirically or subjectively. The following question becomes possible, or inevitable: why and how do so many of us attain a position of dualistic certainty? If sex and gender are 'in reality' (and one has to ask, where exactly *is* that?) a spectrum (admittedly a spectrum loaded heavily towards each end), why and how are they considered to be a split complementarity? Dividing into two leaves a remainder, an odd number. The idea that we constitute an even number, that we are each either male or female, masculine or feminine, is an imaginary fantasy of totalisation.

Gender and the List

Importantly, the polarity male/female is very often reinscribed upon the polarity mind/body, and vice versa. These two pairs are elements from the same List we have encountered before:

> male:female
> mind:body
> spirit:matter
> culture:nature

and so on.

This is one of the most self-evidently tendentious and confusing sections of The List - or so it seems to me, and perhaps to you; and yet for very many people it underpins all their thinking on the subject as a series of parallel pairs so self-evident as to be at times invisible. Stephen Frosh suggests some of the ways in which the List may impact on psychoanalysis:

> Many masculinist assumptions are endemic
> in psychoanalytic theory itself, thus vitiating
> any claim it may have to give a gender-free
> account of sexual difference - notions such as
> the importance of rational control over 'irra-

tional' desire, the centrality of a paternal, law-
giving, culture-creating function in individual and social development, or even the therapeutic necessity of the translation of feelings
into speech, of the body into words. (Frosh
1994: 13)

All of the positions he describes result from parallels drawn
from the List - for example, male is to female as mind is to body.
In a comprehensive demolition of these parallels, Anthony
Wilden points out that lists of binary pairs very often conflate
the *separate* relationships of opposition, difference, distinction,
and contradiction.

Many a so-called 'opposition' (implying conflict) is in fact a distinction (not implying conflict). Distinctions may exist between terms or
persons or systems at a single level; they may
also exist between levels in hierarchies.
(Wilden 1987: 23)

Often in our culture - and for clearly ideological reasons - distinctions between concepts on different levels of a hierarchy are
'symmetrized', treated as if the two terms are on the same level.
Examples from *logical* hierarchies are 'nature' and 'culture', or
'labour' and 'capital', where the second term actually *depends* on
the first, rather than being symmetrical with it. Another way of
expressing this is that the first term is the 'environment' for the
second.[5] Examples from hierarchies of *power* are 'black' and
'white' or 'female' and 'male' (Wilden 1987:   31-6).
'Symmetrizing' black/white or female/male then allows the
symmetrization of conflict, so that men can accuse women of
'sexism' or whites can accuse blacks of 'racism'. In both cases,
the crucial component of effective social power over the other
group which gives an '-ism' its virulence, or indeed its point, is
generally absent.
    Our List, then, includes examples of wildly varying binary
pairs, representing difference, distinction, opposition, and con-

tradiction. Some pairs are from the same hierarchical level, others are flattened out and 'symmetrized'; some are valid, some factitious. The ideologising function of the List is to present all these pairs as equivalent, and to use the authentic and convincing examples to prop up the bogus ones. A classic example of how the list operates is the often-quoted Chinese ur-polarity of Yin/Yang. Originally, Yin is the shaded side of the valley, Yang the sunny side. As the sun passes over from morning to afternoon, the polarities reverse; while at midday all is Yang, at midnight all is Yin. This example of a wholly relative and complementary *distinction* has become - even in Chinese culture, let alone our own - a model for factitious *oppositions* like male/female or masculine/feminine.

This perhaps rather tedious analysis is unavoidable if we are to think intelligibly about the sexed and gendered body - or, indeed, about the body at all. We have already seen pernicious confusions between mind/body, mind/brain and brain/body, for example. A starting point would be to clarify that the relationship between male/female and masculine/feminine is far from transparent. 'Masculine' is not to 'feminine' as 'male' is to 'female'. In other words, the latter pair is - or should be - a *distinction*, while the former is generally treated as an *opposition*.

One of many ways to criticise our culture's treatment of 'masculine/feminine', then, is to pick apart its illogical logic, which treats the two terms, in Jessica Benjamin's phrase, as 'split complementarities' (Benjamin 1996, passim), as an either/or choice not only in logic but equally, and painfully, in life. This feeds and is fed by a general stress in Western thinking on either/or choices, which is now coming under critique from many directions. One example is category theory (Lakoff 1987), which explores the difference between the way we *think* we make categories and the way we actually *do* make them. A category is not a field with a fence round it, so that everything is either (equally) inside it or (equally) outside it; each category creates a continuous gradient ranging from 'very good example of x' to 'very bad example of x', with an infinite number of placings in between.

However, a critique of the bad logic of sexism misses the

point rather completely if it does not acknowledge the *function* of the logical error, the way in which the *generalisation* of masculinity as that to which femininity is the exception underwrites the concrete power relations of society (in a very similar way to what Marx described as the universalisation of bourgeois values). Through the effect of the List, this generalisation also encompasses mind (rather than body) and culture (rather than nature); man, mind and culture share an apparent project of mastery over woman, body and nature. As Elizabeth Grosz says, summarising Irigaray:

> the masculine can speak of and for the feminine largely because it has emptied itself of any relation to the male body, its specificity and socio-political existence. (Grosz 1990:173)

These issues of gender, then, reflect back directly on one of the central questions of this book: why is it that we find it so hard to identify with our bodies? The answer is, it would seem, because to do so is to identify with everything which is marginalised and disempowered in our culture.

The maternal body

> The only behavior displayed *exclusively* by one sex is childbirth... A given individual will almost always display *some* behaviors that are more common in the opposite sex... [F]rom a scientific standpoint, we cannot regard an animal, especially a human, as simply masculine or feminine. Rather, we must specify which structure or behavior we are talking about when we say it is typical of females or of males. (Rosenzweig *et al* 1996: 436)

This very clear statement of current thinking on the issue, as it has reached into the textbooks, perhaps helps clarify the above. It emphasizes though, the theme of childbirth. Notice that what is specified is precisely *childbirth*, not, for example, breastfeeding which is very occasionally done by males (including human males). But we have not yet addressed the whole theme of the maternal body, and the possibility that the child's unique relationship with this body - its individuation *through* and *from* that body - establishes a unique relationship with the female. My own response to this, is that the femaleness of that body is of no relevance to the infant. What is established is the infant's relationship *to embodiment itself* - the semiotic chora, in Kristeva's terms (Kristeva 1984: 27), which establishes the individual pattern of drives and stases on which our subjectivity is founded. The meaning of the fact that the body from which we come is *female* is contingent and retrospective (*nachträglich*), conditioned by cultural factors, by what a particular society makes of the pattern of human reproduction. Behind this, often obscured by it, is the fact that *we are body, coming from body*.

We need to find a way of recognising the central importance of the circumstances of human parturition - how they establish a definitive series of lived bodily metaphors which control our entire psychic experience, as Melanie Klein brilliantly demonstrates, metaphors of inside and outside, of containment, engulfment and expulsion - but at the same time, of insisting that the patterns of gender identity are only secondarily *superimposed* on this template, and differently so in each culture and subculture.

It is beyond doubt that Freud's original theories downplay the role of the mother to an extraordinary extent - one which needs explanation in terms of Freud's own gender politics. In the 1920s, a whole series of theoreticians tried to correct this bias - including Melanie Klein, but also notably Otto Rank, who wrote to Freud:

> I cannot understand why you lay so much emphasis on [my] final birth theory, which therapeutically and theoretically is not nearly so important as the conclusion that *the transference libido is a purely maternal one* and that... anxiety... was originally tied to the maternal genital... (Lieberman 1985: 240, my italics)

Emphasis on 'the maternal body', though, often smuggles in a false naturalism derived from the List, which equates 'bodily' with 'female' (and also with 'archaic', 'primal', etc). Before we can think about 'the maternal body', we have to clarify the extraordinarily complex relationship our culture creates between the categories of 'mother' and 'woman', a paradoxical pair, in which, although one must be a (sexual) woman in order to become a mother, a mother is frequently supposed and expected not to be a (sexual) woman.

There is a great deal more to be said about all this - and about the whole question of the different genders' different experience of embodiment - for example, concerning menstruation. All I have tried to do in this chapter is to throw into question the idea that a consistent psychic bimorphism can be derived in any simple way from our biology. As I said at the start of this chapter, we are simply not in a position to know what difference sexual difference makes.

Is biologism sexism?

Throughout this book, we have been stalking the concepts of 'biologism' and 'essentialism', wondering whether and how it is possible to consider the body without falling into these positions. In discussing gender and sex, we are brought up hard against this question. Perhaps it is time to pause and ask ourselves again - what is 'biologism'? Why should we seek to avoid it?

An '-ism' is the belief that what precedes the suffix is a privileged element of thought, a foundational category taking priority over others. Thus, racism asserts that a person's race is a or the crucial fact about them; sexism asserts the same about sex; essentialism asserts that the category of 'essence' is foundational (so racism and sexism are probably sub-forms of essentialism), and so on.

This is the way we tend to use terms ending in '-ism' - though the discourses involved are highly complex, and, clearly, what is also very important about 'racism' or 'sexism' is that *one* race or sex is privileged *over* another.[6] When we come to 'biologism', there is a further complication: is the category for which privilege is being claimed here that of biology *the study*, or biology as *that which is studied*?

This may seem a pedantic question, but it is actually a fairly crucial one. What biology the science holds to be the case changes with the times; at any particular moment previous positions, or newly emergent ones, can seem quite peculiar. Looking back, we can see how particular positions of biology the science - which at the time seemed to be 'scientific' - are clear reflections of the values of the day. Foucault would say that we are talking about the *discourse* of biology, and how it articulates with other discourses. Perhaps we can usefully redefine our distinction as between biology-the-discourse and the biological world - that is, the world as a network of living things. Unfortunately, though, we must grant that this particular way of perceiving the biological world, as 'a network of living things', is itself a discourse, and in fact a particularly fashionable and no doubt temporary one!

There clearly is such a thing as the biological world, and it clearly is privileged - foundational - in a quite specific sense, in that it is the environment for other worlds such as the social and the cultural. But anything we *say about it* is going to be part of biology-the-discourse, which, like all discourses, is implicated in relations of power, and definitional choices which assign and channel power in specific ways. So the claim of biologism is peculiar, in a way which is probably shared by all essentialisms: a claim of privileged status for a level of reality which cannot be directly known, but only refracted through a discourse which is conditioned by other levels of reality said to be dependent on the first.

As may be already evident, I myself tend very often to privilege the discourse of *power*. After all, our aim in examining the privileging of discourses is not somehow to abolish it - at any given moment some discourse or category is always being privileged. But privilege, if we are to avoid false totalisations, must always be open to challenge, must always be contested, *on the move*, nomadic. We shall return to this question later.

Ripping it off

The following extract from a newspaper article - one of many recent urgent bulletins from the research frontline on this sort of topic - may clarify why feminists in particular are so down on 'biologism'.

> The year was 1964; the place, Baltimore, USA. An eight-month-old baby boy underwent a radical sex change to become a baby girl. When his penis was mutilated following a botched circumcision, doctors advised his parents that gender reassignment would be the best chance for a normal life... Yet by the age of five, his parents knew otherwise. 'It was a disaster,' his mother says now. 'I put this beautiful dress on him and he immediately tried to rip it off.' Joan also rejected Barbie, asked if she could shave like her father, insisted on urinating standing up, and, when her twin brother refused to share, saved her pocket money to buy a toy gun.
> (Krum 1997: 14)

'Even hormone treatment,' the article continues, 'did nothing to quell her instinct to act male.' The incredible powers assigned to biology - that it can program someone to rip off pretty dresses and pee standing up - are probably not quite so drastic in the original scientific papers, whose authors are no doubt aware that in many parts of the world little boys wear pretty dresses and pee squatting down. But the basic confusion operates as strongly in scientific as in popular culture. The powers of biology, the 'instinct to act male' (or female), are understood to operate through two avatars: the genes ('"so much of our identity is in our genes" ...says psychotherapist Dr Emily Hancock' [Krum 1997: 14]), and the brain ('"Despite everyone telling him he was a girl, and despite female hormones, his brain knew he was a male," concurs Dr William Reiner of John [*sic*] Hopkins

Hospital' [Krum 1997: 14]).[7]

It is apparent that several category errors are being made. To be 'male' in this belief system is to act *masculine*. Masculinity is understood as a biological entity rather than cultural, so that maleness/masculinity (together with subjectivity in general - 'our identity') is presented as an absolute quality. It then seems possible to say 'he *was* male', independently of any specific genitalia or hormones (which we might think were appropriately biological locations of sexual difference). Instead masculinity is said to reside in the genes, or the brain - two entities nowadays generally represented as essential and soul-like. Intelligent people only think as stupidly as this *when they need a particular outcome*: there is a profound *desire* for gender identity to be guaranteed, underwritten by biology (representing Nature, or God).

If we followed these ideas to their 'logical' conclusion, we would have to conclude that we have a genetic imperative *to act like those around us who are identified as being of a particular gender*. In other words, little Joanie's genes and/or brain would tell her to imitate Daddy, not Mommy, whatever Daddy got up to (even if he wore a pretty dress?). We would be forced to conclude that not the behaviour, but the adaptation, is programmed - somewhat like baby ducklings who treat the first moving object as 'Mother'. This would leave us with the rather difficult question of how exactly this imperative is coded: not, one presumes, verbally - but then, what is left? Does the sight of the parent's genitalia, or (somehow) the conceptual knowledge thereof, switch on the genetic programme of imitation? The mind boggles at the possibilities for experimental research!

Basically, the biologistic argument will not do. There is clearly more parsimony in taking into account little Joanie's parents, and *their knowledge* that Joanie was originally Johnny.

We can see similar confusions in a much more sophisticated modern 'biologistic' treatment of gender issues. Perry *et al* (1995) try to account for two different responses to trauma in infancy, which they categorise as 'sensitized hyperarousal systems (motor hyperactivity, behavioral impulsivity, hypervigilance)' on the one hand, and 'sensitized dissociative systems (avoidant, depressive, dissociative)' on the other. One of their questions is why more males use the first response (which is connected with phenomena like 'attention deficit syndrome' and 'hyperactivity'), and more females use the second (connected with phenomena like 'dissociation', 'multiple personality syndrome' and so on).

> There is a clear sex difference in response patterns; females utilize dissociative adaptations more than males. Some insight into these clinical observations can be found in examining the relationship between these responses and the underlying purpose of all brain related functions - survival. In order to persist over thousands of generations, each response pattern must have some adaptive advantages. (Perry *et al.* 1995: 282)

The position being taken here is that differential response to trauma must necessarily relate to the *biological* categories of male and female. Yet the behaviours involved quite blatantly relate to the *cultural* differences between masculine ('active') and feminine ('passive'). The choice of strategy is not hardwired (or there is no reason to deduce that it is hardwired), but a response to the cultural situation. As Perry *et al* point out,

> the nature of the trauma seems to be important to the pattern of adaptation: the more immobile, helpless and powerless the individual feels, the more likely they are to utilize dissociative responses. (Perry *et al.* 1995: 286)

Do we actually need a *further* explanation for gender-differential choice of response?

The fashionable new discipline of evolutionary psychology - also known as psychological Darwinism, or as sociobiology - offers supposedly biological 'explanations' of gender difference.[8] These are at least equally specious. The core of these theories is the argument, firstly, that a particular form of behaviour promotes the survival of the genes of the individual exhibiting that behaviour; and secondly, that this establishes the 'cause' of the behaviour.

As Fodor points out in a recent, incisive review:

> the literature of psychological Darwinism is full of what appear to be fallacies of rationalisation: arguments where the evidence offered that an interest in 'Y' is the motive for a creature's behaviour is primarily that an interest in 'Y' would rationalise the behaviour if it were the creature's motive. Pinker's book provides so many examples of this that one hardly knows where to start. (Fodor1998: 13)

Not surprisingly, many of these examples are presented in the area of gender-specific behaviour - a field where culturally-determined contingency can so easily appear to us a 'necessity'. It is also a field where there is a tremendous hunger for apparently 'objective' ways to underwrite culturally preferred attitudes.

As I have already argued, we know far too little about either the brain or gender to be able to theorise meaningfully on causal relationships between the two. As Fodor also says:

> what matters with regard to the question of whether the mind is an adaptation is not how complex our behaviour is, but how much change you would have to make in an ape's brain to produce the cognitive structure of a human mind. And about this, exactly nothing is known. That's because nothing is known about the way the structure of our minds depends on the structure of our brains. Nobody even knows which brain

structures our cognitive capacities depend on. (Fodor 1998:12).

The confusions and misunderstandings here are essentially philosophical; they are problems of *thinking*, which have the function of making possible certain arrangements of power. At this moment in history, biology-the-discourse does *not* tell us that gender is essence. As so often, 'biologism' here is actually the name for a *false* biology.

> A given individual will almost always dis-
> play *some* behaviors that are more common in
> the opposite sex... [F]rom a scientific stand-
> point, we cannot regard an animal, especially
> a human, as simply masculine or feminine.
> (Rosenzweig *et al* 1996: 436 original italics)

So, does the problem lie in the belief that biology matters, or in the belief that our perception of biology can be value-neutral?

'Apparently normal-appearing'

For gender to be 'in the brain' is not so different from the idea of it residing 'in the unconscious'. Analytic theory seems very often to suggest or imply that this is just where gender lives; that the unconscious has very strong, and rather socially con-servative, views about appropriate masculine and feminine attributes. This position is taken perhaps most openly and naively in some Jungian writing, but many Freudians, post-Freudians and Kleinians also write as if the unconscious just *knows* what men and women are supposed to be like. [9]

This position is both profoundly un-Freudian and profound-ly confused. It also depends, ultimately, on a *biological* sense of the unconscious - for where else could the unconscious be get-ting its information?[10] It is, in other words, a further form of biologism. Three psychoanalytic papers by Robert F. Stoller make these confusions very apparent. Stoller closely echoes the case of Joanie/Johnny in a (supposedly) psychoanalytic context, as well as demonstrating how the nature of 'hard evidence' can shift over time.

In the first paper, from 1964, Stoller argues that gender identity derives not only from 'the anatomy and physiology of the external genital organs' and 'the attitudinal influences of parents, siblings, and peers', but also from *a biological force, which, though hidden from conscious and preconscious awareness, nonetheless seems to provide some of the drive energy for gender identity* (Stoller 1964: 220, my italics). To support this claim, he offers two case histories. The first is of 'Jack', who was brought up as a girl, had apparently normal anatomy, but always wanted to be and behaved typically as a boy. 'Typically', of course, is the key point:

> Within a few months of her birth... her mother was already having difficulty. The baby was active and forceful, while her mother, a graceful, feminine, neurotically masochistic, perfect 'lady' increasingly despaired because her daughter was so lacking in gentleness and so much in opposition to many of the feminine qualities the mother wanted to bring forth from her daughter. (Stoller 1964: 221)

Stoller quotes the mother's attitude at length:

> 'The child ate so fast. It wasn't like a little girl, but at least it wasn't a big fuss over every meal. There was no colic. As a tiny baby she moved too fast. She did everything crash! bang! nothing gentle, yet because she ate well and slept well she was a good baby. But there was still the feeling in me - no one else. They all thought I was just very young, and I was worried for nothing. She didn't rebel about eating, but that seemed rather

gluttonous to me, like a little animal just eat-
ing - and playing wildly.' (Stoller 1964: 221)

We can already see that the child has a major problem in the
mother's sense of what behaviour is acceptable in a female or a
male child. So unhappy and awkward was 'Mary' (as she was
then) that at the age of 14, she was given an examination which
revealed that 'she was in fact' a boy, with 'a fully erectile tiny
penis of clitoral size, hypospadias, bilateral cryptorchidism,
bifid scrotum and normal prostate.' (Stoller 1964: 222)
Unusually, she was then *told* that she was a boy; and from that
point on changed her gender role to a masculine one, and
became to all appearances happier and more integrated.

> He only reacted as though the world had
> come to its senses. Although he would seem
> to fit into the category of those rare people
> who have no difficulty in shifting their gen-
> der identity from one sex to the other, this of
> course is not so. He never did shift his identi-
> ty. He always felt (though not consciously)
> that he was a male. He did not shift from
> female to male, but only had the rights of
> maleness confirmed by society. (Stoller 1964:
> 223)

For Stoller, there is something intolerably baffling about all
this:

> First, the child's anatomy did not give the
> visual confirmation of maleness nor was
> there a penis or a scrotum with testes to pro-
> duce genital sensation. Second, the child's
> development defied the parental attitudes.
> Yet there was *an overpowering drive unalterably*
> *and continuously thrusting this child towards*
> *maleness...* [T]his child practically from birth
> on gave unmistakable indications of *a force at*
> *work* which was powerful enough to contra-

dict his anatomy and environment. It was *of such magnitude that even the absence of male genitalia did not raise significant doubt in his unconscious mind as to his maleness.* This force was also strong enough for him successfully to withstand the 'temptation' to submit to the entreaties and seductions of his parents to adopt a feminine attitude. (Stoller 1964: 223-4, my italics)

The most important factor in convincing him that this 'force' was operating, states Stoller, was the personality of the child involved:

It is here, in the clinical data, which must be seen at first hand, that the *calm, sure masculinity* of this child shows itself in glaring contrast to the 'butch'. It is important to emphasize that no one who has seen the child - either in the research team, or his family, friends, teachers, or strangers in society - questions his masculinity or his certainty of being a male. (Stoller 1964: 224, my italics)

The second case Stoller describes (much more briefly) is of a boy, apparently physically normal to puberty, who developed a complete feminised physical appearance.

Until the age of 17, this child was a boy. However, at puberty, he developed all the secondary sex characteristics of a girl, including full breasts, feminine-appearing waist and buttocks, female hair distribution with absence of facial hair, peaches and cream complexion, etc., all in the presence of a normal-sized penis and testes. From the beginnings of memory at age 3 conscious fantasy life consisted completely of playing at being a female. (Stoller 1964: 225)

The physiological changes at puberty were explained by the idea that the testes had suddenly started producing large quantities of oestrogen. At the age of 20, the penis and testes were removed and an artificial vagina created. For Stoller, 'what is inexplicable is the prior history of a feminine identity. So we again fall back on [sic] the biological "force" to explain the fact that the core gender identity was female, despite the fact that the child was an apparently normal-appearing [sic] boy and was also genetically male.'

This second case is completely re-described in a subsequent paper. Stoller begins with a new, psychodynamic account of transexuality, based on several little boys who experienced themselves as female, and who all shared certain family characteristics: 'the special bisexual personality of the mothers, the excessive body contact that the mothers indulged in with their infant sons, the mothers' great pleasure in promoting their sons' femininity, the fathers' almost complete absence from the family and lack of interference with the feminization of their sons' (Stoller 1968: 365). Notice the clear pathologising tone of Stoller's language - there is no doubt that he regards all this as a bad thing. Eight years after the case history, he tells us, this individual

> revealed quite unexpectedly, in the midst of an otherwise rather casual hour, that she had not become feminized as the result of oestrogens produced in her testes but had rather been taking oestrogens since puberty. Thus, she could not have been feminized as a result of a 'biological force' as I had wrongly reported, nor could the development of her secondary sex characteristics be taken as evidence of a 'biological force' that, starting from early childhood on, had so influenced the development of her gender identity that she had felt herself to be really a woman. (Stoller 1968: 365)

In fact, it turns out on closer examination that this person's childhood history exactly matches the psychosocial etiology of transexuality which Stoller has recently developed. 'This patient's case,' Stoller adds in a hasty footnote, 'does not disprove such a ["biological force"] theory; by now, six biologically intersexed patients have been seen who, while they cannot be discussed now, seem to exemplify the presence of such a biological force.' Still, it makes you wonder...

In a third paper Stoller returns to the case of 'Jack'. He reprises the story:

> It was clear that this child was living an impossible existence as a girl. Influenced by *the naturalness of 'her' masculinity* and the believable life-long history given by the parents and the child, I acted on the clinical impression (not attempting to 'read' the masculinity as being a facade or a reaction formation the product of penis envy, disruption in the oedipal conflict, early oral rage, or other explanations that make us rethink the meaning of observed behaviours). I told 'her' to become a boy... 'She' did. From that day on, I was with a boy. *He had immediately known how to be one*, not just how to buy the appropriate clothes or get a haircut. Far more, he fit these accoutrements. To the present, he has been unremarkably, unaffectedly masculine. (Stoller 1979 : 434, my italics)

Stoller seems to be saying, rather as in the case of 'Joanie', that some sort of 'real' maleness in Jack produced in turn some sort of 'real', 'natural' masculinity, an innate affinity for the cultural 'accoutrements' of the masculine role. He distinguishes this 'naturalness' from the presumably 'unnatural' masculinity that results from 'disruption in the oedipus complex' and so on. He seems to have no realisation whatsoever that Freud treats all masculinity and femininity as 'unnatural', as constructed through exactly the sorts of processes to which Stoller refers.

Having now developed his theory of the psycho-social etiology of transexuality (i.e. 'unnatural' mothering), Stoller wants to check what he might have missed in the case of Jack. He interviews the parents, but doesn't find the pattern he's looking for. However he does find, and express, some ideas which may be more striking to us than they are to him:

> S: *Yet from the day she was born, she acted like a boy?*[11]
>
> M: Right. Right. *I couldn't turn that child into a girl.* Almost immediately [after birth] she was never like the girl I expected. I was looking for her to come to my bed and to come into my arms. From the first moment that I saw her as a human being, after delivering her, the first moment I laid eyes on her, she pushed my breast away. The first thing she did was kind of a rejection. Yes. She was fussing at me. She didn't go warm and cozy or cuddly to me. Everything she did was different from what I expected. So I just cuddled her a little more, and she kind of settled down. But her every action was defiant, I mean the small things, not so much when she was a baby but when she was walking around. Barely walking. One year old. A table would be full of papers or books and - whew! All of them! Every action was violent. Every action was all this energy. *Everything was active*, not like a girl, never sitting down and looking at a book, never reading or ever colouring, never.
> (Stoller 1979: 435, my italics)

Stoller does not seem to ask himself whether this is an appropriate description of a 'normal' boy child, or whether it represents a 'normal' sense of gender identity in the mother. He does

not consider the possibility that, within his family environment, a child with 'Jack's' energy and independence *had no
choice but to be a boy.*

Stoller is re-examining Jack's story to check it against the
explanatory models he is now using.

> I know more precisely, as I did not in 1961,
> how effectively post-natal external influ-
> ences can modify gender behaviour. What in
> those days seemed evident to many - that
> biologic forces are peremptory in human
> gender behaviour - is now for me in most
> cases less a rule and more an unlikely
> hypothesis. I still place Jack at the far end of
> what Freud called 'complemental series'...
> But now I attend to interpersonal influences
> that contributed to what Jack brought bio-
> logically to his situation. The two factors
> found in the childhood of very masculine
> women also were present - but in different
> ways - in Jack's early life. First; although in
> his infancy his mother was not damaged
> psychologically or physically so that she
> could not offer and maintain a close and lov-
> ing symbiosis for her 'daughter', Jack's
> mother was nonetheless unable to encourage
> her infant to nestle... *In this case, the failure
> was the infant's...* Jack's father was both simi-
> lar to and different from the fathers of these
> other very masculine girls and women: he
> went along with what he found more than
> trying to make his daughter be like him... To
> this day, *the greatest mystery for me is the natu-
> ralness of Jack's masculinity.* That, coupled
> with his lack of other neurotic problems, his
> successful and creative life, his openness,
> and his honestly are unexplained. (Perhaps a
> psychoanalysis would uncover the roots of

his normality, but one does not get to analyse such people.) (Stoller 1979: 438, my italics)

However, help was at hand:

In 1971, a new class of hermaphroditism was described: 17b hydroxysteroid dehydrogenase deficiency in man, an inherited (?) form of male pseudo-hermaphroditism... In this condition, there is a deficiency of one of the number of enzymes necessary to produce testosterone from cholesterol. Since maleness requires adequate amounts of biochemically normal testosterone during critical periods of foetal development, there results a female-appearing infant who is, naturally, raised as a girl. (Stoller 1979: 439-40)

Jack was tested and turned out to have the deficiency, which 'caused the anatomic hermaphroditism but nonetheless allowed for prenatal androgen priming of the brain.' At last Stoller can rest: he has his explanation. He cares not, so far as we can tell, whether the explanation is physiological, psychoanalytic, or some bastard crossbreed of the two.

Perhaps Foucault sheds some light on this:

The notion of 'sex' made it possible to group together, in an artificial unity, anatomical elements, biological functions, conducts, sensations, and pleasures, and it enabled one to make use of this fictitious unity as a causal principle, an omnipresent meaning: sex was thus able to function as a unique signifier and as a universal signified. (Foucault 1979: 154)

Human biology

I have examined Stoller's work at some length as an example of the sheer hopelessness of a certain kind of task. Trying to establish causal explanations of particular gender identities, I suggest, is like a fish trying to work out what water tastes like. Stoller, like the rest of us, has nowhere to stand from which to view his material: he is himself *in* gender, unavoidably assessing the 'naturalness' or otherwise of other people's performance of gender. He has no possibility of access to any data of the sort which he needs. His work is one long *petitio principi*.

Let us look at a wholly different attempt to wrestle with the issue - one which may perhaps be a relief. At the end of the 'Fish and Ape' case history which we examined in Chapter Five, Reich describes the uncovering in his patient of a confusion concerning gender. Like Perry *et al* (1995), the patient associates surrender, letting go, and being looked after with femininity. 'In this way, his own warded-off femininity was connected with the natural form of orgastic surrender, and thus disturbed the latter' (Reich 1973: 328).

'It is interesting to note,' Reich goes on,

> how society's double standard of morality was reflected and anchored in this patient's structure. In customary social ideology, we also find that surrender is emotionally associated with femininity, and unyielding hardness is associated with masculinity. Accordingly, it is inconceivable that an independent person can give himself and that a person who does give himself can be independent. Just as, on the basis of this false association, women protest against their femininity and want to be masculine, men rebel against their natural sexual rhythm out of fear of appearing feminine; and it is from this false assessment that the difference in the view of sexuality in man and in woman derives its seeming justification. (Reich 1973: 328)

This careful passage throws into doubt some of Stoller's certainties, but, unfortunately, raises as many questions as it answers. Reich sets against each other the 'natural' and the 'social', believing that he is able to tell them apart, and to know which is which. If we are going to maintain - in the face of Freud's entire work - a category of 'natural sexuality', then in a sense we could argue that it hardly matters what specific content we give the category: nothing intelligible will emerge.

But of course it does matter greatly, in terms of the lives available to those to whom the category is forcibly applied. Reich's descriptions of 'natural sexuality', as I have already said, are fairly attractive, and certainly less oppressive than they might be. However, they exclude homosexuality from 'nature' and, like much analytic theory, exclude the whole realm of what are so unhelpfully called the 'perversions'. Starting out as I do from the expectation that most human sexual practices will be *to some extent* creative, playful and problem-solving (just as they are mostly, including 'straight' heterosexual intercourse, *to some extent* oppressive, mystified and deadening), it becomes apparent that we need a radical attitude towards the category of 'nature', perhaps redefining it in this context as 'whatever people do'.

We also need a broader concept of 'biology' and 'body' than the discourses of sexology often allow. It is peculiar how the word 'biology' very often implies both 'reproductive' - as in 'biological urges', which are taken to be urges towards reproductive sex - and 'like (some particular conception of) animals'.

I am urging the possibility and necessity of developing a concept of *human* biology which recognises the human bodymind. The embodied subjectivity of a symbol-using being connotes radically different possibilities of pleasure and transcendence from those available to a non-symbolising being. I am not here drawing an absolute distinction between Homo Sapiens and other animals: it becomes increasingly clear that 'symbolusing' is a fuzzy category (like most other categories), and that there is a continuum of sorts between human and non-human symbolisation and proto-symbolisation.[12]

It remains the case that, so far as we can understand, humans have a vastly greater and more complex use of symbolic representation than other terrestrial species (though possibly not oceanic ones).[13] This fact *transforms our biology*. Rather than devaluing biology, separating it radically from the human and the psychic, we need to *transvalue* it. We need to reinstate the early analytic insight that human 'biological urges' *go beyond the reproductive* - that human sexuality, in transcending reproduction, does not abandon the biological order but extends it.

And jouissance? Can the jewel in the crown of Lacanian analysis be represented within the biological register? In a sense, jouissance *is* the return of the biological repressed - the insistent pressure of unsymbolised experience, of the Real. Symbolisation itself can, in theory, be described within the biological register, as a series of neural states. There simply comes a point at which the process is so tedious that one inevitably reverses the mirroring, and describes the biological in the register of symbolisation! But there is no reason in principle why jouissance cannot be described biologically, or understood as a bodily drive. Although jouissance is described by Lacan within a context of splitting and alienation, it does not itself demand or depend on this context: it is not, so far as I can see, *itself* alienated or alienating.

So we then have the job of explaining why jouissance *becomes* alien, which is another version of the question to which we keep returning - how does it come about that we experience our bodies and their impulses as foreign, even dangerous, to our 'selves'? I shall return to this one last time in my Conclusion.

Character, sexuality, gender and surrender

It is not my aim somehow to abolish the privileging of discourses, but to keep it on the move. And one register of discourse which I find it frequently useful (temporarily) to privilege is that of *character*. Here again we can see that different character positions will respond differently to questions of sex and gender. It is undoubtedly the *hysterical* aspect of each of us, and of culture at large, which draws attention again and again to the unsatisfactoriness of gender. This acts, in a sense, for 'the body' - challenging, subverting, and toppling each attempt to enthrone a fixed category of gender. The hysteric gesture, in fact, is that of ripping off the dress of gender, the mask, the masquerade,[14] while in the same movement sticking it firmly on again (but slightly askew).

From a Reichian perspective, the Lacanian distinction between hysteria and surplus jouissance on the one hand, and obsessionality and phallic jouissance on the other, looks extraordinarily like the distinction between the 'hysteric' character and the 'phallic' character.[15] In Western culture these are privileged character positions for females and males respectively - not in the sense that they are available only to one sex, but that they are *encouraged and supported* each for one sex, and treated as slightly odd and unsuitable in the other (treated, in fact, as evidence of cross-genderedness: the queen, the butch dyke). I have not forgotten my questioning of the recognition of only two sexes, but this arrangement is precisely what the allotting of character structure in this way is intended to support. In exactly the same sense as 'blue for a boy, pink for a girl,' the hysteric/phallic characters are there to tell us what we've got.

Reich is essentially right when he says that, in Western cultures, 'surrender is emotionally associated with femininity, and unyielding hardness is associated with masculinity.' (Reich 1973: 328) He is also right in pointing out that surrender is essential for orgasmic release: surrender of the ego to non-continuousness. We have looked at these ideas in relation to *sexuality*; now, however, we can see that they have to be reinscribed also onto the terrain of *gender*. It is the *ambiguity of the concept of surrender* which in many ways defines both the hysterical character (and much of hysteria) and the feminine role in our culture. To 'surrender' is *both* to let go of control (to 'abandon oneself', to become abandoned), *and* to be defeated, debased, to become less than male. In order to 'win' - to come - we have to 'lose'. I believe that Reich is correct to suggest (though he never develops the suggestion) that the whole panoply of gender can be unfolded as a range of strategies for dealing with this one problem.

Chapter Ten - Body of Knowledge

> It's only what you do not understand that
> you can come to a conclusion about. (Peter
> Høeg 1996: 410)

So what, if anything, after all these words, do we now know? Nothing very definite, I hope. To become definite about all this would undoubtedly be to fall into delusion. My aim has been more to open up questions: to prise open spaces which have been artificially occluded from psychoanalytic thinking. The psychodynamic encounter with the body has been in a state of artificial suspension for more than sixty years; if it wakes up again and resumes life, then no one can predict what forms it will take. So little is yet known - either psychoanalytically or in other forms of enquiry - about embodied subjectivity.

What I have perhaps managed to do is to establish the relevance of the philosophical 'mind-body problem' to analytic metapsychology and, by implication, to analytic practice, and, at the same time, to suggest why the traditional formulation of that problem must be urgently revised. I also think and hope that I have outlined sufficient reason to attend to Wilhelm Reich - not simply as a heretic, which he obviously was, but as the standard-bearer of a certain kind of thinking that is *integral to psychoanalysis*.

Reich's body-centred analysis was very much his own creation, but it was also rooted in his reading of psychoanalytic theory - in *what he heard Freud to be saying* in the early 1920s. Reich never thought of himself as an anti-Freudian, but as truer to Freud's original ideas than Freud himself (Reich 1967). It was by a logical and profound reading of Freud's own work - from *Studies on Hysteria* to *Inhibitions, Symptoms and Anxiety* - that Reich came to his heresies. I hope that it has emerged from my account that his expulsion from the analytic movement was not (just) the shabby silencing of an awkward eccentric, but a key moment in the analytic repression of the body.

> Slowly but surely [psychoanalysis] was cleansed of all Freud's achievements. Bringing psychoanalysis into line with the world, which shortly before had threatened to annihilate it, took place inconspicuously at first. Analysts still spoke of sexuality, but they had something else in mind... Form eclipsed content; the organisation became more important than its task. (Reich 1973: 125)

Reich is looking at the analytic movement from one perspective only; but it is only in retrospect a marginal one. As he also says:

> One group of analysts contends that everything I have to say is banal and has long been known to them, while another group declares that my technique no longer has anything to do with psychoanalysis, that it is misleading and faulty. (Reich 1973: 295)

These are classical paired techniques for silencing the innovator. But what then is Reich's true relationship to analysis? He says in a third passage:

> The goal of my work is the same today as it was twenty years ago: the reawakening of the earliest childhood experiences. However, the method of achieving this has changed considerably, so much in fact that it can no longer be called psychoanalysis. (Reich 1973: 58)

The question then becomes: who is the loser from this separation - Reich, or psychoanalysis? In other words, is Reich's 'changed method' a crazy, dead-end deviation, or does it represent, as I have suggested, a genuine progress - a return to and of the body?

In her book *The Psychoanalytic Mind*, Marcia Cavell begins with the assertion that:

> Psychoanalysis is essentially, and necessarily, a theory about creatures who have minds.
> (Cavell, 1993: 1)

This is diametrically opposite to my own starting point - that psychoanalysis is essentially and necessarily a theory about creatures who have bodies. But it is certainly no less true. There is no question of choosing between 'mind' and 'body'. The way forwards is much more in line with Ferenczi's insight that

> when the psychic system fails, the organism begins to think. (Ferenczi 1988: 6)

Ferenczi had a clear grasp of the body's power to think, to remember, and to act. However he saw it only as an emergency response, a 'traumatic-hysterical' (Ferenczi 1988: xii) crisis in which the body's fixed materiality is 'partially redissolved again into a psychic state.' (Ferenczi 1988: 7). His own realisation of the universal presence of this 'organic-hysterical' phenomenon (Ferenczi 1988: xii) could have allowed him to take the extra step of depathologising it, of grasping that the body does, always and everywhere, think, and that psychoanalysis therefore has to engage with the body's thought - to talk, not only *about* the body, but *with* it. This might also involve a reconnection of analysis with general psychology, which has a much clearer relationship with physiology and neurology.

I have quoted Pribram's description of Freud's *Project* as 'a psychobiological Rosetta Stone'. In some ways, I have been taking the first steps in a search for a contemporary version of such a Rosetta Stone: a descriptive discourse which privileges *neither mind nor body*. Where should we look for such a thing? Like Holt, I am drawn towards information/systems theory and cybernetics, though, like him, I believe that this could end up as a false trail.[1] He shows clearly how applying these ideas to psychoanalysis would be only part of a much larger project of realignment, a new paradigm of knowledge:

> The final contribution of the systems outlook is that it provides an intelligible rationale for the co-operation and interrelation of all the sciences. All of nature may be viewed as hierarchies of systems, one system nested within another in the sense that an atom is a self-contained unit with its own laws, those of physics, but is also a constituent part of a molecule which obeys a new set of laws not deducible from those of the lower hierarchical level. The molecule, itself, is a subsystem in, say, an organelle, which is a subsystem of a cell, and on up through tissues, organs, organ-systems, persons, families, increasingly larger social and political systems on the one hand and larger ecological systems on another. At each level of each of these partly overlapping hierarchies, there are new data, new regularities studied in a distinctive science. No one discipline has any claim to being more important or more basic than another, nor is the subject matter of one in any sense more real than that of another. They are related through complementing one another, not by being reducible one to another. With this understanding, we can stop fearing that chemistry could ever take over psychiatry or that the growth of neuropsychology could threaten social psychology or psychoanalysis. Instead of withdrawing, insulated and isolated from other sciences as psychoanalysis was for too many years, we can confidently co-operate, both learning and teaching in our contacts with colleagues in the biological and social sciences. (Holt 1981: 140)

Such a Rosetta Stone would cast a new light on the unconscious. However valuable Lacan's work may be, his position
that the unconscious is wholly linguistic in nature is an impossible restriction of its scope. The view of the unconscious as a
primarily *bodily* phenomenon, however, is equally restricting.
The unconscious is not language, nor is it the body. It can
appear to be either or both, it seems, because it *inhabits* both -
acts in and through both. Indeed, at least from our perspective,
it acts in and through everything, as Groddeck long ago
argued:

> The It knows neither body nor soul since
> they are both manifestations of the same
> unknown entity... the I, individuality,
> becomes a doubtful concept since the It can
> be traced right back to the moment of fertili-
> sation and even beyond this to the chain of
> parents and ancestors... Life and death... are
> turned into arbitrary, artificial concepts as
> nobody can know when the It makes death
> or life. There is no spatial separateness of the
> It either; it is fused with the environment...
> the consciousness of man loses its central
> position and yields it up to the unconscious,
> yet there is no definite dividing line between
> the two. (Groddeck 1977: 135-6, my italics)

Like a restless spirit, like a soul seeking rebirth, the unconscious uses language to give itself a voice, and uses the body to
give itself a presence. In both, the unconscious is *incarnated*.

The unconscious wants to *talk*. But what it wants to talk
about is the inexpressible, the unrepresentable. With infinite
skill and cunning, the unconscious devotes itself to representing the unrepresentable - itself. Psychoanalysis as a discipline
shadows this project, and also tries to represent the unconscious. Lacan most clearly devotes himself to the paradoxes of
this task.

One of these paradoxes, though, is that of the relationship

between language and experience, or 'mind' and 'body'. This could be phrased as follows: there is a certain 'knowledge' for which, in order to know it, we have to lay down knowledge itself and surrender to not-knowing. The whole concept of *surrender* is intricately entwined with that of the body. It seems that the 'spastic I', the ego which identifies itself with 'mind' and over against 'body', comes into being through processes of abjection, exclusion of the 'improper' (as opposed to the *propre*), which are functionally identical with processes of habitual muscular tension.

What is defended against in these processes is, in one sense, pleasure. But at the same time it represents itself as phobic object (all phobias, I suggest, are essentially terror of spontaneous movement[2]), as hysterical attack (the taking over of the self by uncontrollable otherness), as *jouissance*, as death. I have argued, though, that the horror of surrender to bodily experience is not inherent - we are not split and alienated by the fact of our humanity, but by much more specific psychosocial arrangements. By returning to a bodymind-centred approach, we may perhaps be able to gain insight into these arrangements and even contribute to changing them.

In a sense, this book is a preamble to the work which interests me most: exploring what would be the appropriate form and techniques of a psychoanalysis of the bodymind. This would be - in the words of Reich's metaphor - to stop staring into the mirror at last, and to taste the water.

Notes

[1] It does not appear, for instance, in the indexes of either *A Dictionary of Kleinian Thought* (Hinshelwood 1991) or *A Primer of Kleinian Therapy* (Solomon, 1995). The only relevant discussion I can find in Hinshelwood (Hinshelwood 1991: 73) makes clear that 'body', 'ego' and 'internal world' are used virtually interchangeably.

[2] Cf. also Hillman 197: 25.

[3] Speaking of fantasy, what would have happened if Reich had gone to England rather than Scandinavia in 1933? Nothing useful, probably, since he was so impossibly hard to get on with - but what if...?

Chapter One - Foreign Body

[1] We can contrast this with an equivalent work from a previous generation, Fenichel's *The Psychoanalytic Theory of Neurosis* (Fenichel 1990 [1946]), where the index has 18 references to 'body', 34 to 'affect', and 44 to 'instinct'.

[2] Cf Lakoff and Johnson 1980: 14-21.

[3] See Margolis (1984) for an excellent survey. Young (op cit.: 5-8) gives a brief account of some dissenting views from, for example, Whitehead and Burtt. Dennett (1991, e.g. Chapter 2) is an important source of insight. An account of the philosophical issues explicitly applied to psychoanalysis is Cavell (1993).

[4] For a wide range of examples see Fenichel 1941; Klein 1976; Kohut 1982; Gubrich-Simitis 1987: 79-107; Lacan 1988b: 75.

[5] For example Rapaport 1960, Peterfreund 1980, Rosenblatt and Thickstun 1977.

[6] The sexual imagery also reminds us that one reason for being suspicious of biology is that it may lead us to 'biologism', a form of essentialism: in other words, that a 'crypto-biological' psychoanalysis can end up installing purely cultural features - particularly in relation to sex and gender - as 'natural', 'human' and 'evolutionary'. I address this issue in Chapter Nine.

[7] I have heard two analytic therapists on separate occasions say that they stopped shaking hands with their patients when

they started hearing pregnancy phantasies from them. But why? Would they have stopped *talking* to them if a fantasy of aural conception had developed?

8 It would be more accurate to say that, although the state of metapsychology has been pointed out a number of times (e.g. Rapaport and Gill 1959, Swanson 1977, Rosenblatt and Thickstun 1977), it has created little concern. It is also possible to take the position (like Gill, 1976, or Schafer, 1976) that it is clinical work, rather than metapsychology, which forms the true base of psychoanalysis, and that only 'one theory rather than two' (Klein 1976) is required.

9 See Dixon 1981, especially Ch 7; Silverman 1975; Eysenck 1994: 366-7 (entry on 'subliminal perception') and references there given.

10 It will become apparent that the use to which I put information theory - and, indeed, the version of information theory that I want to use - is very different from e.g. Peterfreund (1980) and other positivist attempts. For a good account of systems theory see von Bertalanffy 1972 (1962), which also explains (30-2) the relationship between this and information theory.

11 I am well aware that 'observation' is not a simple concept; see Chapter Seven for a discussion.

12 We shall return to all these issues in Chapter Seven, and consider also the objection that this sort of work is irrelevant to psychoanalysis.

13 The former is due to the fact that nothing can travel faster than light; the latter is Heisenberg's Uncertainty Principle. Both are fundamental axioms of modern physics.

14 Not in order for them to become conscious, but to *register* them, to *represent* them. See Chapter Two.

15 For a different approach to some of this, see Lakoff and Johnson 1980.

Chapter Two - Body Represented

1 In line with many recent writers, I have throughout silently corrected the translation of Freud's *'trieb'* to 'drive' rather than 'instinct'. I have done the same with other psychoanalytic

texts translated from the German. For justification, see Ornston (1992 pp.93-5).

2 There have been several attempts to define Freud's position in terms of the recognised philosophical alternatives - reductionism, parallelism, etc. My own view is that he takes a basically *functionalist* line - see Margolis 1984, Ch IV.

3 This passage is largely paraphrased in *Instincts and their Vicissitudes*, Freud 1915c: 118/121-2 - just as the footnote is paraphrased in Freud 1920: 306/34.

4 In fact, the physiological analogy which Laplanche criticises so unmercifully - between the cerebral cortex on the surface of the brain and system *Cs* on the 'surface' of the psyche - is not as fatuous as Laplanche makes out. He rightly says that the anatomical position of the cortex is logically irrelevant, unless we imagine 'that external stimuli pass directly through the cranium to the cortex' (1989: 27). But Freud makes it clear that his analogy is based rather on the embryological origins of the cortex in the ectoderm - 'the primitive, superficial layer of the organism' (Freud 1920: 297/26). This double nature of the cortex - ectodermic material which is also, as Laplanche says, 'right at the end of the afferent nerves' (1989: 27) - that is, at the extreme point of 'insideness' - makes it a rather good analogy for the double nature of consciousness, which can be equally well visualised as on the *outside* and on the *inside* of the psyche. See Chapter 7.

5 See also the paraphrase of this argument in Freud 1925a: 242/57-8.

6 Version 3 of the drive, above, is itself a sort of 'downward' conversion theory.

7 Affect is actually very hard to treat from a rigorous scientific viewpoint, and many incomplete and conflicting theories of affect currently exist. For surveys, see for instance Arnold 1968 and Plutschik 1994.

8 See Chapter VII of *The Interpretation of Dreams* where Freud defines affect as a composite of motor innervations and sensations. (Freud 1900: 686/537)

9 The exact relationships within this triad of concepts are hard to establish, in Freud or anywhere else. The closest defin-

ition in Freud is that 'affects and emotions correspond to processes of discharge, the final manifestations of which are perceived as feelings'. (1915a: 181/178)

[10] Even so there is a certain ambivalence in Freud's position: 'Strictly speaking, then, there are no unconscious affects as there are unconscious ideas. But there may very well be in the system *Ucs.* affective structures which, like others, become conscious.' (1915a: 180/177)

[11] As I have mentioned above, the process is at this point understood as 'not of a psychical nature at all,' but 'something physical' (Freud 1894: 53).

[12] In *Civilization and its Discontents*, Freud also talks of 'unconscious anxiety, or, if we want to have a clearer psychological conscience, since anxiety is in the first instance simply a feeling, of possibilities of anxiety'. (1930: 328/135), and in the case of the Rat Man: 'On the contrary, the physician says: "No. The affect is justified."' (1909: 56/175).

[13] On this topic see Cavell 1993, chapter 7, Lear 1990: 89-92, and Schur 1969: 647-9. We shall look in Chapter 7 at some modern neurologically-based thinking about the relationship of reason and emotion.

[14] See for example Freud 1900: 69/5421; 1915a, 176-7/174, 198/193; 1920, 289/19.

[15] See for example Freud 1920: 289/19; 1915a: 195/191; 1915: 199/195.

[16] See for example Freud 1900: 699-700/548-9; 1915a: 199-200/195; 1916-17: 247-9/210-12; 1923: 360/21-2.

Chapter Three -Hysterical Body

[1] Ferenczi suggests that Freud lost the will to do this when he discovered 'that hysterics lie'. (Ferenczi 1988: 93)

[2] Freud was very interested in finding an aetiology for migraine, since he suffered severely from it himself. In fact, many of his researches during this period - into neurasthenia, hysteria, etc. - have a personal motive.

[3] See Sulloway 1980: 139-40.

[4] One thinks here of Miss Lucy in the Studies, whose hyste-

ria was so intimately bound up with her nose and its 'subjective olfactory sensations' (Freud and Breuer 1893: 169/106),
along with its more objective suppurative rhinitis. Also, of
course, there is the 'Irma dream' - the foundational dream of
psychoanalysis - in which Freud looks into the patient's mouth
and discerns there the bones of her nose - the turbinal bones,
bones which in Freud's own nose had recently been subject to
a cauterising operation by Fliess. I have treated the Irma dream
elsewhere (Totton 1996) and related it to Freud's own cancer of
the palate.

5 Freud and Fliess are thinking side by side here. As Fliess
puts it in the preface to one of his major works: 'Woman's menstrual bleeding is the expression of a process that appertains to
both sexes and the beginning of which is not just connected
with puberty... [The two cycles] have a solid inner relation with
male and female sexual characteristics. And it is only in accordance with our actual bisexual constitution if both - only with
different stress - are present in every man and woman (Quoted
Sulloway, 1980: 140).

6 This idea will be taken up in a very different way by Reich.
See below, Chapter Six.

7 There is a great deal of recent research to establish that
much emotional expression is transcultural and apparently
'hard-wired' as Darwin suggests. See for example Plutschik
1994: 153-6; Ekman 1973: 218-9.

8 This list of Ferenczi's is ironically parallel to Darwin's
examples of emotional phenomena which are in his view definitively not subject to individual learning: change of hair colour
from terror or grief, cold sweat, trembling, intestinal secretions,
and 'the failure of certain glands to act' (Darwin 1934 [1872]:
167).

9 Reich started working as an analyst in the year in which
Ferenczi - a senior figure - published this paper. As we shall se
in Chapters 5 and 8, there are further anticipations of Reich's
ideas on therapy and on character in Ferenczi's writings.
Lowen actually refers to Reich as 'Ferenczi's pupil' (Lowen
1958: 10).

10 Reich also used the relaxation approach at first- in the

sense of encouraging the analysand to 'give in to every [bodily] impulse' - before gradually adding physical touch and pressure to his range of techniques (Reich 1973: 311-14).

[11] In fact, Ferenczi actually talks in terms of 'dissociated parts of the personality' (Ferenczi 1994b: 119).

[12] This is in some ways close to Laplanche's work on 'primal seduction' (Laplanche 1989: 89-116).

[13] This implies that not even conscious memory is required for cure. See also Ferenczi 1994b: 119. Despite clients' 'subsequent amnesia' of cathartic discharge, Ferenczi still experienced 'much more of a feeling of reality and concreteness' concerning reconstructed memories.

[14] Reich does not follow Ferenczi in these late developments, and never seems to grasp the idea of retraumatisation.

[15] This passage can be usefully juxtaposed with Ferenczi's reference, quoted above, to the bodily re-education of children.

[16] This would not be most people's experience, so we shall go on to consider how it could be so for Reich.

Chapter Four - Body as Id, Body as Ego

[1] Totton, unpublished paper on Paracelsus; Pachter 1951; Jacobi 1958.

[2] I am convinced that there is a connection between Groddeck's 'palate and priority' paper, and Freud's later cancer; but this is not the place to develop the argument. (See Totton 1996).

[3] To bring out the interplay between Freud and Groddeck, I have used 'It' and 'I' to translate '*Es*' and '*Ich*', rather than Strachey's 'Id' and 'Ego'.

[4] Reich is paraphrasing Freud in 'Mourning and Melancholia': 'It would be equally fruitless from a scientific and a therapeutic point of view to contradict a patient who brings these accusations against his ego. He must surely be right in some way and be describing something that is as it seems to him to be' (Freud 1917: 254/246).

[5] This does not contradict his view that all illness '*comes under the influence of* an unconscious' (1977: 36).

6 This aspect of Reich's thinking anticipates some ideas of D. W. Winnicott, as we shall see in Chapter Seven.

7 For example, Reich does not appear in the index of Peter Gay's biography of Freud (Gay 1995 [1988]), although even his bitter enemy Ernest Jones gives him two references (Jones 1964: 608 and 622). An honourable exception is *The Evolution of Psychoanalytic Technique* (Bergmann and Hartman 1990 [1976]), which gives full attention to Reich's work on resistance analysis.

Chapter Five - Bodywork

1 Some children, of course, are given different instructions, and use the breath in correspondingly different ways.

2 Also Jung, of all people, commented on how 'reactions due to complexes frequently cause a long-lasting reduction in the volume of breathing... I also observed that a large number of my neurotic patients who were tubercular were "freed" from their complexes under psychotherapeutic treatment, learnt to breathe properly again and in the end were cured' (Adler, ed., 1976, 533).

3 See also English 1977.

4 See English 1977: 244.

5 That is, the 'orgasm reflex', a gentle, non-climaxing pulsing of the whole body with each breath which Reich found to emerge in successful bodywork, and which he believed to provide the necessary foundation for full sexual orgasm. See Reich 1973: 330ff.

6 Reich must also have been familiar with the whole German *Gymnastik* movement from 1900 onwards, involving many variations of breath and bodywork, in particular the work of Elsa Gindler (see Johnson 1995: 3-79). Reich's lover in the early 1930s, the dancer Elsa Lindenberg, knew Gindler's work and later started her own school of movement which is still important in Norway (Sharaf 1983: 275; Ragnhilde Vance, personal communication). There is some evidence that Reich himself may have attended Gindler classes (see Franzen n.d., 16).

7 For more on character see Chapter Eight. I am using terms

like 'schizoid' and 'masochistic' here for their familiarity; they are not the terms that I actually work with.

8 Viqui Rosenberg's interesting article 'On Touching the Patient' (Rosenberg 1995), written by an ex-bodyworker who has retrained as a psychoanalytic psychotherapist, portrays bodywork as possibly (and only?) appropriate for 'severe borderline patients', to 'meet the autistic-contiguous anxiety' (Rosenberg 1995: 36). It seems to me that she is limiting her sense of bodywork to reassuring touch, *à la* Winnicott. Reichian bodywork would be a high-risk strategy for such a client.

Chapter Six - Body as Death

1 See, for example, Wilson 1972, Cheney and Sayfarth 1992.

2 This argument might also be extended to say something about the 'uncanny' communicative powers of language - our ability from time to time to understand more than can be said.

3 Of course it is - as always - possible to claim that Lacan is being deliberately ironic.

4 There is a similar quality to the queasy, sleazy flirtatiousness with which he often approaches genital themes - most notably in Seminar XX (Mitchell and Rose 1982: 138-61). See also Jane Gallop, 'The Ladies' Man' (Gallop 1982: 33-42).

5 Cf McDougall 1996.

6 Crudely speaking, Lacan is an hysteric, Reich an obsessive character. A lot of Reich's theory of genitality can be read as the ultimate manifesto of phallic jouissance. (See Fink 1995: 106-7.)

7 'There is no such thing as an I; it is a lie, a distortion, to say "I think, I live". It should be: "it thinks, it lives" . It, that is the great mystery of the universe. There is no I.' (Groddeck 1977: 254). And in even more 'Lacanian' vein: 'The ego is something... in essence illusory, something existing only in our imagination... We all fancy we must have a core at the centre, something that is not merely a shell... We do not realise, cannot realise, that we have in fact no kernel' (Groddeck 1977: 26).

8 As quite often with Reich, one senses here a very close reading of Freud - in this case, *The Ego and the Id* (Freud 1923: especially 378/38).

[9] It is evident that Reich and his followers got confused about this, as people do; but at least one eye witness of the Reichian community in the 1950s (Charles Kelly, personal communication) is clear that those supposed to be 'genital characters' showed no evidence of being enlightened beings.

[10] The complexities of human desire might be unfolded from this perspective, as an almost infinite range of personal strategies around the dialectic of binding and unbinding. on both bodily and psychic levels (themselves in dialectical relationship).

Chapter Seven - Bodymind

[1] This connection has been made a number of times. However, most of these contributions (e.g. Peterfreund 1980) are, from my point of view, unhelpfully positivistic; none of them use Bateson's ideas. The most relevant to my own views is Holt 1981. See Chapter Ten, below.

[2] Western thinking tends to get very confused about the brain, because it sets up a brain-body opposition which it imagines as in some way parallel to the mind-body opposition. The brain is, of course, an organ of the body, one which specialises in information-processing, but information-processing takes place *throughout* the organism.

[3] For the first position see Rosenblatt and Thickstun, 1977, Kubie 1975, and Peterfreund 1980. For the second, see Lustman 1969, and Ostow, in Modell 1963. For the third, see Gill 1977, and Sherwood 1969.

[4] Apart from the references already given, see Klein (1976), Modell (1963), Rapaport (1960).

[5] Here too, Taylor matches Reich's emphasis on *function*: '[A]dvances in the biomedical sciences have led to a greater emphasis on alterations in function, as opposed to changes in structure, as explanations of disease' (ibid 479).

[6] In a fascinating paper, Slavin and Kriegman suggest a rather different field, evolutionary biology, in which Freud can also be seen to be searching presciently for formulations which have only much more recently been achieved. 'We can now

recognise that there was much of value in Freud's essentially legitimate Darwinian convictions: that, in many respects, the mind can be understood as an adaptive organ, the basic structure and function of which was shaped over vast evolutionary time.' (Slavin and Kriegman 1992: 40)

7 I avoid the word 'pathological', but if I were to use it then this would be the place.

8 See Damasio 1996: Ch 10; Varela, Thompson and Rosch 1992.

9 Cf. Slavin and Kriegman 1992: 40n.

10 This account clashes with Lacan's insistence on the drives/development as imaginary.

11 The evidence he gives for this is on pages 70-99.

12 This was first established by Darwin (1934 [1872]), with modern research-based support from - for example - Plutschik 1994: 153-6, Rosenzweig, Leiman and Breedlove 1996 Ch 15, Ekman 1973: 218-9, Ekman and Davidson 1994, although the subjective 'flavour' of each affect varies with culture - see Stern 55, n. There is reason to believe that while deliberate facial expressions are activated through the corticospinal system, involuntary emotional expression is activated subcortically: Rosenzweig, Leiman and Breedlove 1996: 536; Damasio 1996: 140-2.

13 Whenever the occasion arises, I have used 'she' and 'her' to represent the so-called 'neutral' third person pronoun.

14 However, as we have mentioned more than once, Kristeva sees the semiotic chora itself as a location of what later becomes 'neurosis' or neurotic character structure. See Chapter Eight.

15 It's not clear to me whether Lacan's signifying chains are conceived as fully arbitrary - consider, for instance, links between signifiers on the basis of *homophony*. Freud certainly conceives of *associative* chains as non-arbitrary in one sense: out of an infinity of arbitrary elements the unconscious *selects* overdetermined meaningful chains.

Chapter Eight - Body as Character

1 'DSM' is the *Diagnostic and Statistical Manual*, the bible of

(in particular) American psychiatry and psychotherapy - especially since insurance companies have begun demanding a 'DSM number' for every treatment claim.

2 Here Reich seems to be paralleling Fairbairn's ideas on psychic structure. However, this is not Reich's consistent view. Elsewhere he very much emphasises the radical *difference* between ego and id. Nevertheless, the last sentence of the quotation also identifies Reich as an object relations theorist.

3 Elsewhere he also responds to the idea that his method is rigid and overly worked-out. 'If an analyst has developed the ability which Freud recommended [a 'receptive, unbiased attitude'], the handling of the resistance and the transference will ensue automatically as a reaction to the process of the patient. There is no need for strenuous rumination... When the analyst begins to rack his brain... it is a sign of one of two things: either he is dealing with an especially new and unaccustomed type or his unconscious is in some way closed to the material the patient is offering' (Reich 1972: 146).

4 See the partial discussion in Totton and Edmondson 1988: 18-19.

5 We might better say, 'the model for the *armoured aspect* of all character structures'. Each character, to different extents, is embodied as a pattern of *flaccidities* as well as a pattern of *rigidities*.

6 This theory finds its fullest elaboration in Brow 1968, part V.

7 See, among others, Baker (1980 [1967]), Boadella (1987), Johnson (1985), Keleman (1985), Kurtz (1990), Lowen (1958), Painter (1986), Pierrakos (1987), Smith (in Badella and Smith 1986), and Southgate (1980).

8 The developmental sequence runs: 'schizoid', 'oral', 'psychopathic', 'anal', 'phallic', 'hysteric'. The great variety of names given to the character types has come about largely because authors are trying to replace the traditional, pathologising names - usually carried over from 'diagnostic' character theory - with names which are more evaluatively neutral; for example, 'ocular' rather than 'schizoid' (Baker), 'tough/generous' rather than 'psychopathic' (Kurtz), 'crisis' rather than 'hysteric' (Totton and Edmondson). The etiological relationship between charac-

ter position and potential neurosis is, of course, still recognised.

[9] The useful phrase 'character position' (presumably derived from Melanie Klein) seems to originate in Southgate (1980).

[10] This is the barest outline of a theory of creative character and, again, not in my own terminology.

[11] I prefer the more neutral term 'boundary character'.

[12] 'When the baby is born he is in the position of an astronaut who has been shot out into outer space without a space suit; ...the predominant terror of the baby is of falling to pieces or liquefying.' (Bick 1986: 296)

Chapter Nine - Sexed and Gendered Body

[1] In line with most recent writing on the subject, I am using 'gender' to refer to the *social* and *cultural* meanings ('masculine/feminine') which constellate around the *biological distinction* of sex ('male/female'). A person's gender identity may or may not correspond to their biological sex, for a wide range of complex reasons. A footnote such as this is common currency in modern work on gender and sexuality. However, see also Butler (1991) who problematises the assumption that sex *precedes* gender in any simple way.

[2] Cf Riley 1988: 112-14.

[3] We should note as well that Freud here privileges the visual mode over the proprioceptive - what the organ *looks* like rather than what it *feels* like - appearance, we may conclude, rather than reality. It has been argued more than once that this precedence given to vision is a distinguishing feature of patriarchal culture.

[4] It is revealing how Irigaray's enthusiasm leads her to overstate her case, even in its own terms, and forget that some organisms reproduce without sex.

[5] That is, there can be no culture without nature, but there can be nature without culture. (These terms have been criticised as essentialist by - for example - Butler 1991, and MacCormack & Strathern 1980.)

[6] These terms are often used in such a way that only members of the politically dominant race or sex can be said to be

'racist' or 'sexist', rather than simply prejudiced. See the previous section.

7 Until recently the hormones themselves shared avatar-hood with genes and brains, but they have now been relegated to contingent status.

8 See, for example, Pinker 1998; Plotkin 1997.

9 Melanie Klein certainly believed that 'in both sexes there is an inherent unconscious knowledge of the existence of the penis as well as of the vagina' (Klein 1988: 409) - and even, she implies, of the appropriate juxtaposition of the two .

10 The idea that the unconscious ego constructs itself *from what its society offers* is entirely different.

11 How does a one-day-old boy act?

12 See, for example, Oakley 1985: 143 who, bizarrely and unpleasantly, employs vivisection to establish a 'biological continuity of mental capacities between animals and humans' - a conclusion which one might think would militate against the experimental method.

13 Many people believe that dolphins and whales have symbolising capacities.

14 See Riviere 1929.

15 Again, I use these terms for familiarity; I would myself call them the 'crisis' character and the 'thrusting' character.

Chapter Ten - Body of Knowledge

1 Another place to look might be in evolutionary biology and adaptation theory - itself increasingly systems-based. See Slavin and Kriegman 1992.

2 This is fairly obvious in the case of mice, spiders, etc. - which are specifically feared as capable of invading the body. I believe it is an element, at least, in the whole range of phobias. Think for example of ghosts - I'm all alone and *something moves* - of blood, of thunderstorms...

Bibliography

Adams, D., and Lloyd, J. (1983) *The Meaning of Liff*, London: Pan and Faber & Faber.

Adler, G., ed. (1976) *C.G Jung: Letters, Vol II, 1951-61*, London: Routledge and Kegan Paul.

Althusser, L. (1971) 'Ideology and Ideological State Apparatuses (Notes towards an Investigation)' in *Lenin and Philosophy and Other Essays*, London: New Left Books.

Arnold, M.B., ed., (1968) *The Nature of Emotion*, London: Penguin.

Baker, E.F. (1980) *Man In The Trap: The Causes of Blocked Sexual Energy*, New York: Collier Books.

Bateson, G. (1973) *Steps to an Ecology of Mind*, St Albans: Paladin.

Bateson, G. (1980) *Mind and Nature: a Necessary Unity*, London: Fontana.

Benjamin, J. (1996) *Like Subjects, Love Objects: Essays on Recognition and Sexual Difference*, Yale: Yale University Press.

Bentzen, M., and Bernhardt, P. (1992) *Working with Psychomotor Development*, Albany, CA: Bodynamic Institute.

Bergmann, M.S., and Hartman, F.R., eds. (1990) *The Evolution of Psychoanalytic Technique*, New York: Columbia University Press.

Berman, M. (1990) *Coming to Our Senses: Body and Spirit in the Hidden History of the West*, London: Unwin.

Bernhardt, P., Bentzen, M. and Isaacs, J. (1996) 'Waking the body ego: Part II', *Energy and Character* 27, 1.

Bertalanffy, L. von (1972) 'General system theory - a critical review', in J. Beishon and G. Peters (eds.) *Systems Behaviour*, London: Harper & Row.

Bick, E. (1986) 'Further considerations on the function of the skin in early object relations: findings from infant observation integrated into child and adult analysis', *British Journal of Psychotherapy* 2: 292-99.

Boadella, D. (1987) *Lifestreams: An Introduction to Biosynthesis*, London: Routledge and Kegan Paul.

Boadella, D., and Smith, D. (1986) *Maps of Character*, Abbotsbury: Abbotsbury Publications.

Boothby, R. (1991) *Death and Desire*, London: Routledge.

Bowie, M. (1991) *Lacan*, London: Fontana.

Brennan, T. (1992) *The Interpretation of the Flesh*, London: Routledge.

Brown, N.O. (1968) *Life Against Death*, London: Sphere Books.

Butler, J. (1990) *Gender Trouble: Feminism and the Subversion of Identity*, London: Routledge.

Butterworth, G. (1995) 'An Ecological Perspective on the Origins of the Self', in Bermudez, J.L., Marcel, A. and Eilan, N., (eds.) *The Body and the Self*, London: MIT Press.

Cavell, M. (1993) *The Psychoanalytic Mind: From Freud to Philosophy*, London: Harvard University Press.

Cheney, D.L., and Seyfarth, R.M. (1992) 'The representation of social relations by monkeys', *Cognition* 37: 167.

Conger, J.P. (1994) *The Body in Recovery: Somatic Psychotherapy and the Self*, Berkeley CA: Frog Ltd.

Coveney, P., and Highfield, R. (1995) *Frontiers of Complexity: The Search for Order in a Chaotic World*, London: Faber and Faber.

Damasio, A. (1996) *Descartes' Error: Emotion, Reason and the Human Brain*, London: Papermac.

Darwin, C. (1934) The Expression of the Emotions in Man and Animals, London: Watts and Co.

Dennett, D. (1991) *Consciousness Explained*, London: Allen Lane.

Deutsch, F., ed. (1959) *On the Mysterious Leap from the Mind to the Body*, New York: International Universities Press.

Dixon, N. (1981) *Preconscious Processing*, Chichester: John Wiley and Sons.

Eigen, M. (1993) *The Electrified Tightrope*, Northvale, NJ: Jason Aronson.

Ekman, P., ed. (1973) *Darwin and Facial Expression: a Century of Research in Review*, New York: Academic Press.

Ekman, P., and Davidson, R.J. (1994) *The Nature of Emotion: Fundamental Questions*, Oxford: Oxford University Press.

Efron, A. (1985) 'The sexual body: an interdisciplinary perspective', *Journal of Mind and Behaviour* 6, 1-2: whole issue.

English, O.S., (1977) 'Some recollections of a psychoanalysis with Wilhelm Reich', *Journal of the American Academy of Psychoanalysis* 5, 2.

Etchegoyen, H. (1991) *Elements of Psychoanalytic Technique*, London: Karnac Books.

Evans, D. (1996) *An Introductory Dictionary of Lacanian Psychoanalysis*, London: Routledge.

Eysenck, M., ed. (1994) *The Blackwell Dictionary of Cognitive Psychology*, Oxford: Blackwell.

Fenichel, O. (1941) *Problems of Psychoanalytic Technique*, New York: Psychoanalytic Quarterly.

Fenichel, O. (1989) 'Psychoanalysis of Character', in R.F. Lax (ed.) *Essential Papers on Character Neurosis and Treatment*, New York: New York University Press.

Fenichel, O. (1945) *The Psychoanalytic Theory of Neurosis*, New York: W.W. Norton.

Ferenczi, S. (1994a) *Further Contributions to the Theory and technique of Psychoanalysis*, London: Karnac.

Ferenczi, S. (1994b) *Final Contributions to the Problems and Methods of Psychoanalysis*, London: Karnac.

Ferenczi, S. (1988) *The Clinical Diary*, ed. Dupont, J., London: Harvard University Press.

Ferenczi, S., and Rank, O. (1986) *The Development of Psychoanalysis*, Chicago: Institute for Psychoanalysis.

Fink, B. (1995) *The Lacanian Subject: Between Language and Jouissance*, Princeton NJ: Princeton University Press.

Fodor, J. (1998) 'The trouble with psychological Darwinism', *London Review of Books* (January 22nd) 20, 2: 11-13.

Fogel, A. (1993) *Developing Through Relationships: Origins of Communication, Self, and Culture*, Hemel Hempstead: Harvester Press.

Foucault, M. (1979) *The History of Sexuality, Vol I: An Introduction*, London: Allen Lane.

Foucault, M. (1980) *Hercule Barbin, Being the Recently Discovered Memoirs of a Nineteenth-Century Hermaphrodite*, New York: Colophon.

Franzen, G.M. (n.d.) '"It's about time you started responding!": on Elsa Gindler and her work', *Gestalttherapie* 9, 2.

Freud, A. (1986) *The Ego and the Mechanisms of Defense*, London: Hogarth.

Freud, S. (1894) 'The Neuro-Psychoses of Defence', S.E. III, London: Hogarth.

Freud, S., and Breuer, J. (1895) *Studies on Hysteria*, S.E. II, London: Hogarth, and London: Pelican Freud Library 3.

Freud, S. (1900) *The Interpretation of Dreams*, S.E. IV and V, London: Hogarth, and London: Pelican Freud Library 4.

Freud, S. (1905) Three Essays on Sexuality, S.E. VII, London: Hogarth, and London: Pelican Freud Library 7.

Freud, S. (1907) 'Delusion and Dream in Jensen's "Gradiva"', S.E. IX, London: Hogarth, and London: Pelican Freud Library 15.

Freud, S. (1908) 'Character and Anal Erotism', S.E. IX, London: Hogarth, and London: Pelican Freud Library 7.

Freud, S. (1909) 'Some General Remarks on Hysterical Attacks', S.E. IX, London: Hogarth, and London: Pelican Freud Libary 10.

Freud, S. (1912a) 'The Dynamics of Transference', S.E. XII, London: Hogarth.

Freud, S. (1912b) 'On the Universal Tendency to Debasement in the Sphere of Love', S.E. XII, London: Hogarth.

Freud, S. (1913) 'On Beginning the Treatment', S.E.XII, London: Hogarth.

Freud, S. (1914) 'Remembering, Repeating and Working Through', S.E. XII, London: Hogarth.

Freud, S. (1915a) 'The Unconscious', S.E. XIV, London: Hogarth, and London: Pelican Freud Library 11.

Freud, S. (1915b) 'Observations on Transference Love', S.E. XII, London: Hogarth.

Freud, S. (1915c) 'Instincts and their Vicissitudes', S.E. XIV, London: Hogarth, and London: Pelican Freud Library 11.

Freud, S. (1915d) 'Repression', S.E. XIV, London: Hogarth, and London: Pelican Freud Library 11.

Freud, S (1916) 'Some Character-Types Met With in Psycho-analytic Work', S.E. XIV, London: Hogarth, and London: Pelican Freud Library 14.

Freud, S. (1916-17) Introductory Lectures on Psycho-Analysis,

S.E. XVI, London: Hogarth,and London: Pelican Freud Library 1.

Freud, S. (1917) 'Mourning and Melancholia', S.E. XIV, London: Hogarth, and London: Pelican Freud Library 11.

Freud, S. (1920) *Beyond the Pleasure Principle*, S.E. XVIII, London: Hogarth, and London: Pelican Freud Library 11.

Freud, S. (1923) *The Ego and the Id*, S.E. XIX, London: Hogarth.

Freud, S. (1925a) *An Autobiographical Study*, S.E. XX, London: Hogarth.

Freud, S. (1925b) 'Some Psychical Consequences of the Anatomical Distinction Between the Sexes', S.E. XIX, London: Hogarth, and London: Pelican Freud Library 7.

Freud, S. (1926a) *Inhibitions, Symptoms and Anxiety*, S.E. XX, London: Hogarth, and London: Pelican Freud Library 9.

Freud, S. (1926b) 'The Question of Lay Analysis', S.E. XX, London: Hogarth.

Freud, S. (1930) Civilization and its Discontents, S.E. XXI, London: Hogarth, and London: Pelican Freud Library 12.

Freud, S. (1931a) 'Libidinal Types', S.E. XXI, London: Hogarth, and London: Pelican Freud Library 7.

Freud, S. (1932) *New Introductory Lectures on Psycho-Analysis*, S.E. XXII, London: Hogarth, and London: Pelican Freud Library 2.

Freud, S (1933) 'Why War?', S.E. XXII, London: Hogarth.

Freud, S. (1937) 'Analysis Terminable and Interminable', S.E. XXIII, London: Hogarth.

Freud, S. (1950) *Project for a Scientific Psychology*, S.E.I, London: Hogarth.

Freud, S. (1953-73) *The Standard Edition of the Complete Psychological Works of Sigmund Freud*, 24 volumes, ed. Strachey, J., London: Hogarth Press,

Frosh, S. (1994) *Sexual Difference: Masculinity and Psychoanalysis*, London: Routledge.

Gallop, J. (1982) *Feminism and Psychoanalysis: The Daughter's Seduction*, London: MacMillan.

Gay, P. (1995) *Freud: A Life for Our Time*, London: Papermac.

Gibson, J.J. (1979) *The Ecological Approach to Visual Perception*, Boston: Houghton Mifflin.

Gibson, J.J. (1987) 'A Note on What Exists at the Ecological Level of Reality', in E. Reed and R. Jones (eds.) *Reasons for Realism: Selected Essays of James J Gibson*, Hillsdale, NJ: Erlbaum.

Gill, M. (1977) 'Psychic energy reconsidered', *Journal of the American Psychoanalytic Association* 25: 581-97.

Gilligan, C., et al. (1991) *Women, Girls and Psychotherapy: Reframing Resistance*, Binghampton, NY: Harrington Park Press.

Gitelson, M. (1989) 'Theoretical Problems in the Analysis of Normal Candidates', in R.F. Lax (ed.) *Essential Papers on Character Neurosis and Treatment*, New York: New York University Press.

Groddeck, G. (1961) *The Book of the It*, London: Vision Press.

Groddeck, G. (1977) *The Meaning of Illness*, edited by L. Schacht, London: Maresfield.

Grosskurth, P. (1991) *The Secret Ring: Freud's Inner Circle and the Politics of Psychoanalysis*, London: Cape.

Grosz, E. (1990) *Lacan: A Feminist Introduction*, London: Routledge.

Harris, M., and Bick, E. (1987) *Collected Papers of Martha Harris and Esther Bick*, Perthshire: Clunie.

Hillman, J. (1979) *The Dream and the Underworld*, New York: Harper & Row.

Hinshelwood, R.D. (1991) *A Dictionary of Kleinian Thought*, London: Free Association Books.

Høeg, P. (1996) *Miss Smilla's Feeling For Snow*, London: Harvill.

Holt, R.R. (1981) 'The death and transfiguration of metapsychology', *International Review of Psychoanalysis* 8: 129-43.

Hunt, M. (1982) *The Universe Within: A New Science Explores the Human Mind*, Brighton: Harvester.

Hunter, V. (1993) 'Clinical Clues in the Breathing Behaviors of Patient and Therapist', Clinical Social Work Journal 21, 2:161-78

Irigaray, L. (1985) *This Sex Which Is Not One*, Ithaca: Cornell University Press.

Irigary, L. (1996) *I Love to You: Sketch for a Felicity Within History,* New York: Routledge.

Jacobi, J., ed. (1958) *Paracelsus: Selected Writings*, New York: Pantheon.

Jacoby, R. (1986) *The Repression of Psychoanalysis: Otto Fenichel and the Political Freudians*, London: University of Chicago Press.

Johnson, D. (1995) *Bone, Breath and Gesture: Practices of Embodiment*, Berkeley, California: North Atlantic Books.

Johnson, S.M. (1985) *Characterological Transformation*, New York: W.W. Norton.

Jones, E. (1977) *Papers on Psychoanalysis*, London: Karnac.

Jones, E. (1955) *The Life and Work of Sigmund Freud*, Vol II, London: Hogarth Press.

Jones, E. (1964) *The Life and Work of Sigmund Freud: Abridged Edition*, London: Penguin.

Jones, G. (1992) *The White Queen*, London: Gollancz.

Keleman, S. (1975) *Your Body Speaks Its Mind*, Berkeley, CA: Center Press.

Keleman, S. (1985) *Emotional Anatomy*, Berkeley CA: Center Press.

Kernberg, O. (1970) 'A Psychoanalytic Classification of Character Pathology', in Lax, R.F. (ed.) *Essential Papers on Character Neurosis and Treatment*, New York: New York University Press.

Klein, M. (1945) 'The Oedipus Complex in the light of early anxieties' *International Journal of Psycho-Analysis* 26: 11-33 and (1988) in *Love, Guilt and Reparation and other works 1921-1945*, London: Virago.

Klein, G. (1976) *Psychoanalytic Theory: An Exploration of Essentials*, New York: International Universities Press.

Knight, R. (1953) 'The present status of organized psychoanalysis in the United States', *Journal of the American Psychoanalytic Association* 2: 197-220.

Kohn, M. (1996) *The Race Gallery*, London: Vintage.

Kohut, H. (1982) 'Introspection, Empathy and the Semi-Circle of Mental Health', J. Amer. Psychoanal. Assoc. 63: 395-406.

Kristeva, J. (1982) *Powers of Horror*, New York: Columbia University Press.

Kristeva, J. (1984) *Revolution in Poetic Language*, New York: Columbia University Press.

Kristeva, J. (1988) In the Beginning was Love: Psychoanalysis and Faith, *New York: Columbia University Press*

Krum, S. (1997) 'When John Became Joan', *The Guardian* (London), 31st March 1997, p.14.

Kubie, L.S. (1975) 'The language tools of psychoanalysis: a search for better tools drawn from better models', *International Review of Psycho-Analysis* 2, 1: 1-24.

Kurtz, R. (1990) *Body-Centered Psychotherapy: The Hakomi Method*, Mendocino, CA: LifeRhythm.

Kurzweil, E. (1993) *The Freudians: A Comparative Perspective*, London: Yale University Press.

Lacan, J. (1966) *Écrits*, Paris: Seuil.

Lacan, J. (1977) *Écrits: A Selection*, translated by Alan Sheridan, London: Routledge.

Lacan, J. (1988a) *The Seminar of Jacques Lacan, Book I: Freud's Papers on Technique*, ed. J.-A. Miller, Cambridge: Cambridge University Press.

Lacan, J. (1988b) *The Seminar of Jacques Lacan, Book II: The Ego in Freud's Theory and in the Technique of Psychoanalysis*, ed. J.-A. Miller, Cambridge: Cambridge University Press.

Laing, R.D. (1965) *The Divided Self*, London: Pelican.

Lakoff, G. (1987) *Women, Fire and Dangerous Things: What Categories Reveal About the Mind*, Chicago: University of Chicago Press.

Lakoff, G., and Johnson, M. (1980) *Metaphors We Live By*, Chicago: University of Chicago Press.

Laplanche, J. (1976) *Life and Death in Psychoanalysis*, Baltimore: Johns Hopkins University Press.

Laplanche, J. (1981) 'A metapsychology put to the test of anxiety', *International Journal of Psycho-Analysis* 62: 81-89.

Laplanche, J. (1989) *New Foundations for Psychoanalysis*, Oxford: Basil Blackwell.

Laplanche, J. (1995) 'Seduction, persecution, revelation', *International Journal of Psycho-analysis* 76: 663-84.

Laplanche, J., and Pontalis, J. B. (1988) *The Language of Psychoanalysis*, London: Karnac.

Lear, J. (1990) *Love And Its Place In Nature*, London: Faber and Faber.

Lieberman, J.E. (1985) *Acts of Will: The Life and Work of Otto Rank*, New York: Free Press.

Liebert, R.S. (1988) 'The Concept of Character: A Historical Review', in ed. Lax, R.F. *Essential Papers on Character Neurosis and Treatment*, New York: New York University Press.

Limentani, A. (1989) *Between Freud and Klein*, London: Free Association Books.

Little, M. (1990) *Psychotic Anxieties and Containment: A Personal Record of an Analysis with Winnicott*, Northvale, NJ: Jason Aronson.

Lowen, A. (1958) *The Language of the Body* (originally published as *The Physical Dynamics of Character Structure*), New York: Collier Books.

Lustman, S.L. (1969) 'Introduction to panel on the use of the economic viewpoint in clinical psychoanalysis', *International Journal of Psycho-Analysis* 50: 95-102.

MacCormack, C., and Strathern, M., eds. (1980) *Nature, Culture and Gender*, Cambridge: Cambridge University Press.

Margolis, J. (1984) *Philosophy of Psychology*, New Jersey: Prentice-Hall.

Masson, J., ed. (1985) The Complete Letters of Sigmund Freud to Wilhelm Fliess, Harvard, MA: Belknap.

McDougall, J. (1996) *The Many Faces of Eros*, London: Free Association Books.

Meltzoff, A.N., and Moore, M.K. (1989) 'Imitation in Newborn Infants: Exploring the Range of Gestures Imitated and the Underlying Mechanisms', *Developmental Psychology* 25: 954.

Meltzoff, A.N., and Moore, M.K. (1995) 'Infants' Understanding of People and Things: From Body Imitation to Folk Psychology', in eds. Bermudez, J.L., Marcel, A. and Eilan, N. *The Body and the Self*, London: MIT Press.

Miller, L., Rustin, M., and Shuttleworth, J., eds. (1989) *Closely Observed Infants*, London: Duckworth.

Mitchell, J., and Rose, J., eds. (1982) *Feminine Sexuality: Jacques Lacan and the école freudienne*, London: Macmillan.

Modell, A.H., reporter (1963) 'Panel on the concept of psychic energy', *Journal of the American Psychoanalytic Association* 25: 605-18.

Oakley, D. (1985) 'Animal Awareness, Consciousness and Self-image', in D. Oakley (ed.) *Brain and Mind*, London: Methuen.

Ornston, D. G., ed. (1992) *Translating Freud*, London: Yale University Press.

Pachter, H. (1951) *Paracelsus: Magic into Science*, New York: Henry Schuman.

Painter, J. D. (1986) *Deep Bodywork and Personal Development*, Mill Valley: Bodymind Books.

Perry, B.D., Pollard, R.A., Blakley, T.L., Baker, W.L. and Vigilante, D. (1995) 'Childhood trauma, the neurobiology of adaptation and use-dependent development of the brain: how states become traits', *Infant Mental Health Journal* 16, 4: 271-91.

Peterfreund, E. (1980) 'On information and systems models for psychoanalysis', *International Review of Psycho-Analysis* 7: 327-43.

Phillips, A. (1995) *Terrors and Experts*, London: Faber & Faber.

Pierrakos, J. (1987) *Core Energetics: Developing the Capacity to Love and Heal*, Mendocino CA: LifeRhythm.

Pinker, S. (1998) *How the Mind Works*, London: Allen Lane.

Plutschik, R. (1994) *The Psychology and Biology of Emotion*, New York: HarperCollins.

Plotkin, H. (1997) *Evolution in Mind*, London: Allen Lane.

Prigogine, I., and Stengers, I. (1985) *Order Out of Chaos: Man's New Dialogue with Nature*, London: Flamingo.

Rapaport, D., and Gill, M. (1959) 'The points of view and assumptions of metapsychology', *International Journal of Psycho-Analysis* 40: 153-62.

Rapaport, D. (1960) *The Structure of Psychoanalytic Theory*, New York: International Universities Press.

Reich, W. (1927) Contribution to 'Discussion on Lay Analysis', *International Journal of Psycho-Analysis* 8: 174.

Reich, W. (1960) *Selected Writings*, London: Vision Press.

Reich, W. (1967) *Reich Speaks of Freud*, New York: Farrar Straus Giroux.

Reich, W. (1972 [1945]) *Character Analysis*, New York: Touchstone.

Reich, W. (1973 [1942]) *The Function of the Orgasm*, London: Souvenir Press.

Reich, W. (1975) *The Mass Psychology of Fascism*, London: Pelican.

Reich, W. (1983) *Children of the Future: On the Prevention of Sexual Pathology*, New York: Farrar Straus Giroux.

Reich, W. (1990) *Passion of Youth*, London: Picador.

Rickman, J (1957) *Selected Contributions to Psycho-Analysis*, London: Hogarth.

Riley, D. (1988) *Am I That Name? Feminism and the Category of 'Women' in History*, London: Macmillan.

Riviere, J. (1929) 'Womanliness as a masquerade', *International Journal of Psycho-Analysis* 10: 303-13.

Rosenberg, V. (1995) 'On touching the patient', *British Journal of Psychotherapy* 12, 1: 29-36.

Rosenblatt, A.D., and Thickstun, J.T. (1977) 'Energy, information and motivation: a revision of psychoanalytic theory', *Journal of the American Psychoanalytic Association* 25: 537-58.

Rothschild, B. (1994) 'Transference and Countertransference - A Common sense Perspective', *Energy and Character* 25, 2.

Rothwell, J. (1994) *Control of Human Voluntary Movement*, London: Chapman and Hall.

Rozenzweig, M.R., Leiman, A.L. and Breedlove, S.M. (1996) *Biological Psychology*, Sunderland, Mass: Sinauer Associates.

Sachs, H. (1927) Contribution to 'Discussion of Lay Analysis', *International Journal of PsychoAnalysis* 8: 174.

Samuels, A. (1989) *The Plural Psyche: Personality, Morality and the Father,* London: Routledge.

Schafer, R. (1976) *A New Language for Psychoanalysis*, New Haven: Yale University Press.

Schor, N., (1994) 'This Essentialism Which Is Not One: Coming to Grips with Irigaray', in eds. Burke, Schor, N. and Whitford, M. *Engaging with Irigaray*, New York: Columbia University Press.

Schultz, R.L. and Feitis, R. (1996) *The Endless Web*, Berkeley, CA: North Atlantic Books.

258 *The Water in the Glass*

Schur, M. (1969) 'Affects and cognition', *International Journal of Psycho-Analysis* 50: 647-52.

Sharaf, M. (1983) *Fury on Earth: A Biography of Wilhelm Reich*, London: Hutchinson.

Sherwood, M. (1969) *The Logic of Explanation in Psychoanalysis*, New York: Academic Press.

Silverman, L.H. (1975) 'An experimental method for the study of unconscious conflict - a progress report', *British Journal of Medical Psychology* 48: 291.

Slavin, M.O., and Kriegman, D. (1992) 'Psychoanalysis as a Darwinian Depth Psychology: Evolutionary Biology and the Classical-Relational Dialectic in Psychoanalytic Theory', in eds. Barron, J.W., Eagle, M.N. and Wolitzky, D.L. *Interface of Psychoanalysis and Psychology*, Washington DC: American Psychological Association.

Solms, M., and Saling, M. (1986) 'On psychoanalysis and neuroscience: Freud's attitude to the localizationist tradition', *International Journal of Psycho-Analysis* 67: 397-415.

Solomon, I. (1994) *A Primer of Kleinian Therapy*, Northvale N J: Jason Aronson.

Southgate, J. (1980) 'Basic dimensions of character analysis', *Energy and Character* 11, 1: 48-67.

Sterba, R. (1990) 'Clinical and Theoretical Aspects of Character Analysis' in M.S. Bergmann and F.R. Hartman (eds.) *The Evolution of Psychoanalytic Technique*, New York: Columbia University Press.

Stern, D. (1985) *The Interpersonal World of the Infant*, New York: Basic Books.

Stewart, H. (1989) *Psychic Experience and Problems of Technique*, London: Routledge.

Stoller, R.J. (1964) 'A contribution to the study of gender identity', International Journal of Psycho-Analysis 45: 220-5.

Stoller, R.J. (1968) 'A further contribution to the study of gender identity', *International Journal of Psycho-Analysis* 49: 364-8.

Stoller, R.J. (1979) 'A Contribution to the Study of Gender Identity: Follow-Up', *International Journal of Psycho-Analysis* 60: 433-40.

Sudhoff, K., ed. (1922-5) *Paracelsus: Sämtliche Werke*, Munich.

Swanson, D.R. (1977) 'Critique of Psychic Energy as an Explanatory Concept', J. Amer. Psychoanal. Assoc. 25: 603-33.

Sulloway, F. (1980) *Freud, Biologist of the Mind*, London: Fontana.

Taylor, G.J. (1992) 'Psychosomatics and self-regulation' in eds.Barron, J.W., Eagle, M.N. and Wolitzky D.L. *Interface of Psychoanalysis and Psychology*, Washington DC: American Psychological Association.

Totton, N. (1996) 'Freud's Nose', in *Papers from the Universities Association for Psychoanalytic Studies Conference 1995*, London: UAPS.

Totton, N., and Edmondson, E. (1988) *Reichian Growth Work: Melting the Blocks to Life and Love*, Bridport, Dorset: Prism Press.

Van der Kolk, B. (1994) 'The body keeps the score: memory and the evolving psychobiology of post traumatic stress', http://gladstone.uoregon.edu/~dvb/ pg3.htm#CITES [March, 1998]. Revised edition of an article published in *Harvard Review of Psychiatry* 1, 5: 253.

Varela, F., Thompson, E., and Rosch, E. (1992) *The Embodied Mind*, Cambridge, MA: MIT Press.

Verhaeghe, P. (1996) *Does The Woman Exist? From Freud's Hysteric to Lacan's Feminine*, London: Rebus Press.

Wilden, A. (1972) *System and Structure: Essays in Communication and Exchange*, London: Tavistock.

Wilden, A. (1987) *Man and Woman, War and Peace: The Strategist's Companion*, London: Routledge.

Wilson, E.O. (1972) 'Animal communication', *Scientific American*, September.

Winnicott, D.W. (1987) 'Mind and Its Relation to the Psyche-Soma', in *Through Paediatrics to Psychoanalysis: Collected Papers*, London: Karnac.

Wolff, P. (1996) 'The irrelevance of infant observation for psychoanalysis', *Journal of the American Psychoanalytic Association* 45.

Young, R.M. (1994) *Mental Space*, London: Process Press.

Index

ter 133, 192; tension 72, 73-4, 133, 145
music 124-5, 167
mysticism 77, 80-1, 89, 91, 143

`Nasal Reflex Neurosis' theory 50
negative transference 64
neocatharsis 65, 72
neural circuits 147-9
neural synapse 35-6
neurobiology 153-7
neurology 22, 30-4, 152, 153-7, 231; central
    nervous system 29, 188-9
neuronal processes 31, 171
neurophysiology 156-7
neuropsychology 6, 232
neuroscience 6, 7, 146-9, 153-7
neurosis 41-2, 47, 50-1; actual 17, 136; anxi-
    ety 50, 56, 88; and gender 203
nirvana principle 136-7
normality 19, 51, 98
nose 47-51, 239

Oakley, D 247
observation 175
obsessional neurosis 41
ocular character/stage 196, 197-200;
    schizoid 120
Oedipus 88
Oedipus complex 137
oral character stage/structure 191, 192, 196
organotherapy 74
orgasm: anxiety 56, 88, 135-6; reflex 241;
    release 88, 135, 136-7, 228
orgastic potency 100, 136
Ornston, D G 5, 237

Pachter, H 240
pain 42, 75
Paracelsus 80-1, 240
paradox 30, 145-6, 233-4
parameters, analytic 13
pathways 34, 45-6, 151
patriarchy 101, 204, 246
penis 202, 219; removal 212, 220; tiny 218
periodicity 48, 50
Perry, B D 152, 153-5, 188-9, 213-14
perversions 226
Peterfreund, E 151, 235, 236, 243
Pfister O 89
phallic character/stage 190, 196
phantasy 59, 66, 115
Phillips, Adam 103
philosophy 10, 142
phobias 178, 234, 247

physiology 33, 122
Pierrakos, J 245
pleasure 52, 60, 137, 180, 234
Plutchik, R 237, 239
polarities 2, 25-7, 43-4, 205-8
Pontalis, J-B 5
positive transference 64, 181
post-Reichian therapy 8, 113, 189, 191
power: discourse of 211; disempowerment
    208; and gender 203; hierarchies 206
pregnancy 160
Pribram, Karl 37, 231
Prigogine, I 151
primary process 95
privation / prohibition in analysis 15, 73,
    126
privileging of discourses 211-12, 227, 231
proprioception 20, 149-50
protoplasmic vesicle 17
`pseudo-biology' 12, 37
psyche 12, 146; mind-psyche 159; plural 7;
    protopsyche 59; and soma 29-31, 34-6,
    38-9, 44, 78
psyche-soma 157-60
psychic energy 145
psychic reserve 108
psychology: and biology 11-12
psychopathic character stage 188, 196
psychopathology 178
psychosomatics 68, 150
psychotherapy 15, 17, 106-7; parameters 13;
    Reichian 107-19; relationship 115-20; *see
    also* bodywork; transference

quality 29, 32, 35, 42, 146
quantity 29, 32, 42, 145-6

race 201
racism 206, 210-11, 247
Rank, Otto 209-10
Rapaport, D 235, 236, 243
reactive character traits 196
Real, the 25, 123, 128-30, 173, 227
reason 41
recursiveness 152
regression 13, 16
Reich, Wilhelm 3-4, 8, 16, 17, 43, 68-71, 142-
    4, 150, 167, 172, 183, 235, 239, 242, 243; on
    anxiety 56; assessing 97-102, 229-30;
    bodywork 103-16, 118-19, 229; on breath
    104-6; on character 20-1, 178-91, 193-4,
    197, 199, 244-5; and Freud 93-6, 229-30;
    The Function of the Orgasm iii; on gender
    225-6, 228; on Groddeck 91-3; and IPA 18,

Also of interest from
Other Press (US) and Rebus Press (UK)

The Klein-Lacan Dialogues
Bernard Burgoyne and Mary Sullivan (eds.)

The Clinical Lacan
Joël Dor

Introduction to the Reading of Lacan
Joël Dor

Freud's Project: The Roots of Psychoanalysis
Filip Geerardyn

The Subject and the Self: Lacan and American Psychoanalysis
Judith Feher Gurewich (ed.)

Lacanian Psychotherapy with Children: The Broken Piano
Catherine Mathelin

Hysteria from Freud to Lacan: The Splendid Child of Psychoanalysis
Juan-David Nasio

Key Concepts of Lacanian Psychoanalysis
Dany Nobus (ed.)

Out of Order—Clinical Work and Unconscious Process
Martin Stanton

Trauma, Repetition, and Affect Regulation: The Work of Paul Russell
Judith Guss Teicholz and Daniel Kriegman (eds.)

The Water in the Glass: Mind and Body in Psychoanalysis
Nick Totton

Does the Woman Exist? From Freud's Hysteric to Lacan's Feminine
Paul Verhaeghe

The Sovereignty of Death
Rob Weatherill